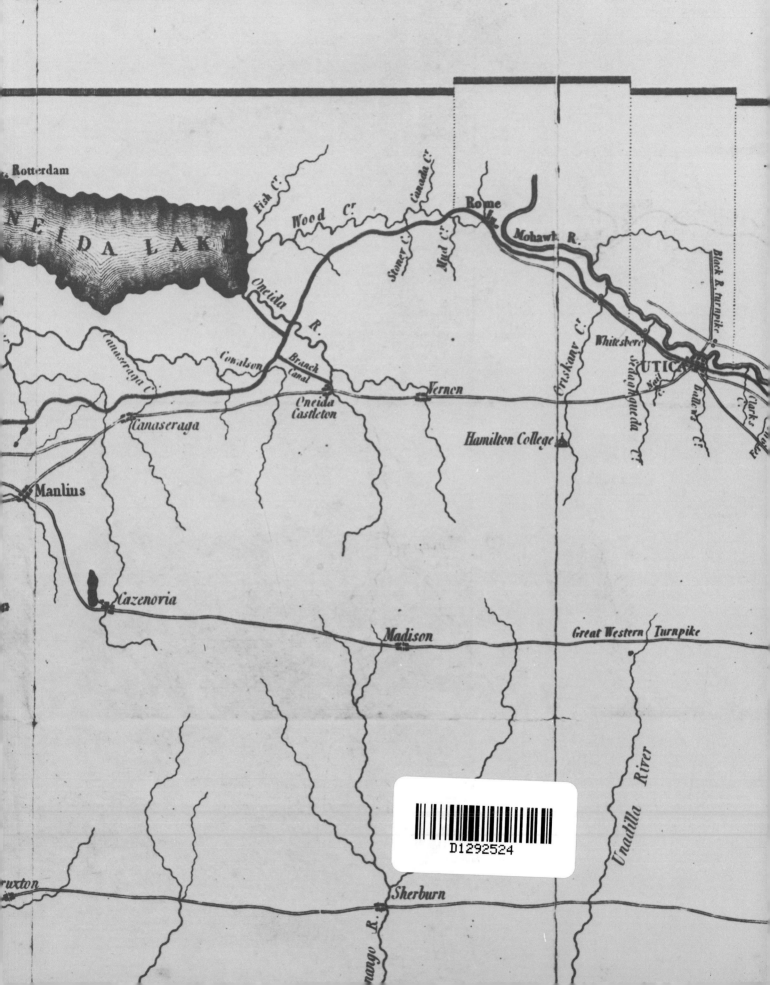

between Lake Erie *and the* Hudson

Rotterdam

ONEIDA LAKE

Fish Cr

Wood Cr

Stoney Cr

Canada Cr

Mud Cr

Rome

Mohawk R.

Oneida

Canaseraga Cr

R.

Conalson

Branch Canal

Criskany Cr

Whitesboro

Sadaaqueda Cr

UTICA

Vernen

Oneida Castleton

Hamilton College

Canaseraga

Black R. turnpike

Ballow's Cr

Clarks Cr

Manlius

Cazenovia

Madison

Great Western Turnpike

Unadilla River

ruxton

Sherburn

nangv R.

Because of our long association
with the residents of Central New York,
we at Key Bank
are especially pleased to offer
this pictorial history of our community.
We recognize
the importance of local awareness
and a sense
of where we've been
and where we're going.
It is our hope
that with this book
we have helped
to meet this need.

Barrett L. Jones
President and Chief Executive Officer
Key Bank of Central New York

C·E·N·T·R·A·L
NEW YORK
A PICTORIAL HISTORY

Henry W. Schramm

Designed by Sharon Varner Moyer

THE
DONNING COMPANY
PUBLISHERS
NORFOLK/VIRGINIA BEACH

        The Donning Company/Publishers
        5659 Virginia Beach Boulevard
        Norfolk, Virginia 23502

Edited by Nancy O. Phillips

Library of Congress Cataloging-in-Publication Data

Schramm, Henry W.
  Central New York.

  Bibliography: p.
  Includes index.
    1. New York (State)—Description and travel—1981—
Views. 2 New York (State)—History, Local—Pictorial works.
I. Title.
F120.S34   1987   974.7   87-22359
ISBN 0-89865-587-0

Printed in the United States of America

Table of Contents

Preface 1

Acknowledgments 2

CHAPTER ONE
The Beginnings, to 1800 5

CHAPTER TWO
The Stage is Set, 1800-1830 19

CHAPTER THREE
Growing Up, 1830-1865 33

CHAPTER FOUR
After Appomattox, 1865-1900 55

CHAPTER FIVE
A New Century, 1900-1920 97

CHAPTER SIX
Triumphs and Trials, 1920-1945 143

CHAPTER SEVEN
The Post War Era, 1945-1987 185

Bibliography 225

Index 228

About the Author 234

Preface

Our Central New York is historically intensive, rich in subject matter and resources. It has been indelibly marked both by great geological processes and by the presence of man for some five thousand years. And, although its written history extends back just three centuries, Central New York and its residents have shared in all the great movements from the Industrial Revolution to the treks west, the massive immigrations, the periods of depression and economic booms, racial movements, wars and political upheavals.

When the decision was made to develop a pictorial history of this area, the first step—not an easy one—was to determine Central New York's geographic borders. We eventually focused on the boundaries of the original Onondaga County of 1782, comprising all or parts of the present counties of Onondaga, Oswego, Madison, Cortland and Cayuga. A case could be made for including Utica and Rome, Ithaca and the Western Finger Lakes as well as Watertown, but this would have impinged on the stories of other regions—the Mohawk Valley of Leatherstocking fame, the Southern Tier, and the eastern border of the Rochester region—territories rich in their own heritages.

From east to west, the communities from Canastota to Weedsport and Port Byron form a necklace of tales of marching soldiers, the Erie Canal and the railroads. Today they are stops along the Thruway. From north to south the roads, rivers and valleys lead from the Canadian border to Pennsylvania and then to the nation's capital. Nearby communities of Auburn and Oswego have long and exciting histories of their own.

We live in an era of instant communication, rapid transit and a world outlook. The fast-food chain in Hong Kong looks like the MacDonald's or Burger King of Syracuse—or Cortland—or Auburn. It was not always like that. Every one of our communities developed a unique history with its own economy and culture established around its particular geography or the whims of surveyors. Oswego could have become greater than Buffalo; salt and limestone made Syracuse different from Canastota; Syracuse University permanently settled there because, unlike the village of Lima, it was on a railroad line.

In turn, each community developed its collections of pictures, lore and attics. Eventually, despite fires, floods, windstorms and spring cleanings, enough remained to be collected, catalogued and concentrated as a window on a particular piece of landscape. The dozens of historical societies, libraries and museums within Central New York offer a particular in-depth view of our yesterdays. In fact, the wealth of material (some estimates are that close to five million items remain to be catalogued at the Onondaga County Historical Association alone) makes selection of what to incorporate even more difficult. Decisions had to be made if Central New York's history was to be truly represented in a limited volume. I hope the right ones were chosen.

Acknowledgments

Writing this book has involved a review of well in excess of ten thousand photographs, drawings, postcards, maps and exhibits, and hundreds of books and articles. It could not have been done without the cooperation of dozens of people: historians, librarians, newspaper writers and editors, photographers, my colleagues at Key Bank of Central New York and people in local business and industry.

Once again the Onondaga County Historical Association's resources offered the guidance of Richard Wright and Violet Hoseler until Vi's untimely death in January 1987 and Dick's retirement to Maryland. Denyse Clifford capably stepped into the void, providing an important bridge to the collection. Tony King, the new president, brought with him an expertise soon evident as the task of restoring the association's physical facilities and collections began.

The Erie Canal Museum's Vicki Quigley placed the entire collection at my disposal, with Don Wilson, the curator, spending many hours aiding me in the selection of representative pictures.

Amy S. Doherty, head of the archives section of Bird Library, Syracuse University, and her associate, Mary Obrien, graciously enabled me to select many pictures from their collection.

Others at the university who were helpful included Dan Forbush, public relations director; David May, director of marketing communications; Lawrence Kimball, sports information director; Mike Holdridge at the Carrier Dome; and C. Purcell of marketing communications. LeMoyne College's Arlene Hathaway, Colgate University's James Leach, director of communications, and Deborah Barnes and Robin Reagan of the office of communications at Cazenovia College offered valuable assistance.

Margaret Horner and Joyce H. Cook of the Local History Section of the Onondaga County Public Library and Hans Plambeck, in charge of the Allied Chemical Section of the Solvay Public Library, were exceptionally helpful. Dan Casey, former president of the American Library Association as well as a fellow member of University College's Thursday Morning Roundtable, offered practical guidance.

Stephen Rogers, Jr., publisher of the Syracuse Newspapers, Diane Murvis, head librarian, and Jean Collin, her assistant, enabled me to avail myself of the facilities and library of the *Post-Standard* and the *Herald-Journal*, while a number of photographers including Carl Single and C. W. McKeen and artist Fred

Heyman provided their assistance. Counsel and help were generously forthcoming from Columnist Dick Case and fellow local historian Richard Palmer.

Malcolm Godell, Cayuga County historian, and Mrs. Leo Pinckney, assistant historian, provided many historic photos and illustrations of the Auburn area, while Tom Hunter, curator of the Cayuga Museum of History and Art, made the institution's entire photographic collection available. Mrs. Betty Lewis of the William H. Seward House in Auburn provided a number of rare pictures.

Oswego's unusual history as a fort, seaport and power center was portrayed through the help of Terry Prior, curator of the Oswego Historical Association; Don Lair of Fort Oswego; retired county historian Anthony Slosek and Linda O'Brien, public relations director of the Oswego Speedway.

Michele Buzley, coordinator of the Friends of History in Fulton, enabled us to present some important aspects of that community. Shirley Heppell of the Cortland County Historical Society was especially valuable in locating some important pictures in the Cortland-Homer area, while Ed Rounds of the *Cortland Standard* steered me toward several other sources. The cooperation of Helen Warner of Key Bank's DeRuyter office and Ernest Baker and the Tromptown Historical Society enabled us to better portray their township.

Betty L. Heinze of Camillus, executor of the estate of Mary Ellis Maxwell, the author of *Among the Hills of Camillus*, and Michael Plumpton of the neighboring community of Marcelius kindly assisted in procuring photos, while authorization for the reproduction of the John D. Barrow paintings was graciously provided by Mrs. Frances S. Milford, president of the John D. Barrow Art Gallery. The Roman Catholic Diocese through its archivist, Carl Roesch, authorized use of several pictures.

The history of the Syracuse Symphony Orchestra was made more readable through the efforts of Sue Harris and Sharon Grutzmacher, while Tom Piche provided me with important subjects from the Everson Museum. Bill Simmons, facility supervisor for the department of aviation at Hancock Field, provided much useful information.

Representatives from area corporations were most cooperative, including Jim Cosgrove of Niagara Mohawk; Connie Grasso, head of public relations at General Electric's Electronics Park and Marleah Farnett of Centro. George Snyder, a former colleague at

2

Barlow/Johnson, a Syracuse advertising agency, provided several historical pictures of the Brockway Truck Company of Cortland, while his daughter, Debbie, made available some rare pieces from the Syracuse Rescue Mission.

A number of interesting pictures of the Weedsport-Port Byron area were made available through the kindness of Howard Finley of the Old Brutus Historical Society while photos of New York State Fairgrounds auto races were provided through the efforts of Glenn Donnelly of Weedsport, president of DIRT (Drivers Independent Race Tracks), Aaron Freshman and Daniel Harpell. Prints from the National Baseball Hall of Fame Museum in Cooperstown were provided through the services of Patricia Kelly.

Jack Murray of the Onondaga County Executive's Office, Congressman George Wortley's office and Tim Carroll of Mayor Thomas Young's office were instrumental in providing essential pictures.

The courtesy of Ed Brophy of Canastota was most appreciated, while photos from the Baldwinsville area were provided through Ruth O'Connell, historian, town of Lysander, and Eleanor Christopher-Mackey, historian, town of Van Buren. The Cazenovia area art was provided through the efforts of Russell Grills of the Lorenzo Mansion and Betsy Michaels of the Cazenovia Library.

Several historic pictures were provided by Jana Telfer, director of communications of the Syracuse Chapter of the American Red Cross, while the Automobile Club of Syracuse through Jack Delaney, its president, and Betty Rothfuss enabled us to show some rare highway pictures. Red Parton and Norman Rothschild, director of the Onondaga County War Memorial, also provided substantial help.

The marketing department staff members at Key Bank Central were especially patient and constructive during the entire period. Margaret Cooke was never sure what would be waiting for her—literally hundreds of captions to type; the drafts and redrafts, much of it from handwritten copy; Richard B. Liddle and Michael McMahon were both kind enough to read the original drafts and provide their input. And Mary Ann Russell did her best to keep the book balanced with other departmental projects.

Branch managers and regional executives throughout the Key Bank system, in addition to those previously mentioned, provided information, arranged appointments, and served as collection points for art and pertinent literature. Among them (and I'm certain I'll miss someone) were Tony Baldino at Liverpool; Frank Caliva at Skaneateles, Bud Chanley in East Syracuse, Bud Clement and Madalyn Stankivitz of the Canastota office; Tom Colvin in Auburn; Dave Dano at Oswego; Harlow Kisselstein, Baldwinsville; Bert Heath in Homer; Ty King of Marcellus; Steve Osborne in Fulton, Beth Walldorff of Cazenovia's office, Linda Ward of Weedsport and Dana Wavle in Morrisville.

William Jackson, superintendent of Fort Stanwix National Monument, and his staff were extremely helpful, while Catherine Baty, curator at the Rome Historical Society, and Mary Reynolds, curator at Erie Canal Village, provided important insight.

The staff at the Donning Company provided important guidance and backup throughout the preparation of the material. Especial thanks go to Franklin Hall, Valerie Von Weich, and Nancy Phillips who painstakingly and patiently edited the manuscript.

The book itself would have been impossible without the photographic skills of Al Edison, whose techniques enabled use of many almost hopelessly damaged or faded pictures. A number of Al's own pictures are also among the photos.

William Tumbridge, former president of the Erie Canal Museum, was kind enough to review the book in its embryonic form and to offer his comments, while Don Wilson, curator at the museum, read the manuscript from a technical standpoint, providing several subsequently adapted suggestions. Oliver Hill of the Onondaga Nation gave thoughtful comments regarding the Iroquois Confederacy.

And so, this book represents an effort to consolidate centuries of complex events and social change graphically and in concise, readable form. My thanks to everyone who helped.

The limestone horseshoe cliff shown above, with its deep, circular plunge pool, is located in Clark Reservation, a part of the state park system, several miles east of Syracuse. The cliff is a true relic of the last great geological incident, which drained the huge inland sea that together with its ice fronts encompassed the present Lake Ontario basin and the land area containing what is now Syracuse and the original Onondaga County. After leaving the falls, the waters sliced through what is now Rock Cut gorge and then flowed to Limestone Creek, the Mohawk River and the sea. Courtesy of Onondaga County Historical Association

The Beginnings to 1800

The sight and sound would have stunned human senses—if there had been anyone to see, hear or appreciate them.

But the great cataract, backdropped by massive ice walls and with a sheer drop twice as high as Niagara, with equal volume, had diminished to a dry, smooth-lipped limestone cliff by the time man first appeared in Central New York some five thousand years ago. The cliff is still visible at Clark Reservation, near Jamesville.

The great stands of melting ice, the tiltings of rock layers and erosion provided Central New York with unique blessings, including the deposits of thick layers of Manlius and Onondaga limestone, salt and gypsum, the easily available raw materials for future economic growth.

The shifting rocks enabled the lands south of the Tully-Cortland areas to drain through the Susquehanna River into what is now the Chesapeake Bay, while to the north the ancient inland sea poured into the St. Lawrence or the Mohawk Valley and then into the Atlantic.

The retreating glaciers put the finishing touches on the unique chain of long, narrow and deep bodies of water known as the Finger Lakes. The etching process left *drumlins*, the tear-shaped hills containing rich lodes of gravel. The former sea bottom heritage includes the rich black dirt so important to agriculture today and the great Montezuma and Cicero swamps.

Streams and valleys formed the north-south and east-west corridors which later enabled man to travel by water, by foot and eventually by stage, canal boat and train.

Forests covered the entire area, providing food and shelter for wildlife. Deer, wolves and bears were plentiful. The lakes and streams offered almost unlimited quantities of salmon, whitefish and perch. The land was ready for man.

The first humans are believed to have reached Central New York in the Lamoka Lake region of Schuyler County. Archeologists in 1937 excavated a primitive village site along the shores of Oneida Lake at Brewerton in northern Onondaga County, discovering pottery and other utensils of a people who are thought to have made their way south from the Canadian Laurentians two thousand years before Christ.

These tribes were eventually succeeded by the Mound Builders, a people whose early tools and clay pottery shards were recovered in the ruins of a prehistoric fortification at what is now Fort Hill in the center of the city of Auburn.

The last prehistory stage of local history was the Woodland Period of full-sized villages, ceramics and an agricultural economy revolving around crops of corn, beans and squash, a period which lasted from 1000 B.C. until white men arrived.

The Algonquins populated the region for centuries until driven out by the members of the five-nation Iroquois Confederacy in the later days of the sixteenth century. Included in the Confederacy were the Mohawks, Oneidas, Onondagas, Cayugas and Senecas. Joined by a sixth nation, the Tuscaroras, the Confederacy today still represents native American interests in Central New York.

The Nations themselves came from other territories: the Onondagas from what is now Jefferson County to the north; the Oneidas from near Ogdensburg; the Mohawks from the regions of Montreal and Quebec, where the Hurons had driven them out.

An Onondaga chief, believed to be the real person from whom the legendary figure of Hiawatha developed, is credited with consummating the union, along with a Huron chief.

Syracuse-area Indians were active in the Pompey and Onondaga Hill regions for centuries, practicing farming and living within highly protected village enclaves.

In 1975, an amateur archeologist, Ferdinand LaFrance, and his nephew Albert noticed an unusual black strip in a plowed field atop a Pompey hill. Further investigation provided evidence that the area had been an Indian settlement in the fifteenth century. It is also believed from the structural remnants that a 577-foot longhouse had been located on the site.

The location of numerous Indian villages in Onondaga County is not surprising considering the agricultural structure of their economy, which led to moves once the land became infertile.

The early settlers learned a great deal from Indian farmers. Their tools were rudimentary, so the Indians had developed unusual methods. Corn, for example, was grown in mounds, along with other vegetables, so that the stalk could be used for climbing beans. Weeds were thus eliminated.

Eventually the white man came, but exactly when?

Much local prehistory was based on fragile evidences. Some of these were the blends of legend and fact comprising the oral history of the Indians, passed from generation to generation. Others incorporated fact, geographic error and bragging by early explorers and soldiers. And still others, such as the Pompey Stone and the Cardiff Giant, were simply hoaxes.

The relatively stable conditions of the Iroquois Confederacy were shattered in 1615 with the arrival from upper Canada of Stephen Brule, a Frenchman who scouted for Samuel de Champlain. With twelve Hurons, Brule penetrated as far as Waverly in Tioga County. He escaped from torture on this occasion, but according to a French historian known as Sagord, eventually was put to death by the Hurons in Canada.

In 1615 Champlain came into Central New York with an army of several hundred Huron and Algonquin warriors, introducing the first guns into the region.

The French wavered between harsh military measures for handling the Iroquois and turning the mission over to the Jesuit priests who steadfastly carried the cross throughout Upstate New York despite torture and a heavy death toll. One of the best known of the latter was Father Simon LeMoyne, who journeyed throughout the region without military support. He came to Canada in 1638 to teach Indians the Christian way. He gained the respect of not only the Hurons, but the Iroquois as well. They, in turn, sent a message to the French in Quebec—"Send a black robe to us."

After a trip of fifteen days, LeMoyne arrived at Indian Hill near Pompey, then the site of the Onondagas' village, in August of 1654. He quickly gained the trust of the Onondaga chieftains, establishing a reputation both as an eloquent speaker and as a peacemaker.

LeMoyne was the first white man to recognize the salt springs for what they were. The Indians in New York and Canada, the priest said, used no salt at all.

The French continued their abrasive tactics in 1696, when Count Robert de Frontenac led an expedition of 1600 French troops, 460 Indians and 400 boats, along with light artillery, in an effort to take over the Onondagas. Arriving at Oswego, they proceeded up the river, portaging at Oswego Falls (now Fulton) and camping at what is now Phoenix. They built a fort along Onondaga Lake and then proceeded to burn the Onondaga village. All of the Nation escaped, except for one old man who had volunteered to stay. He was burned at the stake.

The continued French excesses and their use of Huron and Algonquin warriors drove the Iroquois into a permanent relationship with the British. The French and English had been at war periodically for centuries, with treaties intermittently settling the issues.

Under the rule of Queen Anne of England, Protestant efforts to Christianize the Iroquois were started about 1700, but in no way compared to the intensive campaigning of the Jesuits.

The Moravians, however, with Bishop John Frederic Christoph Cammerhoff and the Reverend David Zeisberger, did come up from Pennsylvania for a missionary tour of the Nations in 1750. They arrived first at the center of the Cayuga Nation on the east shore of Cayuga Lake near the site of present-day Union Springs. They were well received during their stay in Central New York, but there was no followup.

Father Poncet, also a Jesuit, was the first white man to visit Oswego, passing up the river to Onondaga in 1653, a year before LeMoyne. But it was the British who made the first effort to fortify and strongly garrison Oswego, which became a major supply bastion in several wars and the locale of a number of engagements.

Governor Burnet of the New York Colony established a trading house at Oswego on the west side of the river in 1722. The following year 57 canoes ventured from Albany, returning with 738 packs of beaver and deerskins. The French were exceedingly

This view shows the steep flight to the rim of the Great Falls in 1888 at Clark Reservation. The rim was occupied by a resort hotel in 1885; the resort failed a few years later. Courtesy of Onondaga County Historical Association

jealous, countering the British by repairing a fort at Niagara to the west, accommodating a strong trading post of their own.

Foreseeing trouble, Burnet called in the chiefs of the Five Nations for support and in 1726 allocated funds to build a fort which was ready for action the next year. By 1755 the system included interdependent forts at Oswego, Forts Ontario and George. Earlier in 1744, traders and others fled the area when it was thought the French were on the move, but the Treaty of Aix-la-Chapelle restored peace.

On August 14, 1756, Louis Joseph de Montcalm's forces captured and demolished Fort Ontario, taking 1520 prisoners and destroying 7 warships and 200 bateaux. The failure of the French to gain a decisive victory in a skirmish at Battle Island just north of Fulton led to their decision to abandon the area. The British rebuilt Oswego and held it throughout the later wars, where it served as a base of supplies for England's agent, Sir William Johnson; Joseph Brant, the legendary Mohawk warrior; and colonial and eventually Tory troops.

The British, with the help of American colonists and the Iroquois, prevailed over the French in the French and Indian War. Brant, whose sister was said to be Sir William's mistress, was taken under the agent's wing. Sir William was an extremely popular governor and soldier whose word was trusted by the Indians. Brant was even schooled with Sir William's son and made several trips to England. Despite being a pragmatic and brutal warrior, Brant displayed tact, and as a Freemason he protected fellow Masons whom he had taken prisoner. Baptized as a Christian, he translated the Book of Matthew into his native language.

When the Revolution came, the Iroquois found themselves in a bind, wooed by both English and Continental forces. Only the Oneidas decided to remain neutral. Brant, as a captain in the British forces, worked closely with the English, Canadians and Loyalists in leading the Indian warriors in the march from Oswego to Fort Stanwix in 1777, participating with Lt. Col. Barry St. Leger and Col. John Butler in the siege of the fort and in the eventual empty-handed return to Oswego.

The following year Brant and Tory troops descended on Cherry Valley, massacring many of the inhabitants. Others, including women and children, were marched west through the Onondaga lands and Skaneateles before being sent to Canada.

The Revolutionary forces decided to teach the Iroquois and their allies a lesson. In 1779 George Washington approved a campaign to be directed by General John Sullivan, utilizing a third of the available Continental army.

The troops chopped their way northward from the Southern Tier, devastating the Cayuga Nation, but never reaching the town of Onondaga despite some confusion in historic reporting. The Onondagas were actually attacked in April of 1779 by soldiers led by Col. Goose Van Schaick and Lt. Col. Marinus Willett, via Canajoharie and Fort Stanwix.

The 558 soldiers in thirty bateaux traveled over Oneida Lake, landing opposite Fort Brewerton at three in the afternoon of April 20. They spent the night without fire near what is now Cicero, then reached Onondaga Lake the next day. At nine in the morning they forded a two-hundred-yard-wide stretch of water which reached up to their armpits.

At Onondaga Creek they slipped across a log bridge near the present location of West Colvin Street. There they captured a young Indian who provided them with information about the tribe's whereabouts.

Then the historic sources vary. Timothy S. Cheney, in his remarks, said General Sullivan led the attack, taking the Indians by surprise while they were at breakfast. Many reportedly fled into the creek and were killed in the water. Others say Indian lookouts warned their fellows and that the bulk of the women and children escaped into the woods while the men slowed down the invaders before being driven off with relatively small losses. This skirmish was reportedly where lower Onondaga Park stands today.

However, according to historian William M. Beauchamp, Sullivan never came into Onondaga territory, and Van Schaick is given full credit for destroying the village just south of where Seneca Turnpike and Onondaga Creek now cross.

Cheney said that a Negro locksmith, found repairing Indian guns, was seized by the soldiers, hanged and quartered. Others say that a Negro doctor and thirty-three Indians were captured, with twelve Indians killed. One of the prisoners reportedly was a child of Joseph Brant's.

The Continentals returned to Stanwix. Total elapsed time: five and one-half days. Not a soldier was lost.

The destruction of the Onondaga camp was the climax for the Sullivan-Clinton campaign, a campaign which led to George Washington's being known as the "destroyer of towns."

The last local combat during the Revolution was an abortive attempt by an American force led by Colonel Willet to retake the fort at Oswego, which had been abandoned, then reoccupied by the British in 1782. General Washington, while at Newburgh, had called in Colonel Willett for a conference about capturing the fortification.

The colonel, with 400 troops loaded on 120 sleighs, left Fort Herkimer on February 8, 1783, for a surprise attack on Oswego, arriving at Oneida Lake on the twelfth. They proceeded on foot from Brewerton along the Oneida.

Their presence was discovered by the British, who were waiting before the fortifications. Willett had no choice but to retire, losing several men who froze to death during the retreat. But the seeming defeat could have been far more tragic. The scaling ladders carried by the Americans would have reached only two-thirds of the way up the strengthened palisade.

And, besides, the war was over!

Peace with the Iroquois remained unfinished business. The British could go home, but the Indians had to stay behind—all except the Mohawk Nation, which departed for Canada. In 1784 this latter group received from the British a reservation six miles wide from each side of the Grand River, which empties into Lake Erie forty miles above Niagara Falls, and extending one hundred miles inland.

In October of the same year, a peace treaty between the remainder of the Iroquois Nations and the United States was signed at Fort Stanwix, where Chief Cornplanter of the Senecas represented the Indians.

Eventually land settlements were made, with the Six Nations located on reservations. Only two Nations are in Central New York—the Onondagas, sited south of Syracuse with 7300 acres and the Oneidas, with 400 acres four miles south of Oneida. A part of this Nation lives near Green Bay, Wisconsin.

Peace, although to be of short duration, had arrived. Everything was in readiness for the entrance of a new influx of pioneers.

This site of ancient Indian habitation along the shore of Lamoka Lake in Schuyler County was excavated by members of the Archeological Society of Central New York on October 19, and 20, 1946. Courtesy of Cayuga Museum of History and Art

A prehistoric 577-foot-long bark house was found in the 1970s near Indian Hill, Pompey—the longest of the longhouses discovered in the area. These twenty-foot-wide structures were constructed of sapling stakes pushed into trenches, and then covered with strips of elm bark as shown in this drawing. Surrounding palisades provided protection. *Courtesy of Onondaga County Historical Association*

The Great Seal of the Onondaga Nation is said to depict the Nation as a bark lodge or longhouse on top of a high hill. The "People of the Hills," the fire keepers of the Iroquois Confederacy, were thus shown in the highest place, politically above their neighbors on the lower hills to the east and west. The swamp at the base is thought by some to be included in the meaning of the word Onondaga. *Courtesy of Onondaga County Historical Association*

It was Hiawatha who traveled to the various tribes to bring them together, and supposedly demonstrated to the assembled chieftains at a meeting on the shores of Onondaga Lake that a single arrow can be easily snapped, but that when a number are bound together, they are unbreakable.

A more fanciful explanation, developed from legend and embroidered by the stories of early explorers and settlers, tells of Hiawatha's arrival in a white canoe on the shores of Lake Ontario, and his later departure, which may well have derived from teachings about Christ's ascension.

Under the Iroquois Confederacy, the five Nations acted in unison in war, maintaining peace among themselves. The Onondagas held the territorial position, and they maintained the Grand Council fire. All envoys, whether Indian or white, met with the chiefs at this fire, actually the place where the records, belts and memorials of treaties were preserved.

Hiawatha is depicted here at the Grand Council of the Iroquois Confederacy, as illustrated in a 1919 report of the Public Museum of the city of Milwaukee. *Courtesy of Onondaga County Historical Association*

In 1869 an Indian legend seemed to come to life in the village of Cardiff, just south of Syracuse. Onondaga children were told of stone giants who lived here long ago, but who incurred the wrath of the Great Spirit. He destroyed them with lightning, turning them into the stone formations near Jamesville.

One giant was said to have escaped and vowed to kill the Onondagas—one each day. The Indians reportedly dug a great hole, covering it with leaves. The giant fell in and was quickly buried.

When William Newell and his two hands, Gideon Emmons and Henry Nichols, were digging a well on October 16, 1869, they found something unusual. A piece of what looked like a foot—a giant foot.

People came to see the foot—and the attached body—all 2,996 pounds of it. The body was covered with "pores," giving some scientists cause to believe its authenticity. In one day twenty-six hundred visitors paid fifty cents each to view the ten-foot monster lying under the tent (above) raised over the excavation.

P. T. Barnum offered sixty thousand dollars for the giant. Shares were sold to people who should have known better. Then the perpetrators admitted the hoax. A German stonecutter in Chicago had been commissioned by Newell's cousin, George Hall, a Binghamton tobacconist, to carve the creature. Special techniques were used to create the so-called pores. The giant now rests in the Farmer's Museum in Cooperstown.

There was another giant discovery, this one by a gang of workmen widening a roadway near Taughannock Falls on the west shore of Cayuga Lake. They made their discovery two days before the Fourth of July, 1879. But this giant was only eight-hundred pounds, and a mere seven feet long. His creators, more scientifically minded, endeavoured to make their monster from elements found in the human body. Again P. T. Barnum showed interest. Again, it was found to be a hoax. But its mortal remains are among the missing, as they were dropped while en route to an exhibition place and crumbled. Courtesy of Onondaga County Historical Association

The year was 1820. Philo Cleveland, a Manlius area farmer, was clearing boulders. He struggled with an imbedded, oval-shaped rock, finally forcing it loose with a crowbar. Cleveland was ready to toss it into a nearby pile, when he noticed some unusual markings. A quick brush revealed an engraved figure of a tree encircled by a serpent. Further investigation indicated some mysterious lettering: "Leo DeLon," and a date, "VI, 1526."

From there the stone, measuring twelve by fourteen inches, with a thickness of eight inches, was carried to Manlius and then to Albany, where it became known as the Pompey Stone, was studied by experts, and was then established as a prized exhibit at the Museum of the Albany Institute.

A school of thought developed. Predating the earliest French explorations by almost a century, the inscription was believed to be that of Spanish adventurers who had worked their way up the Mississippi in search of a "silver lake." Some early historians took the story at face value.

That is, until 1894, when the Reverend William M. Beauchamp, a noted local historian, and John A. Sweet disclosed that Sweet's uncle and another man had carved the inscription at an Oran blacksmith shop. The joke got out of hand and, once the specialists got into the act, the local men were afraid to admit it. Courtesy of the Onondaga County Public Library

In 1615 the French forces under Champlain skirted Onondaga Lake, finally reaching a well-constructed Indian fortress with a high palisade. The exact location of this fortress has never been truly ascertained. Some say it was at Nichols Pond near Cazenovia; others believe it was located near what is now the Hiawatha Boulevard exit of Route 81 in the northwestern section of Syracuse.

But whatever the location, the Indians held out, despite early panic. The French built a Roman tower from nearby timber, shown at the right of the drawing of the battle, and, moving it close to the palisade, were able to fire directly into the fortress. Garbled orders, however, resulted in failure to take advantage of the confusion. Champlain himself was severely wounded and was carried back to Canada on a crude litter. Courtesy of Onondaga County Historical Association

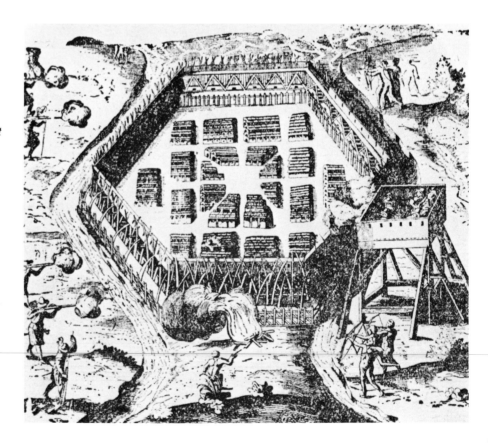

In 1654 Father Simon LeMoyne arrived at the portage on the present site of the city of Fulton, as depicted in a mural painted by an anonymous W.P.A. artist. It now hangs on the wall at the Fulton Post Office. Photo by Dave Dayger

The Jesuit Monument between Aurora and Union Springs marks the first site of Christian worship in the Finger Lakes region. The inscription reads:

> "This valley was the site of the principal Cayuga Indian Village. To the brave French Jesuit missionaries, whose heroism was almost without parallel, Joseph Chaumonot and Rene Menard, who as guests of Chief Saonchiocwa, built here in 1656, the first house of Christian worship in Western New York, Stephen de Carheil, who for nine years ministered here, and his co-labourer, Peter Raffeix, this memorial is respectfully erected."

Courtesy of Cayuga Museum of History and Art

This early map was exaggerated in scale, and displayed many topographic highlights erroneously, even excluding a number of them. Yet it gives some evidence of the great unknown areas of the state and mid-Atlantic territories in relation to the populated regions. *Courtesy of Onondaga County Historical Association*

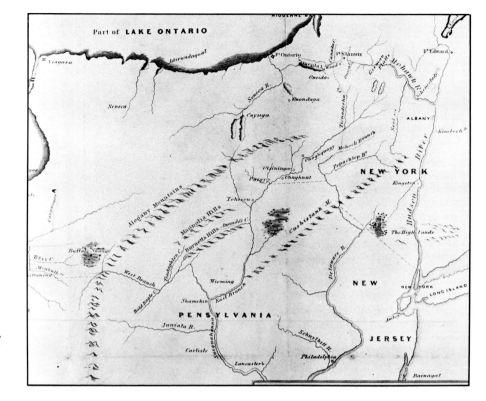

This early drawing showed the first British fort at Oswego, circa 1727. The fortification saw action in three major conflicts—the French and Indian War, the Revolution, and the War of 1812. The bluff to the right is the site of the present Fort Ontario. *Courtesy of Fort Ontario State Park*

A medal struck in the era of Louis XV commemorated French victories in the Oswego area during the early days of occupation. *Courtesy of Oswego County Historical Society*

Joseph Brant (1742-1807), a Mohawk warrior, chief and spokesman, was educated by the British and joined them in the French and Indian War and the Revolution, serving in most of the major engagements in Central New York. He was described in holiday uniform while on garrison duty in 1782 as follows:

> He was a likely fellow of a fierce aspect—tall and rather spare—well spoken, and apparently about thirty years of age. He wore moccasins, elegantly trimmed with beads, leggings and breech-cloth of superfine blue, short green coat, with two silver epaulets and a small laced round hat. By his side hung an elegant silver mounted cutlass, and his blanket of blue cloth, purposely draped in the chair on which he sat, to display his epaulets, was gorgeously decorated with a border of red." He was too sensible to wear such a costume in the wilds of Onondaga.

Courtesy of Onondaga County Historical Association

JOSEPH BRANT—THAYENDANEGEA.

In this painting Gen. Nicholas Herkimer, seated at left, negotiates with Joseph Brant, standing, trying to convince the Indian leader to side with the Continental forces. Instead, Brant and his forces joined the British. At their next meeting Herkimer's forces were ambushed and the general fatally wounded, but they managed to fend off the British. The conflict discouraged the British, while raising the spirits of the Americans who held Fort Stanwix and preserved the western gateway to Albany. *Courtesy of Fort Stanwix National Monument, U.S. Dept. of Interior*

Fort Stanwix, looking southward. The siege of the Rome fortification by British forces in August 1777 failed to budge the Continental defenders and discouraged the combined British, Loyalist and Indian forces from continuing their attempt to link up with General Burgoyne to the east, and is therefore considered by some to have been the decisive battle in the Revolution. Courtesy of Fort Stanwix National Monument, U.S. Department of Interior

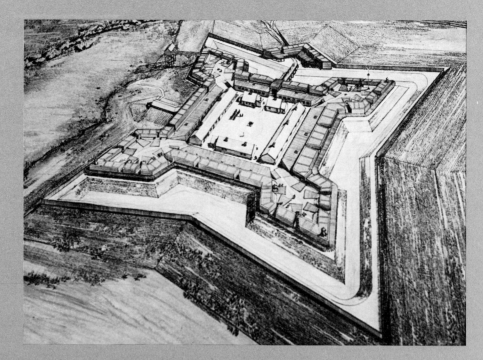

Sunrise at Fort Stanwix August 3, 1777 *was painted by Edward F. Buyck in 1927. Funds to pay Mr. Buyck for this painting were raised by the citizens of Rome. The theme of the painting is the raising of the Stars and Stripes above Fort Stanwix during the siege of August 2 to 22, 1777. Some believe it was the first time the American flag was flown in combat. Courtesy of Fort Stanwix National Monument, U.S. Department of Interior*

The Treaty of 1784 ended the conflict between the Iroquois Confederacy and the Continental forces, but continues to be a source of contention. Courtesy of Fort Stanwix National Monument, U.S. Department of Interior

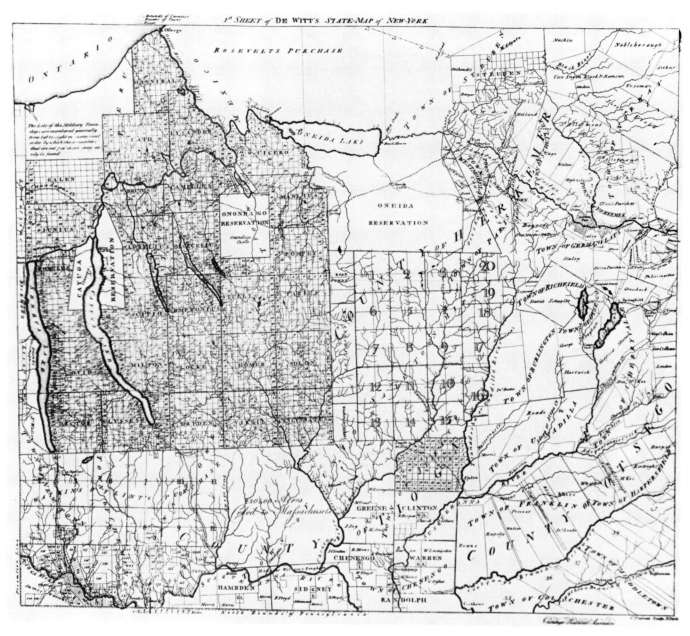

The leaders of the new nation of the United States recognized a debt to the veterans who had shared the risks of revolution in a wild, forbidding land against an especially dangerous foe. A military tract of 1 million acres was established in 1782, including the present counties of Onondaga, Seneca, Cayuga, Cortland and parts of Oswego, Wayne, Schuyler and Tompkins Counties. The land was divided into towns, each six miles square, and further subdivided into six hundred-acre homesteads. The soldiers drew lots for the parcels, which were allocated one hundred to the town. Several were set aside for schools, churches, and for exchange if a soldier drew a lot covered by water. Land entitlements included: privates and non-commissioned officers, six hundred acres; lieutenants, twelve hundred acres; captains, eighteen hundred acres; majors, twenty-four hundred acres, and colonels, three thousand acres. Only regiments commanded by Colonels Philip Van Cortlandt and Goose Van Schaick and Colonel Joseph Lamb's artillery regiment, plus engineer support troops, were eligible.

Many of the men had already camped by land to which they had taken a fancy—some as prisoners of war had found a special meadow or glen they had liked during their cross-country march. The result was a lively sale and exchange of property. Courtesy of Onondaga County Historical Association, Syracuse

Hostilities ceased on April 18, 1783, and five days later a truce party was dispatched to Oswego. Captain Thompson was blindfolded and taken into the British fortifications, where the disgusted British officers under a Major Ross finally accepted the terms. They did not leave, though, Oswego remained a British outpost until it was finally surrendered in 1796. Note the British leaving under their banner in lower right, as the Stars and Stripes goes up. Painting by Charles Henry Grant, courtesy of Anthony Slosek

Clearing the land provided a pleasing opportunity to bring light into the oppressive darkness of too many trees for too many miles. So, as soon as the trees were in leaf, they were felled, first those closest to the house, then those farther out. The leaves on the fallen trees drew the moisture out of the branches, making a complete burn possible in early fall. Potash made from the ashes was an important early by-product for market. The building of the log cabin, the collection of the stumps for final burning and other chores requiring more than one man turned even the most independent settler into a social person. Bees were the answers, with such occasions serving to clear land, raise barns or conduct other heavy labor. Courtesy of Onondaga County Library

CHAPTER TWO

The Stage is Set
1800-1830

The veterans trickled back, a few here, a couple there—traders, fur trappers, wanderers and dreamers. They did not expect an easy life, but they were not fools. They clung to the highlands, away from the swamps and disease-ridden lowlands. Where possible, they sought land by a stream—a source of food, water, transportation and importantly, power for the mills, prevalent in a society just embarking on the Industrial Revolution.

There were Indians, too. Just a few years before, both sides had resorted to the most savage combat, with torture and scalping condoned by both British and Continentals. But the Indians abided by the treaties. They accepted the white man, traded with him, and intermarried. The fear of continuing neighborhood conflict evaporated.

The new settlers moved in from Albany and New England to the east; and from the south through Pennsylvania. They used waterways as far as they could, breasting the Susquehanna and its tributaries, or coming via the Mohawk River and the Little Falls portage from Albany to Stanwix, then along the old military routes to Oswego, Onondaga Valley, and points west.

By the century's last decade, the movement was established. Men and women came into the Cortland-Homer area thirty miles to the south of Syracuse. John Hardenbergh and his family journeyed north from Pennsylvania to build the first crude dwelling in what is now Auburn. Ephraim Webster, a Revolutionary War legend who was to continue the life of a hero and adventurer for another twenty years, came to the land of the Onondagas, recruiting Asa Danforth and Comfort Tyler and their families along the way.

But before roads were built or mills constructed, there had to be more than wilderness.

Some settlers gravitated to salt, or "white gold"—that all-too-rare product which was then worth a fortune if you could get it to market. Comfort Tyler was among them, as was Moses DeWitt and, a few years later, James Geddes.

Others saw the potential in the rich soil.

Still others became the entrepreneurs of the day, providing goods and essential services. Would-be-millers like Tyler hauled the sections of their mills for flour, lumber or paper, over their shoulders dozens of miles across rough terrain.

But many came simply to get away from poverty or trouble. They became the laborers who cut the trees along the Syracuse swamps to fuel the salt kettles. They died by the score, victims of the prevalent "bilious fever," later recognized as malaria.

When arriving, the settler's first order of business was to construct a rude hut. Once shelter was provided, the pioneer felled nearby trees, so that a log house could go up. Although the floor was initially dirt, the thick walls provided a measure of warmth.

A split log floor often replaced dirt, but was seldom level. A board floor and glass windows were signs of wealth. Furniture was simple, with bedsteads often made of poles and strips of bark. Chairs were usually slabs split from logs with holes bored in the corners for rough legs to be inserted.

The old Indian standby, corn, was an important early crop, with wheat a basic as well. Squash and pumpkins were necessities. Flax was an essential fabric ingredient.

In the first days, dairy products often were rare, costly and of bad quality. Until ample pastures could be cleared and planted with good clover, the cattle foraged on weeds and leaves, a poor substitute. And they often disappeared into the woods for days at a time. Cows in many cases gave only a quart or two of milk a day, with the butterfat especially sorry.

Many farmers filled out their larder in much the same ways as the Indians—with nuts, berries, fish and game. Wild pigeons, which could cast shadows for hours at a time when their flocks of billions flew overhead, were manna to the early settlers, saving many from starvation in the early spring, and served as an important food source until they finally became extinct.

Something more was needed. Doctors, as primitive as their methods were, the educator and the spiritual leader were all essential. By 1793 the first physician, William Needham, settled in Onondaga Hollow. And, while the Roman Catholic church failed to follow up the missionary work of the Jesuits, the circuit preacher rode from community to community conducting Protestant services in homes, stores or even mills.

The fee schedule of the Tioga County Medical Society published in December 24, 1806 was typical of the price structure throughout Central New York:

Amputations: Femur, $25; os humeri, $20; reducing simple fracture, $5; reducing compund fracture, $6; dislocation femur, $8; dislocation os humerus, $10; lancing abcess, 50 cents to $3; introducing catheter, $1; trepanning, $20;

lithotomy, $30; introducing suture, 25 cents; obstetric operations, natural, $4; obstetric operations, preternatural, $5; introducing trocar, $2; reducing hernia, $5; amputating breast, $10; phymosis paraphimosis, $1; introducing the variola, $2; dressing wounds in general, 50 cents to $1; consultation with any gentleman of the profession, $5.

Getting to and from market, whether shipping fresh vegetables to a nearby town or salt and grain to the eastern centers, was a major concern once the primitive necessities of life were obtained. Highway routes were surveyed, many following Indian paths along the higher ridges. State funds were insufficient, so turnpikes were built by private enterprise. In 1790 and 1791 a party of pioneers under the direction of a General Wadsworth improved the Genesee Trail from Whitestown in the east near Utica, to Canandaigua. It passed through Skaneateles and Auburn, through Waterloo and Geneva, to Canandaigua Lake. Toll houses were set up every ten miles along the gravel and rock roadway. The toll for a two-horse vehicle was twelve and one-half cents; for four horses, twenty-five cents. Many roads were *corduroy*—tree trunks laid sideways, with dirt and rocks used as fill. They did little to add to comfort, nor did the droves of cattle and flocks of geese often escorted down the right-of-way by farmers en route to market.

The Cherry Valley Turnpike, now Route 20, was also laid out in 1800, connecting with the new Seneca Turnpike at Skaneateles.

Sometimes it would seem the roads sought out the steepest hills. Stories circulated that residents of hamlets would ply the surveyors with food and liquor to assure that the turnpike would pass through their communities. It was said that the route of the Seneca Turnpike was originally to go from Chittenango to Salina, but residents of Onondaga Valley, posing as natives of Chittenango, offered to serve as guides. They led the surveyors on a merry journey until the "one best way to go" was determined.

Villages like Nelson, Cazenovia, Manlius, Pompey, Onondaga Hill, Skaneateles and Auburn prospered and became population centers long before Syracuse was more than a swampy setting for a mill and a tavern. People avoided it like, and because of, the plague!

Early school commenced in the home, but was soon followed by the small log cabin and then the Little Red Schoolhouse in the Town of Salina, north of Syracuse, by 1805. In 1812 school districts were established throughout the state and the perennial fights between district and taxpayer began.

The gigantic County of Onondaga was too huge to last undivided. Interests were too divergent. For example, the port city of Oswego had little in common with Cortland or for that matter, Syracuse. By 1799 Cayuga broke away; Cortland in 1808 and Oswego by 1816. By the mid-1800s, the county was its present size.

Politically the region became active shortly after the state legislature formed the county in 1794. The careers of Asa Danforth, Comfort Tyler and other early settlers became enhanced by their political powers. Danforth, for example, was eventually to become superintendent of the newly created Salt Reservation, a judge, a state senator and an army general.

Tyler had grander things in mind. A state surveyor on the old road to Canandaigua, he became a tavern keeper, supervisor, coroner, sheriff and finally a state legislator, when he met Aaron Burr. He became a conspirator in the attempt by Burr to take over a chunk of Mississippi River territory and establish a new empire. Tyler escaped jail and eventually resumed his career as a road builder.

All was not completely quiet on the Oswego front. The British

Baron Frederick William Von Steuben (1730-1794) supervised construction of a fort in Salina in 1794. He was said to have stopped at a Manlius tavern run by John Shaeffer, the village's first settler. The noisy accommodations left the general sleepless, and he is said to have commented, "Your house is full of gossips and goblins, sir!... Your house isn't fit to stable swine." He changed his tune, however, when he learned the commotion was the result of the birth of Shaeffer's child. As a gesture of apology, the general gave the infant a deed to two hundred and fifty acres of his Oneida County property. Courtesy of New York State Historical Association

were still holding their position at Fort Ontario and occassioned considerable worry on the part of the local residents. In fact, fighting broke out between British, Indian and American troops in 1788, and Ephraim Webster, disguised as an Indian, talked his way into the fort and passed information back to the Americans. So great was the fear that Joseph Brant, Sir John Johnson and their colleagues would again attack, that in 1794 a blockhouse was built in the town of Salina under the supervision of Baron Frederick Von Steuben and several attendant generals. The fort, manned for a time by a detachment of grenadiers, eventually became a salt storehouse. It never saw combat.

In 1796 the Jay Treaty fixed the boundaries between the United States and Canada, and Oswego was finally ceded to the United States.

Salt was recognized at an early date as a valuable source of revenue by the state of New York, so that by 1795 it assumed full control over the salt lands, creating the state salt reservation, with William Stevens appointed the first salt superintendent two years

Cazenovia's history was somewhat different from that of other Central New York communities. In 1792, Theophilus de Cazenove, an agent for the Holland Land Company, bought one hundred twenty thousand acres of land in the highlands some thirty miles east of Syracuse along the state road to Canandaigua. John Lincklaen, shown above, a young Dutch naval officer on leave of absence, agreed to serve as field representative for de Cazenove and eventually became resident agent and land owner, laying out what he hoped would be a great commercial center. Courtesy of the Town of Cazenovia

later. Each manufacturer leased the surveyed lots, paying a duty of four cents for each fifty-six-pound bushel of processed salt. For those days the income was substantial. Fifty thousand bushels a year were shipped out during the last three years of the eighteenth century, a total doubled shortly afterward.

Two systems of salt production coexisted for many years. The boiling method, with the saline solution cooked in large boilers, used huge quantities of wood. This resulted in deforestation for miles around the brine wells. A more satisfactory system of solar evaporation was evolved. The brine was pumped into trays which were exposed to the sun. When rain threatened, a whistle was blown and covers were slid into place over the flat beds.

Other areas throughout the region were growing.

In 1791 Amos Todd, his wife and his brother-in-law, Joseph Beebe, found their way to what is now the village of Homer in Cortland County, building a rude home of poles and timber. Life could be uncertain and uncomfortable. One winter, Amos and Joseph had business in another section of the state, and were unable to return home for six weeks because of deep snow. Mrs. Todd was the sole white person within a radius of thirty miles!

Fayetteville's first settler was Cyrus Kinne, who came with his four sons in 1792 and established a blacksmith shop.

The first settler in the Brewerton area north of Syracuse was Oliver Stevens, who built a log cabin which served as home, store, hotel and eventually a tavern to accommodate boatmen, as well as an Indian trading post.

To the west, Captain John L. Hardenbergh, a tall veteran of Sullivan's campaign, came upon the rushing waters of the Owasco River in 1793 and decided this was the spot to establish a mill—and a community. He, his daughter and their two black slaves selected a spot for their cabin at what is now the fire headquarters on Market Street in downtown Auburn.

Hardenbergh held a church society meeting at his home in September 1796, which led to the erection of the Dutch Reformed Church at Brinkerhoff Point on Owasco Lake, the first church to be built west of Albany.

In 1800 the central part of Syracuse was a dense cedar forest. Pines and other forest trees grew on the occasional higher ground. Streams, ponds and bogs covered most of the area. Inroads were made slowly. By 1803 there were eight frame houses, a few log cabins, a post office and a court. Most of the sixty inhabitants were involved in salt production.

Transportation via the new turnpikes provided a way to market, but the going was arduous for travelers, with the stagecoach providing a painful alternative to walking. So difficult and uncomfortable were the journeys, especially in the winter, that country inns and taverns were established every few miles offering a fire, liquid refreshments, a questionable meal and, at night, a place to share a bed with one or two or more fellow travelers.

A couple of unique and innovative settlers made the difference in Syracuse's future—Joshua Forman, at attorney who had settled near the Onondaga Reservation in Onondaga Valley and James Geddes, a surveyor and engineer. Forman, a judge, was elected to the state legislature in 1807 on the Canal Platform. He carried on the idea which is attributed to Gouverneur Morris, who remarked, "Lake Erie must be tapped and its water carried over the country to the Hudson."

Forman in 1808 secured passage of a joint resolution calling for a survey of proposed routes—either a canal from Oneida Lake joining the Seneca River and leading to Oswego and then west, or any other route deemed feasible—a broad concept including a route independent of Lake Ontario.

James Geddes, a self-taught Pennsylvania farm boy, an engineer, an attorney, and eventually a judge was appointed to conduct the canal survey, to be made at a cost not exceeding six hundred dollars.

In 1809 the zealous Mr. Geddes submitted his report on three different routes, with a section strongly in favor of the interior route. He also traveled to Washington in the company of William Kirkpatrick, then an Oneida congressman, to talk to President Thomas Jefferson about the inland route.

According to W. W. Clayton's *History of Onondaga*, the president was a little more than cool to the idea, and said "You talk of making a canal 350 miles through a wilderness. It is a little short of madness to think of it at this day."

Even so, at Geddes' prodding, the state legislators continued to favor the inland route.

DeWitt Clinton was a state legislator, former mayor of New York City and the twice-elected governor of New York. The political acumen he had acquired assured any program he backed a good chance of passage. When he was named to the Canal Commission, little help was anticipated. But he surprised everyone by coming out staunchly in favor of the method as a cheap means of transportation, despite the concerns of many New York City interests.

Then, for the second time in thirty years, the uneasy peace between former colonials and the Crown broke into open conflict. And once again the events at Oswego were to have a major bearing on the outcome of hostilities. But, except for the production of war materiel and the provision of manpower, the inland area was relatively unscathed. British prisoners of war did march by, and the threat of attack was always there. The Onondagas, however, had cast their lot with the Americans, and Indian support was to prove an important benefit. Little happened at Fort Ontario itself until June of 1813, when a British fleet cannonaded the fortifications, then retired. To the west, the British crossed the Niagara at Black Rock in the winter of 1813, destroying Buffalo. The word got out that the British were advancing. A cavalry company was hurriedly formed in Central New York and rushed off toward the war zone. The settlers collected arms and set up a defense. It was only when the horsemen reached Canandaigua that they found the British advance was a myth.

The following year a British deserter blew his bugle as he approached Auburn from the west. Again the community was convinced the redcoats were on the way.

Meanwhile, numerous contingents from throughout Central New York proceeded to assemble, fighting throughout the campaigns to the west and north.

Sackett's Harbor to the north was an important Lake Ontario naval and shipbuilding base for the Americans. They managed to keep the installation provided with guns and ammunition, culminating with a British defeat at Sandy Creek. At one point a detail of eighty-four men carried five tons of ship's cable over their shoulders from Sandy Creek to the harbor, a distance of thirty miles.

During the war the frigate *Superior* (sixty-six guns) and the *Mohawk* and *Jones* were launched at Sackett's Harbor. A giant ship of the line, the *New Orleans*, was partially completed, but remained a hulk until sold to Syracuse businessman Alfred Wilkinson in 1883 for $427.50.

When the war was finally settled, the state could return its attention to more basic issues. The canal concept was once again on the agenda, with the inland route, safe from the possible inroads of hostile naval forces, gaining support. The needed funds were authorized by the state of New York, with Governor Clinton and State Senator Martin Van Buren teaming up to approve the Canal Act.

The job was tremendous in aspect. A total of 363 miles of canal had to be built, crossing twenty rivers, requiring eighty-three locks to rise approximately six hundred feet—all with just five million dollars and ten years to do it in.

In 1817 the building proceeded, with Governor Clinton wisely selecting the level land between Rome and Syracuse to begin digging. This assured an early favorable public progress report.

On July 4, a Judge Richardson, the canal's first contractor, turned the first spadeful of earth at appropriate ceremonies in what is now Rome. By December, fifteen miles had been completed. A resident of Onondaga Hill, Chauncey J. Parsons, is said to have made the first dig in Onondaga County.

Not everyone can win. The symbolic first turning of earth effectively buried the expansion dreams of dozens of high-road towns, while canal-level crossroads were to embark on their future growth to metropolitan centers—Utica and Rome; Syracuse;

DeRuyter's early settlers came in 1793 and 1794, arriving by horseback, oxcart, or on foot, mostly from New England via Utica and Cazenovia, via the Lincklaen West Road. John Lincklaen named the community after Admiral Michiel DeRuyter, shown above, the greatest of the Dutch naval officers who simultaneously split and defeated the French and English fleets in the Battle of Solebay. Courtesy of Tromptown Historical Society

Rochester and Buffalo being among the winners. Buffalo at the time had a population of seven hundred. Syracuse had far fewer.

The losers were communities along the turnpikes to the south, among them Cazenovia, Pompey, Manlius and Skaneateles. Oswego's bright outlook as the state's greatest city outside of New York was considerably diminished by the inland concept, although the Oswego Canal would eventually provide it with access to the center of the state. The construction of the Welland Canal along the Niagara frontier several decades later, at first thought to be a boon to Oswego, proved most advantageous to Buffalo.

Communities such as Oneida, Canastota, Weedsport and Port Byron were early benefactors as the movement of people and goods began, with the *Montezuma*, the first boat, arriving in Syracuse on April 21, 1820.

In a few years it took only $7.50 a ton to ship goods across the state in just eight days. Previously it required twenty days at a cost of $100 to reach the same destinations.

But construction was not without a price. "French powder," a second-rate gunpowder which sometimes hang-fired, caused

22

many casualties until the new DuPont blasting powder was introduced, dramatically reducing casualties and time.

The canal continued into the Montezuma swamp area, a land of muck and mire between Port Byron and Waterloo. Progress was in inches as thousands of laborers, among them Irishmen imported for the occasion, worked waist-deep building side walls. Free whisky was one factor that helped them keep going. But it did not keep them from dying.

Malaria hit in the hot, fetid summer months. In August 1819 alone, more than a thousand died. Even the most heartless of contractors could not face up to the toll. So, until the September frosts killed off the mosquitoes, work stopped. Once the malaria vanished, the work could be continued.

Other surprises surfaced. When the canal was first filled, in what is now Syracuse, the water disappeared into the ground as it neared the Salina Street area. For a time it appeared that the whole project was in danger. But then it was learned that the porous nature of the soil was confined to a few feet below the surface. Once the area was dug out, filled with blue clay and then tamped down—a method the British in England had pioneered years before—the problem abated.

Another problem was early cement used in lock construction. It was proving useless because it did not harden well under water. Providentially a hydraulic form of cement was found near Chittenango, and the crisis averted.

In the fall of 1825 Governor Clinton and an entourage of several boats proceeded down the length of the canal with barrels of water from Lake Erie to blend with the Atlantic off New York City.

It was a triumphal procession, complete with cannon fire denoting the boat's progress at each community. At Weedsport on October 29, the celebration turned to tragedy as a 24-pounder accidentally discharged, killing the two gunners, David Remington and Henry Whitman.

The Central New York region was veined with dozens of feeder streams and canals which either met the water needs of the Erie's lock system or provided shipping access to communities on lakes and rivers across the state. Construction of the Cayuga and Seneca Canal began in 1826, with twelve locks descending from Geneva to Montezuma. Other connections tied in Fayetteville and Marcellus with the canal and provided access between lakes. And in 1828 the Oswego Canal opened from Syracuse, offering a direct access to Lake Ontario and international shipping. (The canal did not actually achieve full operation until the following spring.)

As could be expected, almost before it was finished the "Clinton Ditch" was too small to accommodate its traffic demands and by the mid-1830s plans called for a seventy-foot-wide improved Erie Canal with high berms (or sides) which would overcome spring flooding. It was not finished, however, until 1863.

But the day of both the canal and the stage was already setting. The earliest steam engines had already been proved. The *Claremont* had sailed up the Hudson. And people were talking about steam-powered railed vehicles.

With their canal mission successfully completed, Joshua Forman and James Geddes became involved in a new project, that of draining the unhealthy swamps in downtown Syracuse and along the shore of Onondaga Lake. Salt workers by the score died each year from malaria. The problem was the annual flooding of the lowlands around the lake caused by obstacles which blocked the lake's overflow into the Seneca River. This resulted in a backup of Onondaga Creek into the Walton Tract and other low-lying areas. Through Forman-Geddes pressure, the legislature put up the $4,500 needed to deepen and clear the channel. Thousands of acres were thus made available for settlement; the primary health problem was overcome, and Syracuse became a place to live.

But much still had to be done. Decades passed before all of the ravines, stagnant ponds and streams such as Yellow Brook were cleared and downtown streets paved. Eventually even the pond which occupied the present site of the Jefferson Street Armory was filled with dirt from the top of Prospect Hill, now the location of St. Joseph's Hospital.

Previously logs and brush were used as fill for downtown thoroughfares, making the shortest journey an ordeal. As late as 1847, quicksand made travel for heavy wagons a dangerous undertaking along West Onondaga Street. At Onondaga and Seymour Streets one horse was mired up to its neck after a heavy rain and was rescued only after strenuous digging.

But that was the beginning of a prosperous community. Hotels, taverns and workers' dwellings were joined by varied businesses, many, such as the Forman law offices, moving in from more healthful Onondaga Valley and the surrounding highlands. Brick-making, mills of all sorts, the development of a barrel-making industry to package the processed salt, all provided more jobs. Even the Onondaga County Court House, first located at Onondaga Hill, was brought near the village, being located at Ash and North Salina Streets.

Many residences were already taking on a prosperous air— white houses of one and a half to two stories with picket fences, green lawns and shrubbery. Brick sidewalks were common.

It was time the community received a permanent name. *Bogardus*, or *Cossitt's Corners* did not quite fit. *Corinth* was a likely name, recommended by Joshua Forman, but the Post Office refused to accept it because another community within the state had already adopted it.

John Wilkinson, a graduate of Onondaga Academy, came up with another suggestion—*Syracuse*.

By 1824, the village with the new name of Syracuse was ready to celebrate the Fourth of July—on July 5.

Lorenzo, the stately 1807 federal-style mansion of the Lincklaen and Ledyard families at the southeast edge of Cazenovia Lake, reflects the expectations of the early settlers for the future of the area. It is now a museum. Courtesy of Cazenovia Library

23

This account appeared in the *Syracuse Gazette* two days later:

At the morn's early dawn the day was ushered in by the thunder of cannon bursting upon the stillness of the hour; and at sunrise a National Salute was fired from Prospect Hill, on the north side of the village. As the spiring columns of the cannon's smoke disappeared the star spangled banner of our country was then seen floating majestically in the air, from the top of a towering staff erected on the summit of this hill for the occasion. At about 12 o'clock, a procession was formed in front of Mr. Williston's Hotel, under the direction of Col. A. P. Granger, marshal of the day. An escort, consisting of Captain Rossiter's company of Light Horse, an Artillery Company under the command of Lieut. J. D. Rose, and Capt. H. W. Dunford's company of Riflemen, with their music swelling and banners flying, preceded the procession which moved to the new meeting house—(the old Baptist Church). Here the usual exercises took place, and an oration was pronounced by J. R. Sutermeister, Esq., which was received by the large assemble with a universal burst of approbation. The procession then formed again and moved through the village to the summit of Prospect Hill, where under a bower a numerous company partook of a cold collation prepared by Mr. Williston (landlord of the Mansion House).

It was a truly interesting sight to see among our fellow citizens who participated in the festivities of this day, about thirty of the remnant of that gallant band of patriots who fought in the revolution. These spared monuments of our country's boast honored the company with their presence throughout the day, giving zest to the festivities rarely to be found in common celebration of this National Anniversary.

Upstate New York was entering its period of greatest growth.

An arsenal along the eastern hillside of Seneca Turnpike, extreme right, served American needs during the war of 1812. In this painting by George K. Knapp, British forces captured at the Battle of Lundy's Lane march from the west en route to prison camps in the east, while valley residents and Onondaga Indians watch. Nicholas Mickles' furnace, at the present location of Elmwood Park, supplied cannon balls and shells which were transported by wagon to Salina and then by boat to Oswego for further distribution at the frontier. Secretary of War John Armstrong, who believed in the inviolability of maps, pulled one of the classic gaffes in military history. He ordered a naval vessel up the "Onondaga River" from Oswego to Onondaga Valley to pick up a shipment of shot. The ship got no further than Oswego Falls (now Fulton). Courtesy of Onondaga County Historical Association

It was in May 1814 that the British,
with a force of nine hundred men captured
and sacked Fort Ontario. The Americans,
three hundred strong, were in no position to
resist effectively, so after an initial skirmish
they retreated in good order, with minimal
losses, to reform at Fulton as a defense for
the stores there. The British failed to follow
up their advantage. Courtesy of Fort Ontario
State Park

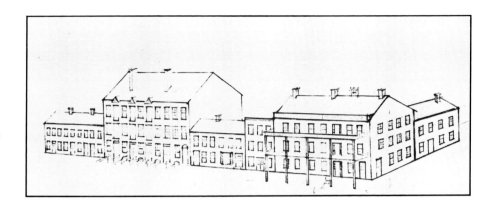

This rendering of early downtown Syracuse shows the buildings facing Clinton Square along the north side of West Genesee Street. The building at the right corner is Williston's Mansion House, with an extension along North Salina Street. The large building, second from left, is the Marvin Block.

In 1804 Abram Walton purchased two hundred and fifty acres of downtown land from the state for sixty-five hundred dollars, the proceeds from the sale earmarked by the state for developing the Genesee Turnpike through the area, which eventually was to link Utica with the west along much of the Erie Canal route. The community became known as Bogardus Corners, named after the keeper of a saloon on what is now the north side of Clinton Square. Courtesy of Onondaga County Historical Association

The old red mill at Onondaga Creek near West Genesee Street is believed to be the earliest downtown bulding. It was probably a flour mill. Art from H. C. Hand, Syracuse From a Forest to a City

Shown here is the Syracuse House as it appeared in the 1830s. It was located at the southeast corner of East Genesee and South Salina Streets—now the site of the Onondaga Savings Bank.

The Syracuse House served for many years as the center of Syracuse life; it hosted the earliest meetings on establishing railroads, housed a number of political conventions, and was headquarters for the first New York State Fair in 1841.

The church at the extreme left of the picture is St. Paul's, the area's first Episcopal church. It was later moved and renamed St. Mary's when it became the first Catholic church in the village of Syracuse. Art from H. C. Hand, From a Forest to a City

Elkanah Watson, a New York banker, had gone to Paris during the Revolution as an aide to Benjamin Franklin. He carefully studied Dutch and French canals, and when he returned home he was a firm believer in the constructed waterway as the ideal system to navigate the nation. At his own expense in 1788 he went from Albany on foot to explore a route and published a pamphlet depicting the value of a canal to the communities west of Albany. In 1791 Watson and several companions explored Central New York and its water route potential. An offshoot of this enthusiasm was the development of a lock system at Little Falls to bypass the obstruction which previously required an expensive portage west to Fort Stanwix. Shipping costs dropped dramatically. Courtesy of Erie Canal Museum

Joshua Forman (1777-1848), a native of Pleasant Valley in Dutchess County who moved to Onondaga Hollow in 1800 to open a law office, was a prime force behind legislative approval for the Erie Canal, and a founder of today's Syracuse through the purchase and development of what is now downtown. Courtesy of Onondaga County Public Library

The painting below, which appeared on the official first-day cover for the 1967 postage stamp commemorating the 150th anniversary of the Erie Canal, shows the ground-breaking ceremony at the beginning of the canal on July 4, 1817, as interpreted in the 1960s by artist J. Erwin Porter of Penfield, New York. After Judge Joshua Hathaway, representing the citizens of Rome, gave a speech, he placed the spade in the hands of a Judge Richardson, the first contractor of the Erie Canal, who thrust the spade into the ground.

The Erie Canal Commemorative stamp was designed by George Samerjan, a New York City artist, who also designed the Adlai Stevenson stamp of 1965 and the Arctic Exploration stamp of 1959. It was modeled by Robert J. Jones and engraved by Howard F. Sharpless of the Bureau of Engraving and Printing. Courtesy of the Onondaga Savings Bank

Although easier than stagecoach travel, boat passage required patience and a willingness to put up with hardships and indignities. The boat's cabin space was shared with the captain, his family and the spare horses or mules used to tow the boat. The communal dining table served at nightfall as someone's bed. Meals were plain, repetitious and heavy—pork or beef, potatoes, turnips, bread, pudding and coffee, served steaming hot regardless of outside temperatures. Cabins were narrow and fetid. The only pastime consisted of watching the world pass by, with constant awareness that there was only a six-inch clearance between the roof and the average bridge. The bridges did not discriminate between male and female passengers; the unwary of either sex could wind up with a sore head and a dumping. All of this for four cents a mile, meals included. Cooking in a canal boat cabin required deft handling in a narrow, combustible space. Courtesy of Onondaga County Historical Association

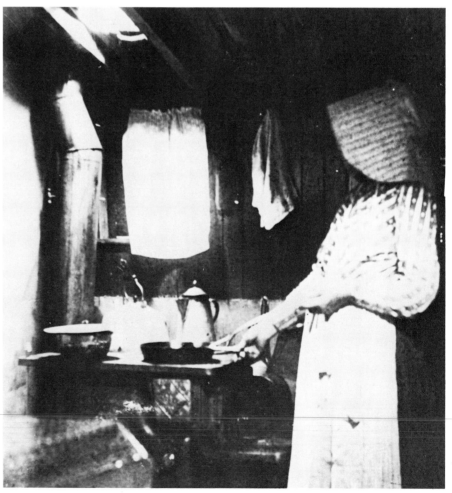

Laundering was a fair-weather sport when the upper deck provided a clothesline. The tillerman's task was boring yet essential. Courtesy of Onondaga County Historical Association

Jethro Wood, a native of Saratoga County who moved to Cayuga County in 1799, invented the iron plow. The significance of his invention was so great that Wood, who died in 1834 at the age of fifty-six, received letters of appreciation from President Thomas Jefferson, and Russia's Tsar Alexander. Courtesy of Cayuga County Historian's Office

The iron plow patented by Cayuga County resident Jethro Wood enabled the world to substantially increase its food production, freeing up millions of workers for factory jobs during the Industrial Revolution. Courtesy of Cayuga County Historian's Office

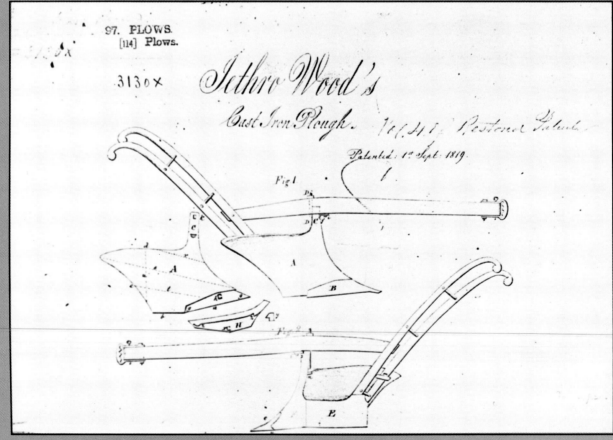

While in New York City, John Wilkinson was impressed with a poem written by Edward Stanley which had won the Chancellor's Prize at Oxford University. Entitled "Syracuse," it described Ortygia, the predecessor of the ancient Sicilian city of Syracuse. Wilkinson did additional research and discovered there was much in common between the Syracuse in Sicily and the village by Onondaga Lake—both had neighboring lakes of a similar size; both had marsh lands and a mix of salt and fresh water. And in both New York and Italy, there was suspicion that underground passages led to the salt deposits. There was even a town north of the Sicilian city named Salina. Through Wilkinson's efforts the name Syracuse was adopted by the village, which had previously been called Bogardus Corners and Corinth. Courtesy of Onondaga County Public Library

A view of the ancient city of Syracuse, Sicily shows the similarity to the typography of New York's Syracuse and its neighboring Onondaga Lake. The amphitheatre is in the foreground. Art from H. C. Hand, Syracuse From a Forest to a City

This toll booth was located on the plank road leading from North Syracuse to Cicero. The hemlock planks (on hills soft maple was used instead), were generally eight feet wide and four inches thick. For each mile 168,980 feet of plank, laid crosswise, and 14,080 feet of four-inch stringers were required, the latter embedded in the ground. The planked west side of the road was for loaded wagons, while the return side was dirt. The toll road had four gates, with a charge of five cents for horses, a penny per head of cattle and twenty cents for a horse-drawn wagon.

This road continued to operate until April 11, 1913, with bicycle races a feature in later years. Other roads were constructed between Auburn and Cato and as a connecting link for dozens of other communities across America. Photo by A. B. Wraught, courtesy of Erie Canal Museum

Growing Up
1830-1865

By 1830 Central New York was developing into a chain of politically and economically maturing communities linked by the Erie Canal, its feeders and criss-crossing turnpikes which joined the region to the coastal cities of the east and south.

The early settlers had to make room for the waves of migrants offering labor, ideas—and sometimes trouble. The supporters of the canal and highway were gradually replaced by the railroader, the mercantilist and the banker.

Tiers of society built up. The Formans, the Geddeses and the Wilkinsons moved from cabins to colonial-style mansions. The middle class arose from the supervisor and small-store owner.

The laboring classes lived in shanty cities near the salt wells. Along the canal, roustabouts, gamblers and denizens of what in Syracuse were known as "Robbers' Roosts" along lower James Street near Salina, mingled with canaleers and warehouse workers. A constabulary was formed in 1826 under H. W. Dunford to deal with the resultant problems. Local laws and ordinances outlawing billiard playing and gambling were invoked.

Enterprising young men were entering the job field.

Millard Fillmore's birthdate was on February 7, 1800, in a log cabin near Moravia, southeast of Auburn. Despite his rise to the presidency, he never quite achieved the fame of another chief executive who had a February birth in a log cabin. During Fillmore's boyhood he spent much of his time near Skaneateles Lake, later teaching school in the area. Fillmore served as the thirteenth president, from 1850 to 1853.

John D. Rockefeller, born on July 8, 1839, in southern Cayuga County, made his first move into capitalism by raising a flock of turkeys from a pair he found in the woods. He kept his earnings in a china bowl. Ezra Cornell was raised in the vicinity of DeRuyter, beginning his career by stringing wires for the Western Union Telegraph Company.

The first awakenings of social consciousness involved welfare and the abolitionist movement, which eventually swelled to vigorous Central New York support of the Union cause during the Civil War.

The early settlers, many primarily of English descent with a New England background, adopted the English system of accepting some responsibility for the pauper: something—but not necessarily too much—had to be done to help.

Before 1826 auctions were held in which the poor were turned over to the person who agreed to care for him, or her, for the lowest fee the county would pay for the pauper's upkeep. In turn, the "buyer" expected to get as much work as possible out of the individual. A bottle of whisky passed about by the Poormaster helped liven the auction and save the county fee money.

As Dr. Robert Bogdan has indicated, humanitarianism was blended with frugality and a strong work ethic in arriving at this plan. And, while pioneers were willing to support local residents who came on hard times, vagrants and strangers were escorted out of town. The arrangement eventually ended when a system of county poorhouses was instituted.

The economic viability of the territory depended to a great extent upon the availability of funds to support growth, to encourage thrift and investment, and to enable money to be transferred. Central New York had banking as early as 1813, when the Ontario Bank in Canandaigua came into being with Nathaniel Gorham as president. The Auburn-Cayuga National Bank and Trust Company, predecessor of the Auburn Bank, opened in 1817. Then in 1832 the banking movement in Central New York was enhanced by the opening of the Bank of Salina, founded by Henry Wells, who was later, with C. D. Fargo, also a Central New Yorker, to establish the Wells-Fargo Express Company. Wells was also the principal backer of Wells College, founded in 1868, which is located at Aurora in Cayuga County.

The Erie Canal also brought a banking bonanza to many communities along the route, as each toll station required a secure depository for its collected funds.

Banking in the early days was perilous. Panics would wipe out fortunes overnight, while others became wealthy by charging five percent interest—monthly.

Many problems could have been avoided, but conflict between President Andrew Jackson and Congress resulted in his veto of the United States Bank Bill in 1837. State and private banks multiplied, often liquidating in short order. The resultant confusion lasted to 1840. Prices inflated. Other panics occurred as speculation in railroad lands and other risky enterprises developed.

The federal government finally succeeded in establishing the National Bank Act in 1863, which brought the modern concept of banking to the United States and enabled the Union to successfully finance the Civil War.

It was also the day of the technologist. People were becoming

By 1825 Cayuga County had a poorhouse, so in 1826 the Onondaga County Board of Supervisors recommended locating one on Onondaga Hill. The poorhouse system was a predominant form of relief for the next eighty years. It saved money, and the poor—whether they were widows (often of well-to-do persons before the days of insurance), unwed mothers, the tubercular, blind, or feeble-minded, the alcoholic, or the insane, orphans or the old—were out of sight and out of mind. In 1857 the census in Onondaga showed 534 inmates, 49 deaths and 11 births; 155 were children under sixteen, 110 persons over fifty; 25 insane; 23 blind; 20 "idiotic and fits," and 105 crippled or helpless. Of all these, more than three hundred were of foreign birth. Courtesy of Onondaga County Public Library

interested in combining a steam engine with a drive mechanism to propel it along a track. Such contraptions, which pulled stagecoaches mounted on flanged wheels over wooden rails, were proving practical in the Baltimore area and in Great Britain. But they were dirty, dangerous, noisy and relatively slow, although not as slow as the stagecoach.

The earliest local application of the rail principle was the incorporation in 1829 of a company to build a horse-drawn line from Onondaga Lake to Syracuse and Onondaga Hollow, then to Homer and Cortland. The trains were to run downhill by gravity, carrying aboard the horses which would pull them up the next hill. But the scheme was never carried out.

However, in 1831, the first state railroad convention ever held was called to order in Syracuse on October 12.

The meeting at the Syracuse House drew delegates from throughout the state. The Syracuse committee members included some familiar names, among them John Wilkinson, now an assemblyman, and Moses D. Burnet, an early banker. The committee passed a resolution calling for a railroad line from Schenectady to Buffalo, passing through Utica and Salina.

By May 1, 1834, the Auburn and Syracuse railroad was incorporated, and two years later the Syracuse and Utica road was chartered. Still, no tracks were in sight.

It was on January 8, 1838, that the Auburn and Syracuse line opened with horse-drawn cars. But it was not until June of the following year that the first steam-powered engine moved through Central New York. The little lines—Auburn and Syracuse, Syracuse and Utica, and the Oswego and Syracuse railroad, were gradually linked together in what by 1853 was the New York Central, connecting Albany with Buffalo.

The train wagons were scarcely larger than the stagecoach, although twenty-four passengers could be carried in each car. In the very first open flat coaches, benches ran crosswise. The roofs were the umbrellas carried by passengers. Sparks from the engine threatened not only travelers, but dry fields and track-side buildings. The iron straps secured to the tops of the wooden rails sometimes worked loose from the rails. The pressure of the car wheels going over them caused the strap to curl up. On occasion the end of the iron band snapped upward through the wooden car floor in what became known as a *snakehead*—a situation not completely alleviated for almost ten years until iron rails universally replaced wood.

As an added incentive to rail travel, passengers sometimes had to join bucket brigades to get water from ditches or wells for the engine tank.

The rail movement was epochal. Canal boats soon were relegated to carrying bulk cargo while the railroad engines, constantly being enlarged, handled passengers, freight and mail quickly and in relative comfort at competitive rates. The day of the long-distance stage was ended. By 1860 streetcars were making commuting easier, with the first horsecars carrying passengers in Syracuse from West Willow to Wolf Street. And significantly, America had a new way to go to war which was to eventually revolutionize the entire concept of land warfare.

Speaking of combat, Oswego served once again as a jumping-off point for a military adventure, known as the Patriot's War, the last against Canada. A group of New Yorkers, including thirty from Onondaga County, illegally joined in an 1837 rebellion by Canadians against British rule. The American contingent was led by P. Schuyler Stone, a Salina chemist, with Niles Gustaf Von

Schoultz second in command.

The group went to Oswego, engaging two schooners and a steamer to carry the force, which, after stops at Sackett's Harbor and other ports, numbered seven hundred.

General J. Ward Birge of Cazenovia was in overall command, but because of a fortuitous illness, turned command over to Von Schoultz. By the time the order to land at Prescott had gone out, only 170 men remained. A grounding of one of the ships further slowed the expedition, and Von Schoultz, with two artillery pieces, set up his forces on high ground surmounted by a large stone windmill.

By this time a detachment of regular army troops from Sackett's Harbor had arrived on the American side and prevented reinforcements from joining the insurgents. Von Schoultz tried to retreat, but the British attacked, and after several days of bloody skirmishes the invaders were captured. Colonel Von Schoultz, Martin Woodruff and Christopher Buckley of Salina were executed; the others imprisoned.

Recreation was limited at a time when the work week was commonly six days, from dawn to dusk. Even so, some unoccupied people managed to get into trouble. In 1844 the village fathers of Syracuse ordained that it was unlawful to keep or maintain "any ball alley, or apparatus, alley, machine, building or enclosure, constructed or used for the purpose of playing thereon or therewith at the game called or known by the name of nine pins, for gain, hire, reward or emolument of any kind, or in any kind or in any manner whatsoever." Playing billiards or pool and any games of chance or betting were also illegal.

The theater did thrive, commencing with the use of second-floor ballrooms of local taverns and hotels as platforms for concerts, lectures and plays.

Circuses featuring racing ostriches, performing elephants, reindeer, chariot events and menageries vied with gaily colored canal packet boat museums and showboats.

Ice skating in winter and boat cruises along the canal in summer benefited residents the entire length of the Erie and its feeders.

William Kirk's Syracuse tavern was popular for its great German Musical Machine which could be seen for just twelve and one-half cents: Arranged in galleries were 128 figures, all of which could be set in motion at one time; two lions reared up to the sound of music; two rope dancers on a tightrope kept time to the rhythm; a military band and figures of distinguished members of European royalty promenaded with their queens; a corps of light infantry and cavalry marched; a dancing party was surrounded by applauding spectators; laborers and mechanics—blacksmiths, coopers, woodcutters, women spinners did their work; and there was a beautiful garden in which children walked and played. All to the tune of twenty airs and waltzes!

Serving as a counterbalance to the roughneck aspects of the canal paths and railroad right-of-way with their saloons, bawdy houses and flophouses were the establishment of permanent churches for many denominations. Following the days of the circuit rider and the itinerant preacher who held services wherever he could collect a gathering, a period of church construction commenced. Other Central New York communities built their churches years before Syracuse. The Skaneateles Baptist Society Greek Revival structure went up in 1808; the Niagara Presbyterian Church in 1803.

The first church to be built in Syracuse was in 1822, when Presbyterians began meeting at a church built by salt-worker

Lewis H. Redfield, above, founded the Onondaga Register, *the first area newspaper to chronicle local events. The initial edition came off the press on September 17, 1814, strongly supporting the Erie Canal concept and Jeffersonian democracy. Competing papers were soon founded in and near Syracuse, including the* Gazette, *the first Syracuse paper, in 1823. An Auburn paper is known to have existed by 1847, with Auburn's daily of today, the* Citizen, *being founded in 1905. In Oswego, the* Palladium *was initially published in 1845, and the* Cortland Standard's *first issue came off the press in 1867. Courtesy of Onondaga County Public Library*

dollars. The story is told that when the contractor for this church was not paid on time, he decided to traumatize the congregation into action. A number of derelicts were enticed to take turns ringing the bell on a continuing basis. The reward was said to have been a sip from a bottle, at which time the bell ringer would return to the end of the line. The bill was soon paid.

The Baptists built in 1824 at West Genesee and Franklin streets. This congregation was eventually located as the First Baptist Church at Jefferson and Montgomery streets.

The first St. Paul's Episcopal Church was constructed in 1826 where the SA & K (Sedgwick, Andrews and Kennedy) Building currently stands.

Catholicism, which had its beginnings in Central New York with the Jesuits, did not thrive during the English period. At first Catholics, like other church people, met in the homes of fellow believers. It was not until 1829 that the Roman Catholic church had a meeting place of its own, built on land on North Salina Street donated by Thomas McCarthy.

Methodists, too, first located in private homes before building at East Onondaga and South State Streets. Their tower was built over the objections of Charles Pease, a cobbler and an especially devout Christian who opened his home to the first meetings. He believed the steeple was all vanity. And he was twice vindicated. It fell during construction, and then was struck by lightning.

The stagecoaches were often crowded, with passengers sitting on top of the roof. Stiff, hair-stuffed leather seats did little to add to the ease of travel. Springs were nonexistent, and the rolling motion of the coach body, suspended from the wheels by leather straps, was enough to make the hardiest sick. When the coaches arrived in early Syracuse, the horses were kept on a tight rein, for if they strayed off the road, they would soon sink up to their shoulders in the mire or frog ponds bordering downtown. H. C. Hand in his autobiographical book, Syracuse From a Forest to a City, carries the ditty of the coachman:

He tightens the reins and whirls off
with a fling
From the roof of the coach his ten feet
of string;
Now lightly he flicks the "nigh"
leader's left ear,
Gives the wheelers a neighborly slap
with the stock,
They lay back their ears as the coach
gives a rock
And strike a square trot in the tick
of a clock!

There's a jumble, a jar and a
gravelly trill
In the craunch of the wheels on the
slate-stone hill
That grind up the miles like a grist
in a mill.
He touches the bay and he talks
to the brown,
Sends a token of silk, a word
and a frown
To the filly whose heels are too
light to stay down.

Courtesy of Richard Palmer

The earliest Jewish congregation was the Society of Concord, which established its first temple in the Syracuse community in the early 1840s, to be followed in 1844 by Beth Israel, representing the European Jewish community.

The abolitionist movement began as a gentle breeze, gathering strength until it became a full-blown storm by mid-century.

In 1810, 153 blacks resided in Onondaga County, of whom 41 were slaves who lived with their white owners. The region initially accepted slavery as a way of life, practiced by some friends and neighbors. Then some had second thoughts.

Mrs. Caroline Hargin recalled that her father, Gen. John Ellis, had traveled from Onondaga to Virginia to buy four slaves to work on the farm—Sam, Cries, Peter and Chloe. They were liberated by Mrs. Ellis after the general's death.

Other prominent settlers, including Jasper Hopper and a Judge Curtis, kept slaves. Pompey had its slaves, as did residents of Jamesville. Judge Joshua Forman also owned an elderly slave, but made provisions for her when he died. James Geddes is also said to have owned several slaves.

But by 1830, slavery had ceased to exist locally.

Most residents were not really interested in the issue, especially in 1835 when Gerrit Smith, a wealthy Peterboro philanthropist (he was believed to have given financial aid to John Brown), William Lloyd Garrison and other abolitionists met in Syracuse to form an antislavery society. They found strong opposition from John Wilkinson, Vivus Smith and other local leaders who frowned on the society's concept of disobedience to the law.

Local churches split on the issue. Coming out strongly in favor of the abolitionist cause was Samuel J. May, of the Church of the Messiah, who arrived in Syracuse in 1845. He was to become the conscience of the abolitionist movement.

Daniel Webster appeared in Syracuse in 1851 to speak before local residents from the balcony on the east side of the Courier Building. (The corner structure still stands west of City Hall at Montgomery and East Genesee Streets). He addressed his remarks to abolitionists in the crowd who had met earlier at Market Hall.

"Let me tell you, as often as you meet in convention in that hall and pass the resolutions you did (to break the federal fugitive slave laws), it is treason! It is treason!"

Little attention was paid to the warning.

The fugitive slave statute raised some new issues, holding people who helped a fugitive liable to six months in jail and a thousand-dollar fine. The antislavery society promised resistance.

The opportunity came on October 1, 1851, with the arrest and subsequent freeing of a slave refugee called Jerry (his real name was William Henry), who came from Missouri to Syracuse, where he found work in a cooper's shop through the efforts of supportive townsmen.

Another celebrated slave incident had occurred in 1839 when J. Davenport, a wealthy Mississippi planter and his wife arrived at the Syracuse House accompanied by Harriet Powell, a maid of exceptional beauty, who appeared to be an equal to her mistress. Gossip began that she was a slave. Several black servants at the Syracuse House suggested she escape.

Some local people assisted in the getaway. Harriet Powell was escorted to the home of a Mrs. Sheppard near Marcellus, a station on the Underground Railroad to Canada. An alarm was sounded. An Oswego-bound packetboat was stopped and searched. Spies kept the homes of Gerrit Smith at Peterboro and James C. Fuller at Skaneateles under surveillance.

The career of stagecoach driver Jason C. Woodruff rivaled the legends of Horatio Alger. As a young man with training as a blacksmith, Woodruff left his native New England with eight cents in his pocket. He landed in Utica, commenced driving stagecoaches and became the line's manager. Then he went into milling, banking, and the livery business, succeeding in each. In 1852 Woodruff was elected mayor of the city of Syracuse. Courtesy of Onondaga County Public Library

Harriet was passed from safe house to safe house until arriving at Kingston, Canada. Despite an abortive attempt to kidnap her, she married and raised a successful family. The Davenports were said to have gone bankrupt a year after the incident.

In 1841, Jermain Wesley Loguen, born a slave in Tennessee, arrived to pastor the AME Zion Church, founded in the same year. So successful was Loguen in his efforts to transport runaway slaves that Syracuse became known as "the Canada of the United States."

Many white persons joined in the effort. In fact, the president of the Syracuse and Utica Railroad gave orders to stop the train if a fugitive was put aboard to be returned to the south, take off his irons and set him at liberty.

It would be impossible to explore the antislavery movement in Central New York without mention of Harriet Tubman, an Auburnian who was born a slave in Maryland about 1821 and who served as a leader in the Underground Railroad and as an active participant in the black movement in the Civil War.

Abolitionism was only one aspect of Central New York's political precociousness. In addition to the moves which led to the freedom for slaves and adventures into Canada, the Syracuse area makes not one, but several claims, that it, and not Jackson, Michigan, or Ripon, Wisconsin, was truly the place where the Republican Party was formed.

Gen. Amos P. Granger of Syracuse wrote and offered a series of resolutions in the Auburn Whig Convention of 1853 which could be termed as fomenting the G.O.P. ideals.

It has been said also that the idea was conceived under a great tree at the Syracuse home of Vivus W. Smith on the southeast corner of West Onondaga Street and South Avenue. Horace Greeley, Thurlow Weed and others were meeting at the time with Smith for a series of political discussions.

Then, at the Rowe Hotel in Camillus on January 27, 1852, a call went out to form the Free Soil party to oppose the fugitive slave law. The party nominated David Allen Munro for supervisor. It was heralded in later years as the first Republican meeting preceding the organization of the party at Jackson, Michigan, in 1854. The next year Munro was nominated and elected to the State Assembly on the Free Soil ticket.

An upcoming community of eleven thousand in the midst of farm country, Syracuse's location on both railroad and canal established it as a logical site for the first New York State Fair in 1841.

Elkanah Watson and James LeRay DeChaumont of Jefferson County were successful in parenting the New York State Agricultural Society in 1832. Nine years later, in 1841, the state legislature finally came through with the eight thousand dollars for the "promotion of agriculture and household manufactures in the State" through an annual fair. The two-day event was held on September 29 and 30.

A suitable fair site, with the old two-story Onondaga County Court House serving as the exhibit hall, was located in a square bounded today by North Salina, Division, Townsend and Ash Streets. The new wooden railroad depot on Vanderbilt Square in downtown Syracuse provided a center for award presentations. And the Syracuse House was the focal point for lodging, banquets and speeches.

The high-spirited gathering was held despite a crushing ordeal for Syracusans, who had suffered the worst catastrophe in its history just two months earlier when a tremendous warehouse explosion, felt in Fulton, fifteen miles away, killed thirty persons and injured scores of others.

The fair, a tremendous success, attracted between ten and fifteen thousand spectators; the railroad proved its worth by bringing in hundreds of livestock from Albany and points east. As President Joel Nott of the State Agricultural Society said, it exceeded the most sanguine expectations.

The event, which was to go on the road for the next half century, came back to Central New York in 1846 with a successful exhibition in Auburn on a tract at Capital Hill, a location named because of that community's hopes of serving as the State Capital. (Syracuse had similar aspirations in 1850, with the Prospect Hill site to the northeast of downtown suggested. Neither Central New York suggestion was taken, and Albany remained the capital.)

Then in 1849 the James Street Hill, a mile from Clinton Square in Syracuse, became the fair site, with Vice President Millard Fillmore and a popular political favorite, Kentucky's Henry Clay, guests of honor.

The hilltop location at what is today Highland Street, featured a spectacular first, the erection of a fifty-foot-high ferris wheel dominating the grounds.

The fair did not return to this region until 1858, when a grounds was selected along Onondaga Creek a mile south of the Syracuse business center. Daily attendance was close to twenty thousand despite rain, with a tent city sporting all sorts of midway shows and amusements sprouting up outside the fair itself. Former presidents Martin Van Buren and Millard Fillmore took their turns on the rostrum.

The first glimpse into the future for the fair came in an editorial in the Syracuse *Daily Standard* suggesting the state could do worse than select Syracuse as a permanent site.

Central New York in the 1840s was an innovative place. The Syracuse region was notorious for its poor road system, with

The early locomotive cab was open to the weather. Some engines had crude frames on which oilcloth could be stretched to protect the driver from rain, sun or snow. Snow itself was a tremendous problem until the engine plow was developed.

Here a railroad fan admires the engine of the DeWitt Clinton, the first locomotive on the New York Central, during a Syracuse exhibition in the 1930s. Courtesy of Onondaga County Historical Association

movement outside of the city almost impossible during the spring thaws. Especially poor was the route north to Cicero. Consequently, there was considerable excitement when in 1846 the first plank road in the United States was built along the sixteen and one-half miles from the community of Central Square to Syracuse.

Medicine did not necessarily keep pace with other progress. Anesthesia, hypodermics and the clinical thermometer were beginning to come into general use toward the end of the era, but the practice, sanitary procedures and the understanding of the causes of disease were still in the previous century.

Medical practice often involved phlebotomy (blood-letting), the use of drugs such as mercury and arsenic in heroic doses, and rude, crude, brutal surgery without benefit of anesthesia or sanitation.

Dr. Cyrus Thomson did not agree with the accepted practice, for which he was not appreciated by the organized profession. His forte was botanical medicine using herbs applied at the Botanical Infirmary which opened in 1830 at what is now Erie Boulevard West and West Genesee Street.

Syracuse came of age in 1848. The trigger was an incident at Sigel's Coffee House (later known as the Cook Coffee House) at South Warren and Washington streets. One New Year's Eve two years earlier, hooligans among the Salina salt workers came to the tavern bent on trouble. It took the militia to break up the bloody riot. And responsible elements from both the villages of Salina and Syracuse agreed to join under a single city charter. The name was to be Syracuse.

Americans in the 1850s remembered the need for eternal vigilance. Veterans of the War of 1812, the War with Mexico and the Indian confrontations to the west were still there as reminders of the uncertainties of international relationships.

Consequently, militia service was a part of life for most young men. Unit names were romantic: the Light Dragoons, the Onondaga Light Guards, the LaFayette Grenadiers and the Washington Artillery, among them.

In August of 1853 Syracuse hosted the state militia encampment at Camp Onondaga, with troops passing in review and undergoing training in the forty-acre camp (eighteen acres of which were tented). Some thirty thousand Syracusans and visitors watched the spectacle.

The troops were ready when the Civil War broke out. The Fifty-First Regiment of Syracuse offered its services on April 15, 1861. The war itself could not have come as any great surprise. The Underground Railroad had been under a full head of steam for years. The discontent of the southern states was reported in the press. Only the spark was needed. And the action at Fort Sumter provided that.

Formed up at the fairgrounds, the units moved out of Syracuse with high hopes. Homemade flags were presented at the railroad station as bands and speeches saluted the troops. Families provided hampers loaded with food for the journey to Elmira, where the soldiers received basic training and were provided with uniforms, guns and ammunition, and were pointed south.

More than twelve thousand were to serve from Onondaga County, with Oswego County providing more than ten thousand soldiers and sailors. And they fought in almost every engagement and skirmish from Bull Run to Appomattox.

A soldier's day in camp began at five-thirty in the morning. Roll call was at six; breakfast at seven; drill from nine until noon, then dinner. Drill was held until four, then supper at five and roll call at nine with taps at ten.

Food was substantial if unimaginative. Bread and smoked bacon for breakfast; bread and salt or beef roast and boiled potatoes for dinner and supper—except when boiled beans sometimes took the place of the noontime potato. And there was coffee—plenty of coffee—several quarts a day for many men. Extra treats such as pies or fresh bread could be bought at a substantial price from outside vendors.

The troops in the field slept in tents. Each soldier had a piece of cloth six-feet-square, which buttoned to another. The two were stretched over a six-foot pole, placed in four-foot-high crotched sticks. The sides were fastened down with wooden pins and a third piece of cloth fastened on one end of the tent, leaving the other end open.

Once the battle broke, the routine and humors of camp life were quickly forgotten. George N. Cheney, who had good-naturedly written of the first night at camp where the neophyte soldiers had to be told to get their boots off their bunks, and where one washed in a creek using a handkerchief as a towel, was the first to fall at Blackburn's Ford, a preliminary skirmish to the First Battle of Bull Run.

One of the most unusual stories to come out of the war was that of John T. Williams of Syracuse, a freckled redhead who had signed up in the early days of the war with John Butler's Zouaves, the first company to come out of Syracuse. He was captured by the Confederates while on a scouting mission. Threatened with hanging as a spy or spending the rest of the war in prison, he signed up with the rebels. It was a bad bargain—for them. Williams had an objective: to learn what he could of the southerners' battle plans and get back to his own line. He succeeded, reporting a Confederate attack plan to northern officers, with a resultant saving of many Union lives at the Battle of Bentonville.

Several women, accompanying their husbands, served at or near the front during the war. One of the most noted was Jane Higgins, wife of Captain Benjamin L. Higgins, a chief of the Syracuse Fire Department, who accompanied her husband when he and the rifle company he had recruited from among the firemen left for Elmira. As she said, when her husband found her seated on the train, his objections were overcome when she provided him with a good lunch.

She popped up in camp or along picket lines throughout the war, working in hospitals and making herself useful as a cook.

The captain was promoted to colonel in the Eighty-Sixth New York Volunteers for gallantry at Gettysburg, where he was wounded. Then, on November 7, he was hit again, a poisoned minie ball passing through both thighs and into his boot. His wife, who had nursed him through his previous wound, was again called to his side. It was thought the injury was fatal. He asked for a big bed, like at home. Mrs. Higgins proceeded to build one out of spare mattresses and sheets.

Her nursing helped him through the crisis, and the colonel and his wife returned to Syracuse in triumph. Mrs. Higgins' service is recognized in the monument for the Eighty-Sixth on Sickles Avenue in Gettysburg.

Then it was apparently all over. But the last act had not as yet been played. The nation still faced the ordeal of Abraham Lincoln's death and the vindictive reconstruction to come.

In just a few years, the nation was to be unified by rail. A new banking system gave strength to the economy. And a long period of relative worldwide peace loomed ahead.

Hamilton Institute, later Madison University, was formed as a Baptist school in the village of Hamilton in 1817 by twelve dedicated men. By the post-Civil War period it was firmly established and ultimately became Colgate University. Courtesy of Colgate University

The concept of an agricultural fair was furthered not only in New York, but throughout America, by the same Elkanah Watson who was an advocate of a canal system across New York State.

As a gentleman farmer living near Pittsfield, Massachusetts, Watson decided to display his pair of rare merino sheep under a tree in the village square. So well received was the little show that it led to the formation of the Berkshire Agricultural Society in 1811. Returning to New York State in 1816, Watson became the Johnny Appleseed of county fairs, including one on Onondaga Hill on November 2, 1819, which listed two hundred dollars in prizes. *Courtesy of Onondaga County Public Library*

A view of the New York State fairgrounds on Capital Hill in Auburn in 1846. Courtesy of H. W. Schramm, from Empire Showcase

An early view of Auburn shows Auburn State Prison on the left, surrounded by farmland. The center of town lies to the right. Courtesy of Erie Canal Museum

One of the earliest photographs of Clinton Square, Syracuse, was taken before 1850. The Third National Bank Building now stands where the Star Building (at left) is located. Courtesy of Erie Canal Museum

The first Catholic church in the village of Syracuse was St. Mary's. This frame structure, acquired from the congregation of St. Paul's Episcopal Church, was moved from its location at East Washington, East Genesee and South Warren streets (the present site of the SA & K Building), to the current location of the Cathedral School on Montgomery Street. Courtesy of the Catholic Diocese of Syracuse

The city of Oswego, then a busy seaport serving the milling and coal industries of Canada and the United States, was devastated by fire on the morning of July 30, 1850. Courtesy of Erie Canal Museum

Some of Dr. Cyrus Thomson's ideas as practiced in his Botanical Infirmary, founded in 1830 and shown here a half-century later, at the corner of West Genesee Street and Erie Boulevard West, were a little strange. The Thomson recipe for a cancer cure begins: "Fill a brass kettle full of red clover"; the ingredients for his cure included such substances as cayenne pepper, undistilled whisky, Indian tobacco, and a variety of herbs.

The following verses written in 1844 describe his system:

'Tis now my object to unfold,
In a brief way to you,
My system, or the gen'ral rule,
Which you must keep in view.
See when the patient's taken sick,
The coldness gained the day,
And fever comes as nature's friend,
To drive the cold away.
The body now has losts its fire,
The water bears the sway;
Quick must the air be rarified,
Or it will turn to clay.
Then place the patient in a room,
A lively fire prepare,
And give him Nos. and one and two,
As warm as he can bear.
And place his body o'er a steam,

With hot stones from the fire,
And keep a blanket round him wrapped,
To shield him from the air.
The body now receives the heat,
To overpower the cold:
If there be inward fire,
Life will the vic'try hold.

But if there is no inward heat,
For you to kindle to,
Then all your labor is in vain,
You must bid him adieu.

Courtesy of the School of Architecture, Syracuse University

There were unusual people on the medical scene in the 1830-1865 period. Shown here is Dr. Hiram Hoyt, a brilliant surgeon and phrenologist and considered by many to be somewhat unstable mentally. Others, including some of his colleagues, thought him a genius.

In one celebrated instance, a child had suffered a severe head injury and required an operation. Doctor Hoyt invited witnesses to an unusual demonstration. He raised a flap of skull and the youngster, who appeared to be dead, regained consciousness. When it was lowered, the child lapsed back into a coma. The doctor viewed this as proof that there is no immortality of the mind, and observed that when "the brain cannot act there is no mind." The youngster recovered.

Then there was Dr. Isaac Magoon, the first doctor to establish a practice in Camillus. He

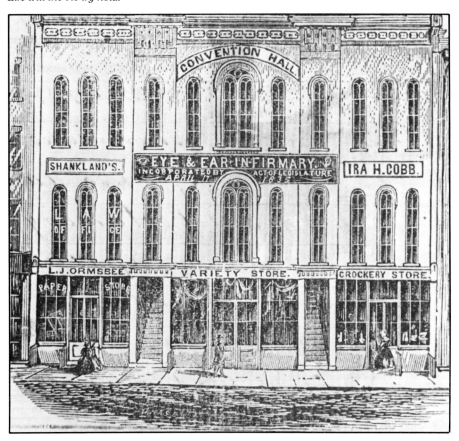

was good-natured, considered lazy, and was so fond of telling stories that he was often suspected of forgetting the purpose of his professional visits. On one occasion he is said to have begun his stories, when the anguished parent interrupted, asking him to attend the patient. The doctor reached into a crib, felt the pulse of a child there, and said, "Yes, it is very ill" At that point the parent again interrupted: "That's not the sick one." *Courtesy of Onondaga County Historical Association*

A Syracuse-area portrait artist (unidentified) painted himself at work in the pre-Civil War period, before the photographer took over the task of immortalizing the individual's likeness. Courtesy of Onondaga County Historical Association

The Connoisseurs *was painted by Central New York artist Sanford Thayer in 1845. Thayer, who learned his craft under the tutelage of Charles Loring Elliott, was later to influence the works of Henry Ward Ranger and Francis Bicknell Carpenter, who was the portraitist of Abraham Lincoln and whose* Emancipation Proclamation *hangs in the House of Representatives. Courtesy of Onondaga County Historical Association*

Central New Yorkers took to the air at an early date.

In the summer of 1847, a Mr. Wise made a balloon ascension in Syracuse from the west side of Salina between Fayette and Jefferson streets. Then he announced he was going to ascend from Auburn the following day and would bring the Auburn paper to Syracuse before the fastest train.

The next morning a southeast wind was blowing and no one expected to see the balloonist. But he rode some freak air currents, landing from a great altitude where his conveyance "looked only the size of an apple." A dray brought him from his First Ward landing spot to the Syracuse House, where he delivered the paper, as promised.

A special flight later in the day almost ended in the Erie Canal, but Wise threw out his coat and then his boots, sufficiently lightening the craft to clear downtown. He came down safely in a West Genesee Street garden.

A balloonist here draws a goodly crowd to Clinton Square. The Onondaga County Court House is at upper left. Courtesy of Erie Canal Museum

These shackles, worn by a slave refugee known as Jerry when he was arrested in Syracuse, symbolize the slavery issue. The Jerry case became an important footnote to the entire slavery issue. Jerry was arrested on October 1, 1851, under the Slave Act and was taken under heavy guard to the United States Commissioner's office for arraignment. The community was jammed with delegates and visitors attending the Liberty Party State Convention and the county fair. The Congregational church bell rang, calling the abolitionists to action. Soon almost everyone (some twenty-five hundred persons) was in, or in front of, the Townsend Building on Clinton Square.

Noting the friendly audience, Jerry (whose real name was William Henry) made a bid for freedom. He plunged downstairs and lurched in chains to East Water Street near Hanover Square where he was subdued, placed in irons and jailed in the police station at the Journal Building on Clinton Square, shown above.

The abolitionists, armed with clubs and a battering ram, mobbed the building. Jerry was freed and smuggled out of town.

Charges were placed against the conspirators, but no one ever went to jail.
Courtesy of Onondaga County Historical Association

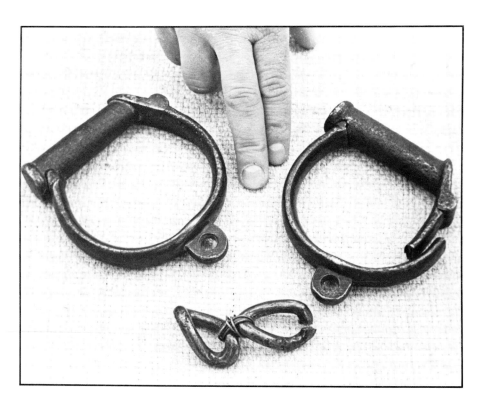

The "Moses of her people," Harriet Tubman, at right above, before and during the Civil War led more than three hundred blacks from slavery to freedom and served as well as a nurse and a Union spy.

Known as Aunt Harriet, she had a price of forty thousand dollars on her head, dead or alive. She made Auburn one of the centers of the Underground Railroad, and lived a long and industrious life before dying at the age of ninety-two in 1913. Courtesy of Onondaga County Historical Association

Harriet Tubman, far left, in 1885 at her home for aged and indigent Negros in Auburn. Courtesy of Onondaga County Historical Association, Syracuse, New York

The Syracuse Bank printed its own currency in 1859, as exemplified by this five-dollar bill. New York State's Bank Law went into effect in 1838, and in the next decade the fly-by-night operators were eliminated. But many states were not as progressive. Too many people were authorized to print bank notes. In 1861 between five and ten thousand different kinds of bank notes were in circulation. Counterfeiting was rife, and credit could easily be disrupted. A federal banking system was an obvious necessity. Many business firms issued money, or scrip, to their employees for purchase of food or other necessities from company stores; such scrip, much of it backed by nothing, was called shinplasters, after the pieces of brown paper applied to cut shins and held there by vinegar, tar or tobacco juice. Courtesy of Onondaga County Historical Association

Edward Judson, born in 1813, was a craggy-faced native of Oswego who had earlier been in the timber business and who had helped found several Syracuse banks. He came out strongly in support of then-Treasury Secretary Salmon Chase's plan for a federal system, which ultimately helped the Union finance the Civil War. Judson's reward was the first federal charter in New York State, issued for the First National Bank of Syracuse. It would have been the first in the nation, except for a mistake in the application when it was sent to Congress. Courtesy of Key Bank of Central New York

MISS JULIA L. NORTHALL,

Respectfully announces to the citizens of Syracuse and vicinity, that she will give a

CONCERT

Thursday Evening, August 27, 1846,

AT THE

EMPIRE HOUSE HALL,

For which occasion she has engaged the popular and favorite Vocalist,

MR. EDWARD SHEPPARD.

PROGRAMME:

PART I.

SONG—Mr. Sheppard, "I'm Afloat,".......Russell.
BALLAD—Miss Northall—"The spell is broken,".
Bellchambers.
DUETT—Miss Northall & Mr. Sheppard—"Come where the Violets blow,"...........Iucho.
SONG—Mr. Sheppard—"My dog and my gun," Brown.
CAVATINA—Miss Northall—"By that consuming, quenchless flame," (from the Opera of Anna Bolena,)...................Donizetti.

This fine composition is highly descriptive—describing the thrilling tones for mercy from the unfortunate Queen of Henry the VIII, previous to her being beheaded.

PART II.

BALLAD—Miss Northall—"The heart of thy Nora is breaking for thee," ....Glover.
BARCAROLLE—Mr. Sheppard—"A Rover's life for me,"........................Auber.
SONG—Miss Northall—"Thou art lovelier," Miss Hawes.
DUETT—Miss Northall and Mr. Sheppard—"Master and Scholar,"...........Horn.
CANTATA—Mr. Sheppard—"The ship on fire," Russell.
SPANISH SONG—Miss Northall—"What Enchantment,"......................Blanco.

☞ Doors open at 1-2 past 7. Concert to commence at 8 o'clock.

Tickets, 50 Cents,

For sale at the usual places, and at the Office of the Emp. House.

Syracuse Daily Journal Print.

A playbill from 1846 outlines a concert presentation by Julia Northall and Edward Sheppard at the Empire House Hall in Clinton Square, Syracuse. Courtesy of Onondaga County Historical Association

The Morris Centrifugal Pump works in Baldwinsville are shown in a woodcut, circa 1860. The Erie Canal is in the foreground. The company is still in operation. Courtesy of Erie Canal Museum

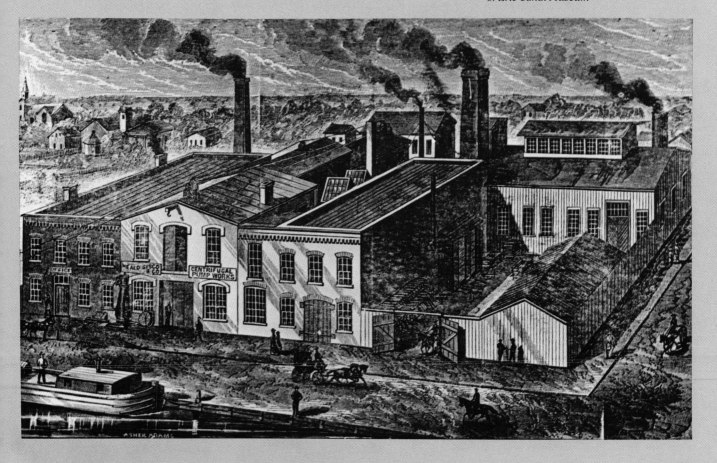

At the Battle of Gettysburg Color Sgt. William C. Lilly of the 149th Regiment of New York Volunteers repaired the regiment's flag staff with strips from his knapsack so the banner, which had suffered eighty hits, could again be raised. The deed is represented in the design for the Soldiers and Sailors Monument at Clinton Square, Syracuse. Sergeant Lilly was killed at Wauhatchie, Tennessee on October 28, 1863. Courtesy of Erie Canal Museum

The repair of the 149th New York Volunteers flag at the Battle of Gettysburg, was celebrated in this painting as well as the Clinton Square Monument in Syracuse. Courtesy of Onondaga County Historical Association

Col. Henry Barnum presented the regimental colors of the 149th Regiment of the New York Volunteers to the Onondaga Historical Association. This was the same flag battered and repaired at the Battle of Gettysburg. Courtesy of Onondaga County Historical Association

51

Col. Augustus I. Root, a native of Syracuse, participated in every major battle except Antietam and was killed at Appomattox Court House on the eve of Lee's surrender. Courtesy of Erie Canal Museum

Gen. John J. Peck had several horses shot out from under him at Gettysburg. Courtesy of Erie Canal Museum

Doctor Mary E. Walker taught school in Minetto after studying at a seminary in Fulton, then became a student at Syracuse Medical College in 1853, receiving her degree two years later, the only woman in her class.

She and her husband Albert set up medical practice in Rome, but she was not accepted by the local community. Her lifestyle and dress, which included the wearing of trousers, were not well received by many.

When the war broke out, she joined the military to serve as a surgeon. Despite continuing complaints by her superiors, she rode alone on horseback into enemy territory to minister to the wounded. Captured by the Confederates in April of 1864 and imprisoned in Castle Thunder at Richmond, she was exchanged several months later as a surgeon for a Southern major. That October she finally was named an acting assistant surgeon.

On November 11, 1865 Dr. Walker received the Congressional Medal of Honor for meritorious service, signed by President Andrew Johnson. The original citation was supposedly written by Abraham Lincoln on the back of an envelope. In 1917 the Board of Medal Awards ruled the award unwarranted, and she and almost a thousand other recipients were ordered to return the medal. She refused. It was restored in 1977. Courtesy of Oswego County Historical Society

Among the women serving in the Civil War was Mrs. Elmina P. Spencer of Oswego, who foraged for supplies for the sick and wounded in the van of the 147th Infantry Regiment (from Oswego) at Gettysburg. She often joined her husband, a hospital attendant, close to the lines. She was also welcomed for her coffeemaking ability.

Mrs. Spencer, who sometimes rode horse-back near the fighting, was fired at by snipers and at City Point was temporarily paralyzed when a boat blew up and she was struck in the side by shrapnel. The photo of Mrs. Spencer above was taken more than thirty years later. Courtesy of Oswego County Historical Society

William H. Seward, seated, then secretary of state, is portrayed in 1867 signing the treaty acquiring the territory of Alaska for the United States. The oil painting by Emmanuel Leutze hangs in the Diplomatic Gallery in the Seward House in Auburn. Courtesy of the Seward House

After Appomattox 1865-1900

The postwar era was ushered in by the solemn arrival of President Lincoln's funeral train—his second visit to Syracuse and the drafty little railroad station at Vanderbilt Square.

Lincoln's life and assassination were closely entwined with that of William Henry Seward, a native of Florida, New York, who made Auburn his home when he entered law and politics following graduation from Union College in 1824. Elected governor in 1838, Seward proved an astute politician, championing educational improvements, prison reform, railroad construction and canals. Controversies with southern governors over slavery soon brought him into the national spotlight as a leader of the antislavery movement.

In 1846, two blacks, Henry Watt and William Freeman, were brought to trial in Auburn, accused of murder. Seward, representing both, eloquently defended them even though the case was lost.

Seward ran for the United States Senate in 1848 on the same ticket as his Upstate neighbor, Millard Fillmore, who was successfully elected vice-president. An accomplished orator, Seward wanted the Republican presidential nomination in 1856, but was advised to wait. It was to prove a mistake. He made some political errors and lost support, so that Lincoln, instead of Seward, was the 1860 nominee.

Although disappointed, Seward campaigned hard for Lincoln and was rewarded with the post of secretary of state. During the Civil War, after initial tests of power with the president, he became a loyal and harmonious secretary.

Seward, a farsighted believer in expansion, sought to acquire Hawaii and the Virgin Islands as territories. Stymied by Congress and others in government, he looked toward the northwest and saw the potential for Alaska as a stepping-stone toward acquiring western Canada. After a substantial fight with hostile congressmen he succeeded in winning the case, and Alaska, at a cost of $7.2 million in gold—far less than was to be dug out of the territory during the Yukon gold rush several decades later.

Upstate New York had always been a politically active area. Syracuse as a convention city has veered toward the Democrats, the Whigs, the Republicans, and back to the Democrats.

In 1868, the state GOP convention held in Syracuse was the national focal point for the Grant-for-President boom which led to his nomination by acclamation at the national convention.

Even after the Civil War was over, some fighting did not stop.

This time it was local, and it was soldier against fireman. During the demobilization days thousands of troopers were encamped at what is now Oakwood Cemetery in Syracuse. Among them was Company B of the 149th Regiment.

July 4 was traditionally a day when local firemen, including those of Continental Number Three, held dances to raise money. They put up their posters, and then, several days later, were surprised to learn that the soldiers were planning a similar event—a day earlier.

The firemen decided to act. The Continental hired the Dresher & Maurer Band and paraded up the street to Pfohl's Hall at Butternut and Salina, where the military party was underway. In minutes the assault was launched. The Continentals wrecked the ground floor saloon; then James G. McIntosh, the firefighters' assistant foreman, led the way up the stairs to the drill hall.

The soldiers had a premonition that something was happening. They broke open lockers belonging to the national guard. Armed with bayoneted muskets and the skill to use them, the squad proceeded down the stairs into the charging fire laddies. McIntosh took the full brunt and was fatally wounded. Several others were slashed and the firemen were soon in full retreat. The coroner's inquest found the firemen at fault. Public outcries, similar to those against the Cook Coffee House riot, led to reform in the operation of local fire organizations and the ultimate establishment of a paid force.

The salt industry, which had been the mainstay of the Central New York economy for forty years, had peaked in 1863 when nine million bushels were produced.

As the salt industry limped along, William Cogswell, a chemist who came from the Oswego area, recognized the potential for mixing salt and limestone to produce soda ash. He acquired the license to process developed by Ernest and Alfred Solvay of Belgium and established the Solvay Process Company west of Syracuse. Cogswell received the necessary financial support from Rowland Hazard of Rhode Island.

Salt left another legacy which was to prove even more important. The peripheral businesses and satellite industries needed to support the production and transport of salt required innovative measures, drawing skilled craftsmen and engineers from Cornell and other technical schools.

John S. Greene specialized in making the giant salt kettles.

Mills to grind the salt products for finest uses required special tooling. Boatbuilders congregated along the Erie establishing boatyards and drydocks in such places as Port Byron to the west. Railroads amassed their own breeds of technicians, including mechanics who could rebuild steam engines in the roundhouse. Coopers and barrelmakers were prevalent north of Syracuse, where they supplied the salt fields. The old steel rolling mills produced fifteen thousand tons of rails a year—two minutes to make a rail, one hour to cool it.

Mowing and reaping machines were turned out at Sweet, Barnes & Company on Wyoming Street. But this was long after John Jethro Wood, a farmer living in Moravia, produced the first cast-iron plow, enabling food production to expand to meet the needs of a world where more people were forsaking the farm to work in factories. Wood was acclaimed by such personages as Thomas Jefferson and Tsar Alexander of Russia.

William A. Sweet first produced steel in Syracuse in 1870; his firm was later purchased by the Sanderson Brothers of Sheffield, England. Thus Central New York began a long tradition of quality tool steel, still produced at the Crucible Specialty Metals Solvay Works, a division of Crucible Materials Corporation.

Cornell graduate Charles E. Lipe set up a machine shop at 208 South Geddes Street now still there but a crumbling ruin. Half the building was taken over by John E. Sweet, a member of the Cornell engineering faculty, where he proceeded to make steam engines.

Lipe himself invented the two-speed gear for bicycles which eventually became a prototype for the automobile transmission. He was joined by H. Winfield Chapin. The firm of Brown-Lipe-Chapin produced differentials, transmission gears and clutches and was later taken over by General Motors.

Henry Ford was a frequent visitor to the Lipe plant during the development of his own line of cars.

A Cortland County native, Alexander Brown, worked at Lipe for awhile, inventing what was to become the L. C. Smith typewriter.

The Lipe shop was the meeting place of Herbert H. Franklin, a die-casting specialist, and John Wilkinson, grandson of the man who named the city of Syracuse. Wilkinson, also a Cornell engineering graduate, had an idea for an aircooled gasoline engine—no pipes, no frozen radiators. The upshot was the Franklin car, which was to become, for thirty years, the largest industry of Syracuse.

Central New York had its share of unique industries. The Will & Baumer candle empire formed through the efforts of Anton Will in 1851 resulted in the reputation of Syracuse as the candle capital of the world, supplying most of the beeswax candles for the Roman Catholic church. Local potters commenced producing a fine line of ironstone china, forming the Onondaga Pottery Company in July of 1871. This company was the forerunner of Syracuse China. Even in Staffordshire, England, the *Times* of that city proclaimed in 1875 that the quality of the Syracuse product was of the highest.

An Auburn bank clerk, William Seward Burroughs, attended a lecture, "Mathematical Short Cuts," in 1872. Nine years later he was ready to market the first practical adding machine. This venture was the forerunner of the twentieth-century Burroughs Corporation.

Banking continued to support the regional economy during the postwar period. But even with the new national banking system lending some stability to the financial picture, speculation and the escapades of such entrepreneurs as Jay Gould in

Even as Lincoln's sorrowful train in 1865 pulled out of the Syracuse depot at Vanderbilt Square, shown here, a new day had truly arrived. In a matter of months the old station had been dismantled, carried away in a single day by those who were happy to take the free lumber.

The old station had been a community gathering place, and in 1858 housed the greatest noise ever to occur within the city limits. Thirteen steam engines in tandem sounded their whistles to salute the laying of the Atlantic cable. The result—many women and children were "in a state of shock for days, some going into a swoon." Art from H. C. Hand, Syracuse From a Forest to a City

attempting to corner the gold market led to recurrent panics. On September 24, 1869, the gold market corner forced the price up from 150 in the morning to 162½ by noon, then plunged to 133. Many people were wiped out. It took the government and the sale of four million dollars of its gold to break the corner.

Then on September 18, 1873, Jay Cook, the financier, went bankrupt. On the next day Fisk and Hatch suspended, and three large New York City banks failed. The panic caused the stock market to close until September 30. That was also the year of the money panic when a giant Philadelphia banking house stopped payment. Because of its interconnections, other banks, manufacturers and one railroad could not meet their obligations. Speculation and overproduction coupled with previous high wages led to inflation, layoffs and a depression.

To the west, three factors led to the decline of Oswego trade in the later years of the century—the failure of Congress to renew America's reciprocity agreement with Canada, the shift of the milling industry closer to the western grain supply and the abolition of tolls on the Erie Canal, a step completed in 1883.

And, as the century drew toward a close, the Spanish-American War was to further tax the banking system's strength.

Women's summer styles during the Civil War period were modeled in a romantic setting, with the backdrop as complex as a medieval painting. Courtesy of Onondaga County Historical Association

The post-Civil War decades brought into focus electricity and the internal combustion machine as sources of power. Suddenly, horsepower, steam power and water power were to have impacts which continue to this day. Cornell Professor William A. Anthony and George S. Moler built the first electric dynamo at Ithaca in 1875. The power was transmitted to arc lights on the Cornell campus via an underground cable. The dynamo was driven by an engine designed by John Sweet, blending the old and the new.

Syracuse received its first jolt of electric lighting in 1878 when an arc lamp on top of the Wieting Opera House was illuminated by a dynamo in a nearby store.

Before long the Fulton Street steam plant was sending electricity throughout the city of Syracuse, a marked improvement over illuminating gas which had lighted city streets since 1849.

The electric utility industry was really born when the power generated at the Edward Adams station at Niagara Falls was sent as alternating current twenty-two miles to Buffalo on November 16, 1896. Within a few years lines stretched across Upstate so that all of Central New York could share the hydroelectric benefits of Niagara.

The early electric trolleys first replaced the horsecars in the late 1880s. They were to be a mainstay of local traffic in most communities until the age of the motor bus a half century later. But the suburban railway, with rights-of-way for high-speed traffic, served to bond the larger cities with the countryside. The Syracuse and Suburban line to Manlius was the first to be built, with the initial run moving along the Genesee Street track to Fayetteville in 1898. It was said at one time that a person could ride the interurban from Albany to Chicago without once using other forms of transportation.

The telephone came to Syracuse in 1878, with a gala demonstration (also at the Wieting Opera House) which drew a capacity audience to hear vocal and instrumental music phoned in from Auburn. The first exchange was located in the Gridley Building on Clinton Square in 1879, serving just sixteen subscribers. Twenty years later the company had its headquarters on Montgomery Street, where the Onondaga Historical Association is now located, serving 12,100 customer lines and 200 trunk lines, individually processing 21,000 calls each day.

As engineers, chemists and industrialists began to come into the area from out-of-town colleges, the community was becoming increasingly aware of the new stress on education. Syracuse was beginning to feel left out in the pursuit of higher learning which had already arrived at Ithaca, Hamilton, Cazenovia and Cortland.

Cornell had been established as a land-grant college, through the support of Ezra Cornell. Wells College, a women's school, was founded in 1868 in nearby Aurora. The leading businessmen of Syracuse saw a way to sponsor an institution without having to start from scratch. In 1866 the Methodist Episcopal church resolved to raise two million dollars, mostly for sectarian schools, as a way of observing the church's centennial.

Geneva College, a small Methodist school, had been founded in 1851 in Lima in western New York. The village was tiny and at considerable distance from a rail line. The church decided it preferred a more centralized location.

The city of Syracuse was interested. In 1867 local businessmen and philanthropists raised four hundred thousand dollars to meet a contingency grant of a hundred thousand dollars established by the city of Syracuse. In 1870 the Methodist convention was held in the city and obligingly voted to locate the school there. A downtown site was selected, the state legislature approved the proposal, and in 1871 the college began operations.

But not everyone was happy. The little school in Lima determined to stick it out. And, although its faculty and student body were skeletonized by the new institution, the trustees fought up and down the Methodist hierarchy and in the courts. Plucky little Genesee existed for several additional years, but finally the last meeting of the Genesee College Board of Trustees was held on June 15, 1875. The citizens of Lima were distraught. They never forgot to honor its memory, nor to view the founding of Syracuse with disfavor.

The medical college of Syracuse University was located in 1877 in three buildings on Orange Street, being brought there from Geneva. A main reason for the shift was the founding of St. Joseph's Hospital several years earlier.

That led to a move by the Episcopal church, under Bishop Frederick D. Huntington, to establish the Hospital of the Good Shepherd in the university section. Syracuse was on the way in becoming not only a college town, but a medical center as well.

Despite the growth of the area's medical services, patent medicines continued to provide for the needs of many local residents. Lydia Pinkham's Vegetable Compound for Women's Complaints, Ayer's Cherry Pectoral and Mrs. Winslow's Soothing Syrup were among the quarter-billion-dollar volume of annual patent medicine sales in late nineteenth-century America. Obviously the recipients were satisfied. Mrs. Winslow's formula was liberally laced with morphine. Hostetter's Bitters was seventy percent alcohol by volume—140 proof.

Homemade and natural remedies provided relief, as well—but needed a cast-iron constitution to stomach the taste—sulfur and molasses, castor oil (mixed with cold coffee) and a variety of salts, brews and teas.

Nursing schools were early units at both Good Shepherd and St. Joseph's Hospitals and were subsequently established at Woman's and Children's Hospital, founded in 1887 by fourteen Syracuse women to specialize in ills of the child and the woman.

It was during the mid-nineteenth-century era that Central New York cities and towns commenced to take on their characteristic architectural styles.

Syracuse started as a cluster of log cabins and eventually clapboard shacks and frame houses; then a brick period followed after most of the then-business district along the Erie Canal was leveled by a great fire in 1834. Some of these later buildings are still standing today.

The more well-to-do of the early settlers imported their housing designs from the Dutch colonial style of the Hudson Valley and the British colonial style of New England.

Architects such as Archimedes Russell, Joseph Lyman Silsbee and Horatio N. White contributed their talents to provide the unique architecture of Clinton Square.

Gothic Revival cottages graced many locations throughout the region, including Cazenovia and the John Munro House in Elbridge. Greek Revival structures included Roosevelt Hall on West Lake Road in Skaneateles, with its six massive pillars and two wings dominating the hilltop overlooking the lake.

The Victorian home complete with towers dotted almost every city and village in the Upstate area, participating in communality of style that spread from coast to coast.

New arrivals from overseas soon established various ethnic neighborhoods, providing them with distinctive foreign flavors. Irish, Italian, German, Polish, Ukrainian, Jewish and, most recently, black communities developed in almost every Central New York city.

In Syracuse, tides of Irish immigrants built the canals, then found work in the salt industry, settling in the western area; Italians built the West Shore Railroad and later became employed at Solvay Process, forming enclaves in the village of Solvay and on the city's near north side. Germans centered their community to the north, where they established beer gardens and bakeries. At one time the language spoken at most fire stations in this area was German. Polish and Ukrainian immigrants settled in the near west side while Jewish arrivals focused on the near eastern areas.

This ethnic composition was demonstrated at one of the city's biggest post-Civil War events: the parade and peace festival of May 1, 1871, sponsored by northside Germans to celebrate both the welding together of the Germanic states into a unified nation and Germany's victory over France in the Franco-Prussian War.

The events began with a one-hundred-gun salute from a twelve-pounder perched on top of Liberty Hill behind Haberle's Brewery above Butternut Street. The two-mile parade along decorated streets included military units, civic societies and the fire departments.

The tides of immigration created wholly new layers of spiritual needs upon the original framework of early nineteenth-century Protestantism.

The Roman Catholic Diocese of Syracuse, headed by Bishop Patrick A. Ludden, was formed in 1886 to provide for the spiritual welfare of seventy thousand Catholics. Greek and Russian

At the end of the war, William H. Seward, shown here when he was governor of New York State, was a participant in one of those weird side lights of history. Seriously hurt in a carriage accident several days before Lincoln was shot, Seward was recuperating in bed at his home on the evening of April 14, 1865.

Lewis Powell, a Confederate who had lost two brothers during the war, entered the Seward home on a pretext. He forced his way to Seward's bedside, then knifed him a number of times in the face and neck before escaping.

The events, which placed Seward on the disabled list for several months, were too much for his wife, who died from the shock several weeks later. Seward himself was back at his desk, although in weakened health, within a month. Courtesy of The Seward House

Orthodox churches served thousands of believers with newly formed congregations.

The old-line Protestant denominations, including Baptists, Methodists, Presbyterians and Congregationalists, and the Episcopal church centered among those of English or Scottish descent, while the German Lutherans and the denominations which rose out of the Abolitionist Movement all experienced growth.

By the early 1880s the Evangelical Movement swept into the region. Dwight L. Moody came into Syracuse in 1884 for a November meeting at the armory which attracted a huge crowd, the forerunner of a seven-week 1886 crusade which resulted in eight hundred decisions for Christ.

Life along the docks, canals and railways, in the hop fields and in the salt works and steel mills was strenuous. Laborers came from throughout Europe, often leaving wives and families behind. The mixture was highly volatile, accentuated by the brutalizing effects of the Civil War. Hard play followed hard, dangerous work. Saloons, brothels, gambling dens, horse racing and bare-knuckle prizefighting were the outlets of choice for many. Police kept trouble from spreading into respectable neighborhoods, but were warned by their superiors not to go looking for trouble, "because you'll be sure to find it." Certain "sin city" sections became almost institutionalized. In a six-block area of seventy-four buildings,

Secretary of State William H. Seward for most of his adult life lived in this mansion along Auburn's South Street. Aside from the loss of some trees, the home has changed little since this 1870 photograph. Almost *everything about the house has a story, even the ivy along the paths and walls came from Sir Walter Scott's home at Abbotsford, Scotland, given to Seward by Washington Irving. Courtesy of the Seward House*

twenty-five were respectable, fourteen were saloons, twenty-four houses were of "ill fame" and eleven others combined the services of both.

A new breed of evangelism was coming out of England, via New York City. These people not only remained in the periphery of trouble, but came to grips with it on the sidewalks in front of Syracuse taverns. Whatever the hour, whatever the weather, the Salvation Army was reaching the drunk and the derelict, telling them of the message of salvation, asking them to turn their backs on sin, and offering a cup of coffee.

The bar owners soon lost their sense of humor. Fights broke out as reformed thugs mixed it up with the unrepentent. The police were urged to do their duty, and they complied, marching off the unlicensed Salvation Army troops to jail.

But they kept coming by the trainloads from New York and points east, keeping the campaign alive, and filling the jails until eventually State Supreme Court Justice George Kennedy declared the arrests unconstitutional. The Army was free to hit the streets.

The good work was continued by others as well, including Edward "Ned" Lee of Oswego, who was said to have been a born troublemaker, and Henry Burton Gibbud in Syracuse.

"Muscular Christianity" had its time in Syracuse at the early Rescue Mission founded there in 1887. The mission began in the works of Jerry McAuley who, like Ned Lee, had a record, having served his time in Sing Sing. Converted while behind bars, he dedicated his later life to provide the down-and-outer with the same blessing, founding the Water Street Mission for that purpose.

He soon had a disciple—Henry Burton Gibbud, who had served in the New York City Bowery in the 1880s as a street missionary.

Syracuse churchmen recognized the need for a mission. And they recognized in Mr. Gibbud and his wife the means to it. The couple were invited to Syracuse in June of 1887. In early September a mission had been opened on Railroad Street.

The name *Rescue* came to Gibbud as he explored downtown and was told of the 1851 Rescue of the fugitive slave Jerry. He decided that *Rescue* was central to the mission's purpose.

Again, at one meeting a disturbing element gathered in the hall. The leader rose up as some of the men began to get rowdy. "Drunk or sober you'll be welcome. . . Here are hands to give you a hearty shake of welcome. . . But these same hands are here to take you by the nape of the neck and put you out. . ."

A big fellow, especially drunk, took issue. He climbed a chair and began to shout. In seconds he had landed in a chair across the aisle. The man stayed put. And the meeting proceeded peaceably.

The great Chicago Fire of 1871 underlined the massive potential for catastrophe even the smallest fire could ignite in the combustible world of wooden structures, oil-soaked factory floors and open stairwells.

Central New Yorkers were acutely aware of the danger. Paid firemen were on the job in Syracuse shortly after the Civil War, while by 1870 an automatic telegraph alarm system had been installed.

The first horse-drawn ladder truck came into service the same year.

Weedsport bore the brunt of its worst fire on December 14, 1871, just two months after the Chicago fire, when a four A.M. blaze wiped out everything on both sides of Brutus Street, including a furnace plant and a hoop-skirt factory. The hero of the day was a man-powered 1822 fire engine, which was set in the creek to the east of downtown and prevented the spread of flames in that direction. (The engine, called the *Neptune*, was restored in 1950).

Syracuse faced a series of set fires immediately following the Chicago blaze. One which especially frightened the populace was a fire started in a double dry-goods store on South Salina Street, for which Adam Fralick received a life sentence. (He committed suicide rather than serve time). Night watchers were established by citizens to circumvent any further arson attempts.

The Leland Hotel fire in 1890 resulted in six deaths and eleven severely burned persons, in what at the time was the largest hotel in the city. Although it had been condemned as a fire hazard, the Leland remained open. The midnight blaze caught most people asleep, but the hotel staff did their best to arouse the guests. Henry Bucker, the elevator man, brought down twenty people in the lift, until it finally stopped running.

The West Fayette Street water main had been shut off, and in moments the entire structure was in flames. Cora Tanner, an actress, slid down a rope, let go, struck a ledge and bounded off into a life net. But she lived.

The greatest fire loss of property occurred on March 14 and 15, 1891, when a fire commenced in the Hier & Leighton Cigar Factory at West Fayette and Franklin streets. Fortunately the loss of life was limited to one man who was trying to save a sofa in his apartment when a wall fell on him.

Discovered at six in the morning, the fire was already out of control, spread by a strong gale blowing from the west. In addition, water was in short supply and one of the city's engines was out of service. Soon all the buildings between Clinton and Fayette streets were burned to the ground. The United States Hotel and thirteen other structures were involved. Calls went out to Oswego, Rome and Utica for help.

A spark from West Fayette Street went through an open window in the Christian Cook Block on the south side of East Washington Street, extending from Warren around East Genesee to Montgomery streets. No firemen were immediately available. But then the Oswego and Utica companies and two New York Central firefighting locomotives arrived.

Even so, the Journal Building and then the Montgomery Flats Building at Washington and Montgomery streets were razed. The Myers Block, formerly the site of Syracuse University, and the Courier Building, were barely saved.

Firemen were especially joyful when, on July 3, 1894, the nineteen-mile-long city water system pipeline from Skaneateles Lake was put into service, providing a dependable source for firefighters previously limited to water from the canal or creek, local wells or nearby reservoirs which can and did run dry. That was not the only benefit. With Onondaga Creek water no longer supplying the drinking needs of the community, disease fell off as well.

The development of the agricultural exhibition as an Upstate institution furthered the county and regional fair industry throughout Central New York. Weedsport held the first Cayuga County Fair as early as the mid-1840s. A half-mile race track at the northwest corner of West Brutus Street and Oakland Road was built around 1864. And in 1877 the North Cayuga Agricultural Society commenced holding fairs at the site.

DeRuyter joined the fair towns in 1888, and by 1900 Moravia was a fair site.

But the major event, the New York State Fair, was not held in Central New York from 1858 until 1890, when a parcel of land in the

On October 10, 1872, William H. Seward died on this couch in his library at the Seward House in Auburn. His death occurred just days after his announced support of the Republican ticket with General Ulysses Grant as its candidate for president. Courtesy of the Seward House

town of Geddes west of the city became the fair's permanent home site. James Geddes, a descendant of the Erie Canal pioneer, must be given major credit for bringing the fair to Onondaga County.

As president of the State Agricultural Society, then the sponsor of the event, Geddes sent personal letters to each of the 122 life members of the society. He tactfully pointed up the advantages of geography, canal and rail proximity and sought their support for a permanent location as against the wearisome traveling exposition which prevented establishment of buildings and sites.

The society agreed, and despite Geddes' death in May 1887, the community formed a land company and put together a package. A one-hundred-acre tract comprising the Smith and Powell stockfarm and nursery was acquired for thirty thousand dollars. Some of the contributors were Dey Brothers Department Store; Lyman C. Smith, the typewriter manufacturer; John Crouse & Company; Solvay Process; Francis Hendricks and other leading individuals and corporations.

By late summer of 1890 the stage was set for the first permanent Syracuse fair.

The theater retained a dominant position as a means of entertainment. Dozens of playhouses served the communities, with the Wieting Opera House on Clinton Square in Syracuse considered Central New York's premier theater. Performers including Charles Dickens found Syracuse a worthwhile stopping place while en route to and from New York and points West. Edwin Booth, Sarah Bernhardt, the Shakespearian actor John McCullough, and J. K. Emmett were among the many to play to standing-room-only audiences.

It was on March 9, 1868, that Syracuse was treated to one of its greatest cultural events. Charles Dickens appeared before an appreciative audience of Central New Yorkers who traveled through a late winter thaw to come to the Wieting Opera House to hear one of the world's truly great literary geniuses. They paid two dollars each for the privilege of hearing him read from *The*

This rendition of Oswego, circa 1850, looks toward Lake Ontario, with the fort on the right and the lighthouse to the left. Courtesy of Erie Canal Museum

Pickwick Papers and *A Christmas Carol*.

Dickens, although he had kind things to say about Central New York, was not thrilled with the muddy streets, depressing weather and the "close and sour" room at the Syracuse House. Wine, he found, came in two prices—six and fifteen shillings—for what was really the same wine. The Hall was "a marvel of dirt" and he did not enjoy the "old buffalo for supper and an old pig for breakfast and we are going to have I don't know what for dinner."

The story is told of J. K. Emmett's disappearance the day of a sold-out house. Desperate telegraphing and good luck located him in Troy, 150 miles away, in less than satisfactory condition. He was literally poured on the next train for Syracuse.

When the car arrived in the city, Emmett saw the producer standing along the platform, and promptly went out the other side. Meanwhile, the crowd at the Wieting was impatiently milling around the lobby.

The manager, thinking the worst had happened, stopped at a nearby bar before facing the audience. And there, standing alongside him, was Emmett. The actor was said never to have performed better.

Care of the stomach and palate, both before and after the theater performance was paramount in the nineties. Typical of the holiday fare offered by hotels in this era were:

Shrewsbury Oysters
Cream Turtle Soup—Clear
Chicken Patties à la Reine
Young Turkey, Chestnut Dressing With Cranberry Sauce
Roast Opossum Virginia Style
Asparagus in Butter Sauce
Tenderloin of Beef Epicurienne
Calf Sweetbreads à la St. Cloud
Pineapple Fritters à Chartreuse
Frozen Egg Nog
Mallard Duck, Fried Hominy, Haunch of Venison, Currant Jelly
Salad à la Russe
Coconut Soufflé Pudding, Port Wine Sauce
Truffles
Tutti Frutti Ice Cream
Fruit, Crackers and Cheese

While not a downtown invention, the salt potato later became a free-lunch and clambake institution. The salt marbles came into being when John J. "Sport" Keefe who ran a saloon on Wolf Street in the 1890s, would get a bucket of brine from the nearby salt yards, dump in a batch of tiny potatoes, then boil the little fellows in their jackets.

Warren S. Norton said, "You got your beer for a nickel, then you got your potatoes and went over to the five-pound butter crock..."

The literary efforts of several local men had an impact on the Central New York community during the last decade of the century.

They included Stephen Crane, author of *The Red Badge of Courage*, who studied briefly at Syracuse University, L. Frank Baum, born in Chittenango, and Edward Noyes Wescott, a Syracuse banker. Each was to achieve fame as a writer by the end of the nineteenth century. Baum is best known for the *Wizard of Oz* and the related Oz series, while Wescott created the person of horsetrader and banker David Harum, which became one of the all-time best sellers.

When it comes to team sports, baseball has been a Central

New York favorite for at least 130 years, preceded only by the earlier Indian game of lacrosse, which may go back to the early fifteenth century or before. Football is a relative newcomer, with Syracuse University fielding its first team in 1890.

The Syracuse Baseball Club was organized in 1857, then had to curtail activities the next year because of the state fair which took up the time of most of the players.

The city became a big-league town in 1879 when it was granted a National League franchise. But the Syracuse Stars, with only twenty-two wins as against forty-eight losses, was out of the league by September. The fifty-cent admission price was too much. Patrick Henry McCormick, who pitched in fifty-five games, could not save the franchise, although he won eighteen of the twenty-two victories.

The Stars again made the move up to the big leagues in 1890 when they were accepted in the American Association. This time they did finish the season, winding up in sixth place (out of eight teams).

The team did better in the New York and International Leagues.

In 1887 they fielded a pitcher by the name of Robert Higgins—nothing unusual, except that Higgins was black. On June 9 of that year, the situation exploded when Douglas "Doug" Crothers of the St. Louis Nationals, in town for an exhibition, refused to have his picture taken with the Stars because of Higgins.

Crothers was fined by his club, then threatened with a month's suspension. He followed up by punching his manager. But Crothers served only eight days out of the lineup.

As a result of the incident, on July 14 the International League's board of directors decreed that "no more contracts with colored men" would be undertaken. The league, incidentally, allowed Jackie Robinson to play with the Montreal Royals in 1948, thus breaking the color barrier for all time. Robinson, as a member of the Royals, played a number of games in Syracuse.

Forty miles to the southeast, John J. McGraw was born in the village of Truxton in 1873. A Hall-of-Famer and manager of the New York Giants, McGraw led them to 10 pennants and 2,840 winning games before retiring in 1932.

Auburn, always a strong minor-league community, graduated many of its New York State and Empire League players into the majors. Union Springs and Weedsport were other communities that fielded strong teams in the early days.

Billiards was an important competitive sport also, with the first public match for a stake ever played in the United States taking place in Malcolm Hall in Syracuse on May 13, 1854. The four-ball game was won by Joseph N. White over George Smith.

Cycling got its start as a sporting event in 1868 with a twelve-hundred meter race run on three-wheeler velocipedes at St. Cloud, Paris. In 1884 Syracuse was one of the cities that Tom Stevens passed through en route to Oakland, California, as he completed the first successful intercontinental crossing by bike. This was followed by many races centered in the Syracuse area.

By the end of the decade, there were twenty thousand bicycles in Syracuse, with only seven thousand registered—a sore point with the police.

The era was to end as it began—with the sounds of bands and marching men.

By April 26, 1898, five days after war had been declared against Spain by Congress as an answer to the sinking of the battleship *Maine*, the Forty-first Separate Company of the State

Oswego is shown in 1870, looking east across the busy First Street Bridge over the Oswego River. The courthouse, upper center, and the church, extreme right, still stand today. Courtesy of Erie Canal Museum

Militia had offered its services. On May 1, the unit commanded by sixty-five-year-old Capt. John G. Butler, who had led the Zouave contingent out of Syracuse in the Civil War, departed for Camp Black at Hempstead, Long Island. There it became Company C of the New York Volunteers. Other units quickly followed and were sent to camps throughout the east.

Oswego also raised a company. As its unit traveled to Camp Black, it was greeted by large crowds at Fulton, where the Grand Army of the Republic Chapter and the Sons of Veterans met them at Broadway, while at Phoenix a band and fireworks honored them. In Syracuse the travelers were saluted by the cries, "Remember the Maine, and to hell with Spain."

They were cheered again as they arrived in New York City. Then the cheering stopped. It was on to camp, training routine, boredom and debilitating bouts of malaria and typhoid, which were to cost the United States far more casualties than the Spaniards. Except for a few professionals who saw action with their regular army or navy detachments in Cuba or the Philippines, the volunteers were camp soldiers.

Two events of significance occurred for Central New York's troops. In the battle of Las Guasimas, Trooper Gustave A. Kolbe of Troop K, First Cavalry, was killed on June 26. The trooper's body arrived in Syracuse two months later to the day, and was tendered one of the greatest military funerals ever given in the city. Then in September, Captain Butler returned the old Forty-first safely home, with twenty thousand Syracusans at the station to meet them.

Company D reported back to Oswego without the death of a single man. Again, it was bands and cannons at Phoenix, Fulton and Oswego.

Casualties for Central New Yorkers had been heavier in the Patriots War sixty years earlier.

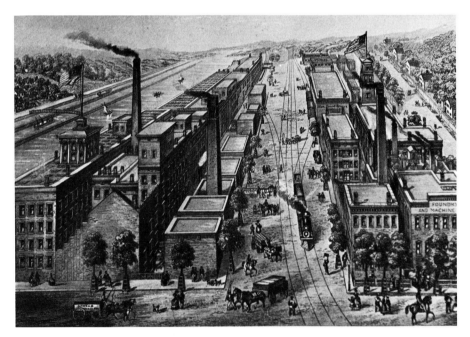

A forest of masts extended down both sides of the Oswego River channel to Lake Ontario in the days of sail at Port Oswego. This drawing is from the late 1860s. Oswego's prominence in the post-Civil War years was as a port city, with the value of its imports at one time ranking ninth in the Union, being mostly lumber and barley.

As an export outlet, sixty percent of all of Canada's imported coal cleared the port. The Delaware and Lackawanna, the Delaware and Hudson and other lines provided the link between the Pennsylvania coal fields and Canada. Courtesy of Onondaga County Public Library

Oswego's manufacturing included that of milling, while the T. Kingsford & Son Starch Factory in 1870, shown above, was the largest starch producer in the world, with a huge installation on the western bank of the Oswego River. Seventy-five percent of the shade cloth produced in the United States was made in two plants along the river, and a million and a half bushels of Canadian barley were malted annually in malt houses in the city. Courtesy of Onondaga County Public Library

The canal, railroad and turnpikes provided access to market for the production of Jacob Amos & Sons in the firm's downtown Syracuse mill, circa 1870. Courtesy of Onondaga County Public Library

In September of 1871, the College of Liberal Arts began operations in the Myers Block at the corner of Montgomery and East Genesee streets in downtown Syracuse. The student population totaled forty-one; the faculty, five. (It was to reach 1,613 by the turn of the century). Then, in May of 1873, the Hall of Languages was dedicated on a barren, windswept highland in the southern quadrant of the city. Courtesy of Onondaga County Public Library

In 1866 Cortland's Village fathers put up seventy-five thousand dollars to get legislative approval for a state normal school, (now SUNY at Cortland) at the site of Cortlandville Academy. In spite of strong opposition from Binghamton, Homer and McGraw, Cortland won the competition. Although ten acres of land were offered on Court House Hill, the final decision was for another location between two churches on Church Street, on the site of the present county courthouse, providing what was believed to be a better environment for the embryo schoolteachers. The cornerstone was laid on September 17, 1867, and Cortland Normal School, shown above, opened in March 1869. The structure burned in 1919, with the new campus buildings opening in 1923 at West Court Street and Graham Avenue. SUNY-Cortland in 1986 had a total of 6,703 students with, 5,584 undergraduates. Courtesy of Cortland County Historical Society

Cazenovia Seminary, pictured here in 1880, was the forerunner of today's Cazenovia College, a two-year coeducational institution. The school was founded in 1824 as the Seminary of the Genesee Conference, the second Methodist seminary to be established in the United States. It originally opened with eight students in the Madison County Court House, then in Cazenovia. By 1874 the school had an enrollment of seven hundred, with distinguished graduates including Leland Stanford, one-time governor of California, president of the Central Pacific Railroad and the man who drove the golden spike linking America by rail. The school faced declining enrollments, and in 1942 church sponsorship was dropped. It became the Cazenovia College for Women in 1961 and in 1982 once again became a coeducational institution, with a current enrollment of eight hundred on a campus of twenty-one buildings. Courtesy of Cazenovia College

This rendering of the Hillside Farm of Mr. and Mrs. Elisha Mabie of Manlius reflects the change from the 1816 log cabin to the dairy farm of the 1870s, with its numerous outbuildings providing for a relatively self-sufficient existence. Courtesy of Onondaga County Public Library

This rare view of the weighlock building in action, circa 1880, looks west. Wharves and hoists enabled canal boat cargoes to be conveniently stored in canalside warehouses, shown at left. By draining water from the lock alongside the building, the boat could be weighed on scales at the bottom of the lock, and appropriate fees charged. Courtesy of Erie Canal Museum

St. Joseph's Hospital, shown about 1875, was the first of its kind in Syracuse. It was the result of the persistence of the Sisters of the Third Franciscan Order of St. Anthony's, who begged, borrowed and cajoled to acquire the former Jacob Samsel dance hall and saloon at the top of Prospect Hill as a place to care for the ill. On May 6, 1869, just a few months after the building became their property, the hospital's first patient arrived. By the year's end, a hunded and thirty-four patients had been treated. St. Joseph's still occupies its hilltop location.

Prospect Hill is believed to have been the site of a July 4 cannon explosion from which two injured men were taken to Dr. Hiram Hoyt's office, where he treated them, keeping them overnight—thus providing the county's first hospital service. Courtesy of Erie Canal Museum

Little was wasted in the farming community. The ragman's horse slowly meandered through the roads and streets of Camillus and nearby towns, as rags were sought for use in area papermills. This photo shows a good day's harvest in Camillus circa 1874. Courtesy of M. Jane Maxwell Estate

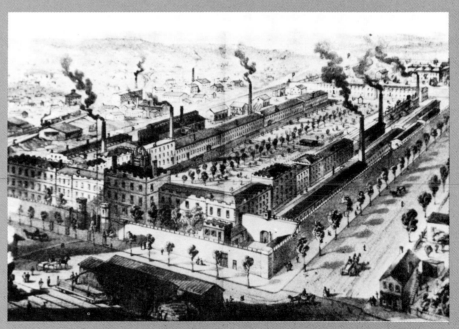

The buildings constituting Auburn State Prison have always intrigued artists and photographers. This picture was drawn in the 1890s, long before the days of the aerial photograph. Except for the smoke, the 170-year-old penitentiary looks basically the same today. Art courtesy of Cayuga County Historian's Office

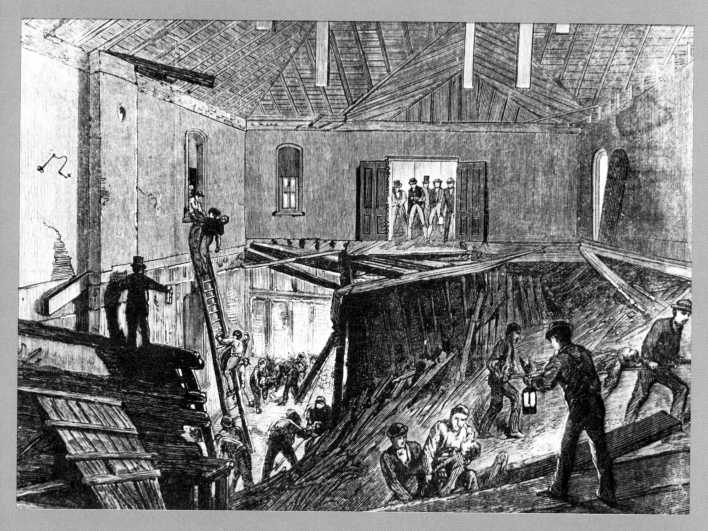

Tragedy strikes at unusual times and places. For residents of Syracuse the evening of June 23, 1874, was especially tragic.

The children of the Central Baptist Church at the corner of Montgomery and Jefferson streets were giving a performance of their "Little Olde Folks' Concert" before a large and appreciative audience in a second-floor assembly parlor.

The time was twenty minutes after nine. A wooden truss between the floors and its supporting iron bars were insufficient for the weight above. Something snapped.

The floor fell instantly, carrying with it ceiling, timber, furniture—and the audience and players. For a few seconds witnesses remember only silence, then a great chorus of cries and screams.

In moments police and firemen were on the scene, along with a vast crowd (some estimate it at close to ten thousand) seeking to help extricate the injured.

Fourteen persons were killed. One hundred and forty-five were hurt. Courtesy of Onondaga County Historical Association

The Excelsior team, a semiprofessional squad, formed in 1874 and in the following year became the Syracuse Stars. They proved themselves by shutting out the Chicago and Boston teams of the newly founded National League behind the pitching of Syracusan Patrick Henry McCormick. He then shut out the St. Louis Browns for fifteen innings, throwing his new pitch, the curve ball. Although an independent team, the 1877 Syracuse Stars pictured here proved worthy competitors for the best in the National League during exhibitions and two years later joined the league to become the first major leaguers in Central New York. Courtesy of National Baseball Library

Olean was the first step up the organized baseball ladder to the New York Giants and baseball's Hall of Fame for John McGraw from Truxton in Cortland County. Shown here in the late 1880s, McGraw was "Muggsy" to players behind his back, "Mr. McGraw" face to face. During his youth, McGraw often traveled the few miles to Homer and southern Onondaga County to play in semi-pro games. He walked five miles to pitch for East Homer in 1889 for two dollars.

In 1938, four years after his death, the Giants played a benefit game in his honor at the Truxton ball field. Courtesy of the National Baseball Library

Salt works pump houses, surrounded by salt vats and covers, were located along the northeast shore of Onondaga Lake during the late nineteenth century. New and more accessible supplies of salt were found to the west. The Watkins Glen region and the area near Genesee, where rock salt could be mined in commercial quantities at lower cost, created competition which could not be ignored by Central New York producers. Even more competition came from the finds in Michigan and a fortuitous strike in Goderich, Canada, where oil-well drillers accidentally hit a tremendous lode of high-quality salt. By 1914 New York sold its holdings along Onondaga Lake for a mere eight thousand dollars. Courtesy of Onondaga County Historical Association

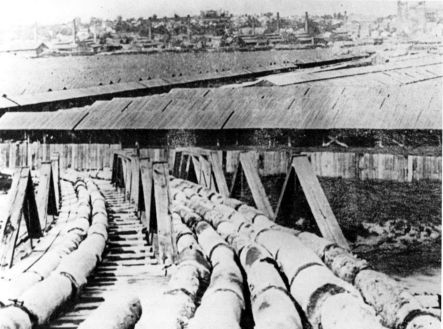

Log pipes were used to convey brine from the pumping stations to the solar vats, when evaporation converted it into high-quality salt. Courtesy of Erie Canal Museum

These salt vats at Syracuse were operated under the principle of solar drying. When rain threatened, a whistle blew and workers pulled covers over the trays. The photo was taken around 1898. Courtesy of Erie Canal Museum

William Cogswell (1834-1921), the chemist and innovator, saw the potential for producing soda ash from limestone and salt, utilizing a then-new process developed by the Solvay Brothers in Belgium. His perseverance led to the establishment of the Solvay Process Company in 1881. Courtesy of the Solvay Public Library

By 1881, with a license from the Solvay Brothers in hand, William Cogswell could commence digging for the quantities of salt required for commercial production of soda ash. Early results in Jamesville, Cardiff and other nearby locations were poor. Finally, in 1885, about the time financial backer Rowland Hazard's patience was beginning to wear thin, drilling in Tully near Christian Hill hit the needed salt at 1,216 feet.

Shown here is one of the Tully salt wells, which provided the saline needed by Solvay Process in the manufacture of soda ash. The solution was piped more than twenty miles to the Solvay plant.

Eventually some forty wells and a network of wooden pipes supplied the Solvay works, while quarries worked twenty-four hours a day to provide trainloads of limestone. The dusty plant to the west of Syracuse became the mainstay for a century. Courtesy of Solvay Public Library

Workers are shown here with a cart-load of wagon wheels outside the W. N. Brockway Carriage Works in Homer in the 1880s, long before the company changed from horse-powered vehicles to truck production. The Brockway Motor Truck Factory was established in 1912 and continued producing quality fire trucks, delivery vans and school buses until the early 1970s. Courtesy of Cortland County Historical Society

The old Syracuse City Hall, circa 1880. It was succeeded a decade later by the present city hall structure. Courtesy of Erie Canal Museum

In this Syracuse scene of the 1880s, a steam engine charges between the SA & K Building, left (now seven stories), and the Vanderbilt House. Note the steam fire pumper on Warren Street, left, in front of Larned Building. Construction on the tower of City Hall can be seen in the center above the plumes of smoke. Courtesy of Erie Canal Museum

Nursing services and the general practice of medicine had benefited tremendously from the Civil War. Clara Barton traveled around the country in 1881, establishing American Red Cross chapters. She conducted a meeting in Syracuse's Larned Building on October 4, resulting in the formation one week later of a Syracuse chapter, forerunner of the Central New York regional organization and its blood bank which now serves twenty-six Upstate counties. Courtesy of Syracuse and Onondaga County Chapter, American Red Cross

Grover Cleveland, was raised in this house on Academy Street, Fayetteville. He later became the reform mayor of Buffalo and was nominated in 1882 by the Democrats for governor of New York State, his first important elective post on the way to two terms in the White House. Courtesy of Onondaga County Historical Association

The longhouse at the Onondaga Reservation is shown during the last years of the nineteenth century. The longhouse is the center of formal Indian society, serving as a meeting place for the Indian Nation's governing body. Courtesy of Onondaga County Historical Association

Aunt Dinah Johns of the Onondaga Nation may have seen George Washington during his visit to Fort Stanwix in 1784. She died in 1883 at the age of 109 years. Courtesy of Onondaga County Historical Association

The Keaton House at 13 Main Street, Cortland, believed in putting out the welcome carpet in this family view in 1885. Courtesy of Cortland County Historical Society

The antismoking campaign of the 1980s had its precedents more than a century ago, long before the medical dangers were understood. The artist's complaints were of stale odor, ashes, restlessness and expense. Courtesy of Onondaga County Historical Association

Cigar manufacturing was a major Syracuse industry in the 1800s, building on production of tobacco on area farms. Many Cayuga County farmers also specialized in the crop. Here are workers at a local factory in 1920. The woman at the extreme right is obviously a clock watcher. Courtesy of Erie Canal Museum

The temperance war of the 1870s and 1880s
was explicitly treated in cartoons depicting
the evils of drinking and the saloon, culminating in the arrival of the Salvation Army and
the Rescue Mission movement. Courtesy of
Onondaga County Historical Association

He got into mischief everywhere, finally winding up in the Onondaga County Penitentiary in 1874. Then his conversion commenced. The kind act of a woman visitor, who gave him a bouquet of fragrant flowers, was to change his life forever. That lady, he said, "is what they call a Christian." After several visits by her, he made up his mind to quit drinking, to forego his earlier ways. He wandered east.

In Albany he was befriended by the Rev. Charles Reynolds, chaplain of the penitentiary in Albany and superintendent of the Tract and Mission Society. Lee became converted, then dedicated his life to mission work, traveling from Albany to Syracuse to Buffalo, stopping at every canal town from Canastota to Baldwinsville to Weedsport and finding the latter two especially troublesome spots, with gangs of roughnecks taking the front seats at his gatherings.

But Ned was tough. After receiving a threatening letter at Weedsport, he appeared on the platform at the next meeting, then announced sharply that the threats must end. He backed up his words by pulling out a borrowed revolver from his pocket and laying it on the top of the desk.

"I will put some of them in their coffins if it continues," he added, then quietly replaced the gun in his coat and resumed the meeting. It was language his audience understood. Courtesy of Anthony Slosek

Edward Lee's birth was in the First Ward of the city of Oswego on May 2, 1846, in a neighborhood called the Flats. It was one of those places the police did not visit after dark. Orphaned at an early age, Ned was soon building a reputation as a vagrant, vandal, thief and drunk. He kept bounding from jail to jail, across the East and the Midwest, escaping from one, landing in another, with time out for navy action along the southern coast and front-line service in the army during the Civil War.

Henry Gibbud (1857-1901) was the first director of the Rescue Mission, established in Syracuse in 1887. Before coming Upstate, he could be found on the coldest nights on New York's Bowery with a large can of hot coffee strapped to his side, going into hallways and cellars, giving a word and a cup. Every hospital, every police station, every jail knew him. Courtesy of the Rescue Mission

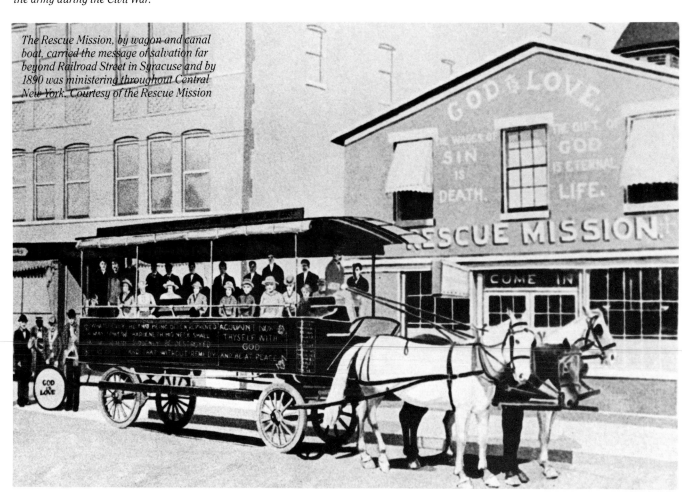

The Rescue Mission, by wagon and canal boat, carried the message of salvation far beyond Railroad Street in Syracuse and by 1890 was ministering throughout Central New York. Courtesy of the Rescue Mission

The Erie Canal steamboat Georgie shown here about 1900 tied up at Weedsport, was owned by a Captain Hanyon, and carried passengers between Weedsport and Port Byron. One old-timer is said to have sought out city-dwelling travelers to sell them bouquets of ''Japanese Parasols'' at twenty-five cents a bunch. They were really clusters of Queen Anne's lace (wild carrots). Courtesy of Old Brutus Historical Society

The Weedsport Fire Company posed in front of the old firehouse on aptly named Furnace Street, circa 1882. Note the steamer in the background. Courtesy of Old Brutus Historical Society

The roller-skating craze hit the region in the 1880s, with the first Alhambra built to house a rink in Syracuse on lower James Street near the Oswego Canal. Each of the several rinks fielded polo teams, while skating races and exhibition skating also attracted devotees. The wheeled variety vied with ice skating along the Erie Canal as a favorite sport. Shown here is a roller skating team known as Gere and Delaney, who demonstrated their roller skating skills to Central New York audiences at the Alhambra. Courtesy of Onondaga County Historical Association

The second Alhambra on James Street near Warren was an important center for roller skating, circuses, political conventions and sporting events. The pianist Ignace Paderewski and other notables performed in concert here. It burned in early 1954. Courtesy of Erie Canal Museum

This is believed to have been the first Kirk Park track in Syracuse. Note the high-wheeled sulkies and the dust storm following the trotters' progress in the 1880s race. Photo by John Clancy, courtesy of Onondaga County Historical Association

In an unusual exhibition, a parachutist descended in a gondola during a late nineteenth-century fair in Central New York. Courtesy of Onondaga County Historical Association

The stone bridge and mills dominate the landscape looking north between Marcellus and Camillus in this photo circa 1900. Courtesy of Onondaga County Historical Association

Syracuse University was to be graced in 1889 by Crouse College, a red Longmeadow sandstone building of Romanesque design created by Archimedes Russell. Courtesy of Onondaga County Historical Association

The ornate chapel in Crouse College at Syracuse University is still a center for student recitals. Courtesy of Erie Canal Museum

This 1920 photo shows from left, Archimedes Russell's red sandstone Third National Bank Building to the north; Joseph Silsbee's gothic Syracuse Savings Bank Building between James Street and Erie Boulevard, and the tall, narrow Gridley Building by Horatio N. White, constructed of grey Onondaga limestone. Courtesy of Onondaga County Historical Association

The circus in 1890 Syracuse meant costumed elephants and a downtown parade at Salina and Jefferson streets, with a tiger and trainer on top of the wagon. Courtesy of Onondaga County Historical Association

Stephen Crane struck a proper author's pose in 1893. The former Syracuse University student wrote The Red Badge of Courage but was better known as a baseball player and party-goer while in school. Courtesy of the George Arents Research Library, Syracuse University

The Syracuse University 1892 baseball team included author Stephen Crane, the player seated in the center, holding the bat case. Courtesy of the George Arents Research Library, Syracuse University

Stephen Crane had a unique way with words, and a number of latter-day Crane specialists believe it was he who penned the report which appeared in the New York Tribune on May 31, 1891 with a Syracuse dateline.

It told of a unique occurrence on the Lackawanna Railroad line from Brighton Corners through the limestone cut, where quarry trains ran to Jamesville. Apparently on the night of May 30, a train en route to the quarry suddenly came upon a swarm of giant insects attracted by a huge spotlight. The bugs, with snapping sounds, threw themselves at the locomotive. Thousands of the insects charged onto the tracks, creating a fearful din and making it impossible for the train to push through. It had to back up and plunge full speed ahead to clear the massed bodies.

Crane never admitted to the story. And trainmen can not remember the incident. Courtesy of Fred Heyman

Frank Baum was born in Chittenango on May 15, 1856, the son of a family which owned a barrel factory. The Baums moved to Syracuse in 1860. Eventually the author settled in California, where he penned The Wizard of Oz, the story of Dorothy, whirled away on a Kansas tornado into a land of strange and enchanting personages. The movie, with Judy Garland as Dorothy, has achieved classic status. Courtesy of Onondaga County Historical Association

John D. Barrow, a Skaneateles artist, bequeathed this self-portrait with a gallery of his landscapes of the Finger Lakes area and nearby farmland to the village of Skaneateles when he died in 1906. There was one catch. Neither the gallery nor the collection could be changed in any way, a situation leading to the deterioration of both building and paintings, until the courts ruled in the 1970s that the collection could legally be refurbished. Courtesy of the John D. Barrow Art Gallery

John D. Barrow's oil painting of the Skaneateles village waterfront is one of the local artist's most famous pieces. Courtesy of the John D. Barrow Art Gallery

John Barrow, the Skaneateles artist, was photographed as he was developing preliminary sketches for his landscape oils which are now displayed in the unusual Barrow Gallery at the village library. Courtesy of Onondaga County Historical Association

The New York Central, the Delaware, Lackawanna and Western (DL & W), and other rail lines continued to bring the world to Central New York. Every boy wanted to be a railroad man, preferably an engineer, although some settled for fireman, conductor or gate-crossing attendant. Such interest was furthered by the exploits of Engine 999, the famous locomotive of the Empire State Express that made the run from Batavia to Buffalo on May 10, 1893, at 112.5 miles an hour, the fastest man had ever traveled. The great effort commenced at the Syracuse Station, where hundreds watched Engineer Charles Hogan and Fireman Ike O'Dell prepare for the run. The train is shown here at Weedsport in 1899. Courtesy of Old Brutus Historical Society

The proud signature of Syracuse China is revealed on the underside of this plate featuring the trademark of "The Premier Egg Cup Co." The forerunner of Syracuse China was the Onondaga Pottery Company, founded in 1871. By 1875, its products were already known and acclaimed abroad. Courtesy of Onondaga County Historical Association

Intricately designed bowls (including one popular model depicting the head of a Revolutionary Minuteman) were features of clay pipes produced in the three pipe factories in Camillus in the 1800s. At the time it was a tradition that at Catholic wakes clay pipes and tobacco would be provided for the men. Young ladies would collect the pipes, place a ribbon on them and hang them in their rooms. Courtesy of M. Jane Maxwell Estate

84

A shirt was chosen at the Milton S. Price store at West Fayette and South Salina streets in Syracuse in the 1890s. Courtesy of Onondaga County Historical Association

The Milton Price mansion was razed in 1893 to make way for Dey Brothers Department Store at the southeast corner of Jefferson and South Salina streets in Syracuse. Courtesy of Onondaga County Historical Association

A horse-drawn hook and ladder rig approaches the West Shore railroad crossing in Syracuse in the 1890s. Photo by John Clancy, courtesy of Onondaga County Historical Association

The sporting scene witnessed a ring tragedy in November of 1894 when Robert Fitzsimmons, the world's champion at the time (standing at right), took on Cornelius Riordan in an exhibition bout at the Grand Opera House. Riordan was killed, and the champion was charged with first-degree manslaughter. A well-publicized trial which brought the nation's focus on Syracuse followed in May, with the fighter being exonerated. Courtesy of Onondaga County Historical Association

The stage of the Wieting Opera House, on Clinton Square in Syracuse, featured most of the great actors, singers and speakers of the day over a sixty-year period, from the Civil War era into the 1920s. Courtesy of Erie Canal Museum

Reflections of canal life appear in this photo taken along the Erie Canal towpath near Camillus in 1896. Courtesy of M. Jane Maxwell Estate

An afternoon's outing for young ladies in 1898 often meant bicycles and straw skimmers. These ladies were known as Weedsport's "Silly Six" for reasons which remain a mystery to modern residents. Courtesy of the Old Brutus Historical Society

A crew poses with its traction engine in the late 1890s. Such equipment bridged the gap between horse power and gasoline engines on farms. The man standing at left holds the all-important engineer's oilcan. Courtesy of Onondaga County Historical Association

*This nineteenth-century view looking east
down Main Street, Marcellus, vividly shows
the task facing teams heading up the
Seneca Turnpike hill. Courtesy of Al
Edison and the Marcellus Historical Society*

Stearns bicycles, which were made in Syracuse, are shown on display at a bicycle show in the 1890s. The exhibit was a fore-runner of today's automobile shows, which first appeared around 1905. Courtesy of Onondaga County Historical Association

Crates of Syracuse-produced Stearns bicycles were shipped by the wagonload to San Francisco in 1899. Courtesy of Onondaga County Historical Association

This young lady at the turn of the century thought bicycling a serious business. Courtesy of Onondaga County Historical Association

One of the great days of area bicycle racing occurred in 1897 at the Kirk Park oval, shown here, with Syracuse Eddie Bald the favorite as he took on one Tom Cooper, looked upon as the villain. Bald easily won his mile heat, but Cooper, caught in the back of the pack on a dusty track rutted by earlier trotting horse races, threw up his hands and pulled off the course to the boos of fans. Syracuse Eddie easily won the final.

Track conditions and crowded heats resulted in numerous spills, with Chic Scoville of Syracuse and a rider named Haynes from Buffalo suffering serious injuries which put them out of action for a month. Haynes broke a rib when he somersaulted four time after running over a wheel of a downed bike in the home stretch.

I. A. Powell of New York City was seriously cut when he fell and his pedal tore into his leg and side, but he was back in competition the next day in Saratoga. Barney Oldfield of Toledo, C. A. Church of Philadelphia, H. R. Stevenson of Syracuse and F. A. McFarland of San Jose, California, were others among the racing pros. Courtesy of Onondaga County Historical Association

Kirk Park's half-mile dirt track provided a rough racing surface for these six competition cyclists. The bikers at left are tandem racers.

Bicycling attracted more than nine hundred cycling club members and thousands of fans to the trotting track at Kirk Park on the south side of Syracuse for the Empire State Meet. A smoker and grand march were featured events at the Alhambra.

The cycles were heavy and clumsy. Those with brakes were considered in a class for "safety bikes." Heavy frames were needed to absorb the pounding over cobblestones, ruts and holes in board sidewalks. But even these monsters were far better than the high-wheel versions with their tendency to pitch the rider over the handlebars in the infamous "header."

The races were one- and two-mile sprints, with heats and a final to determine who took home the prize—a gold watch, a diamond ring or cuff links—which were easily pawned by the hungry amateurs.

On race day the visitors took off for a ride through Onondaga Valley, Jamesville, DeWitt and the Genesee Turnpike (now East Genesee Street) to downtown for the smoker and band concert. Then everyone adjourned to Kirk Park, where the stands were packed with visitors wearing the colors of the various clubs. Courtesy of Onondaga County Historical Association

Eel weirs in the Oswego River are shown in this view of Fulton before 1900. Courtesy of Historical Society of Fulton

The brickyards at Warners, west of Syracuse, could produce as many as 1 million bricks at a time, taking about a month for the baking and cooling processes. In 1947 six million bricks a year were produced at Warners. The first bricks were made from native clay trod by oxen. Here, piles of bricks are ready to be placed in archways for firing. Courtesy of M. Jane Maxwell Estate

Edward Westcott, who was a teller at the First National Bank of Syracuse beginning in 1873, subsequently founded a firm of bankers and brokers.

He was to die in 1898 before his book, David Harum, *was published. It became a best seller, with the locale generally accepted to be in Homer and Cortland County. The book cover shown here was from the second edition.*

The book was adapted into a movie starring Will Rogers, which had its world premier in Cortland in 1934. Another spinoff from the book was a radio serial, The True Tales of David Harum. *Photo from Henry W. Schramm collection*

The David Harum Tavern in Homer picked up on the popularity of Edward Noyes Westcott's turn-of-the-century best seller. Although the author never claimed it, the Homer-Cortland area was believed to be the locale of the story. Courtesy of Erie Canal Museum

Syracuse Standard

ESTABLISHED 1829. SYRACUSE, N. Y., WEDNESDAY MORNING, FEBRUARY 16, 1898. PRICE TWO CENTS.

THE BATTLESHIP MAINE BLOWN UP IN HAVANA HARBOR

A Terrific Explosion Destroys the Pride of the American Navy and the Lives of One Hundred Men.

The Ship On Fire and Sure to Sink—All the Officers Escaped—Captain Sigsbee's Report Of the Terrible Disaster.

THE BATTLESHIP MAINE.

CAPT. SIGSBEE'S REPORT.

WAITING FOR WOODFORD

A Message from the Minister at Madrid Expected.

DE LOME INCIDENT CLOSED

But the Text of Spain's Apology Has Not Yet Been Received.

LORD NEVILL A CRIMINAL.

A Scion of One of England's Proudest Families Sent to Prison for Five Years.

APPEAL OF SILVERITES

The People Called Upon to Crush a Conspiracy.

GOLDBUG AND MONOPOLIST

Are Said to Be Forging Chains With Which to Fetter the Nation.

OFFICERS OF THE MAINE.

SPAIN'S APOLOGY.

It Will Say that Spain Has Acted in Perfect Good Faith in Cuban Affairs.

Another Feat in Newsgetting.

Syracuse the Only City in the State Except New York and Buffalo to Know That Spain Had Disavowed the De Lome Letter.

For thirty-three years, except for frontier warfare between Indians and the professional army, Central New Yorkers had been at peace. The sinking of the Battleship Maine in Havana Harbor on February 15, 1898, and the resentment against Spain stirred up by the press, quickly led to an enthusiastic public response. Young men throughout the area flocked to the colors. Courtesy of the Syracuse Newspapers

Honorary fire chief Hamilton Salisbury White, in the light coat, is depicted here racing to a Syracuse blaze. An innovative amateur, he spent a fortune providing the city with many pieces of fire-fighting equipment and is credited with inventing the boot-and-trouser combination enabling a fireman to jump from bed into boots and trousers, then down the brass pole. He died of smoke inhalation and exhaustion while fighting a fire in 1899. Courtesy of Onondaga County Historical Association

Miss Fanny Crosby, despite being blind from the age of five, wrote more than twenty-five hundred hymns and other songs. Born in 1823, she was seventy-six when this photo was taken during a visit at the Hitching's Fruit Farm, in Onondaga Valley in August 1899. Courtesy of Onondaga County Historical Association

The Cazenovia countryside along West Hill is shown here before the days of paved roads. Courtesy of Erie Canal Museum

The mucklands near Canastota provide a perfect growing environment for onions and celery. These are celery field workers in the late 1800s. Courtesy of Erie Canal Museum

This view of downtown Cazenovia around 1900 looks to the west. The Lincklaen House, still in existence, is on the corner to the right. Courtesy of Erie Canal Museum

The transmission of power from Niagara Falls to meet the needs of Upstaters had been first demonstrated with a line to Buffalo in 1896. Then came the plan to transmit it 150 miles to Syracuse. A Niagara Falls Power Company crew is shown inspecting the early lines, which passed Rochester and the hills of Wayne County, arriving in Syracuse in 1906. Two years later a line of steel towers was built along the eighty-one miles from Rochester to Geneva, Auburn and Syracuse, much of it adjacent to the present Route 5. The company bought up every available metal windmill tower at Sears Roebuck to Meet the need. Courtesy of Niagara Mohawk Power Corporation

C·H·A·P·T·E·R F·I·V·E

A New Century
1900-1920

The twentieth century was born with appropriate pomp and ceremony around the world. In Central New York it was ushered in by the advent of the automobile age and other advances.

High-tension lines from the new Niagara Falls generator station were crossing the state, providing a perpetual source of electric power.

The population in Syracuse had grown to 108,374, more than three times grater than the 31,700 residents at the close of the Civil War. Among them were a thousand blacks who came to build the Woodland Reservoir.

A network of speedy suburban trolleys interconnected almost every upstate community. Milk, mail and passengers were carried to nearby destinations in one or two hours—not days—at a mile-a-minute clip.

The Wright Brothers were conducting experiments in flight which were to have substantial local impact.

President McKinley, the victor of the Spanish-American War, was in the White House at a time when the economy was relatively stable. While the salt-processing industry had dwindled to next to nothing, and the Erie Canal was being succeeded by a new and bigger State Barge Canal and the burgeoning railroad travel, Sanderson-Halcomb Steel, the Solvay Works, Columbia Rope and the Alco locomotive factories in Auburn vied with paper mills in Fulton for economic attention.

At the state fairgrounds a group of forty workmen with fifteen teams of horses began construction of a mile-long race track. It was to take seventy days and ten thousand dollars to complete.

The great streets—James and East and West Genesee in Syracuse, Genesee in Auburn, and Main in Cortland, reached their zeniths as examples of Victorian, French and Corinthian architecture.

Gordon Wright uniquely combined a hotel, the Mizpah, into his architectural concept for the First Baptist Church along Jefferson and Montgomery streets, creating a first.

The Upstate community was enjoying two major exhibitions in the early part of September 1901. On the sixth, President McKinley was visiting the Pan American Exposition in Buffalo, while the state fair was readying for the appearance of Abbott, the second fastest trotter in the world, for a world-record attempt on the new track.

The president was in a reception line in the Exposition's Temple of Music. The time was seven minutes past four as a thoroughly ordinary-looking young man moved up in front of McKinley, who extended his hand. The man reached out. From two feet away, he fired a pistol through a bandage covering his right fist. Then he fired again.

One of the bullets went into the president's abdomen.

The man, twenty-eight-year-old Leon Czolgosz, an anarchist, was immediately seized and jailed.

For a while McKinley seemed to rally, and the state fair opened on schedule that Monday. For the rest of the week McKinley's condition was reported as stable. It was quite a shock when at a quarter after two on the morning of Saturday, September 14, the president expired.

Not everyone was disappointed. Congressional Medal Award recipient Dr. Mary Walker of Oswego vilified the dead president from the speaker's platform, saying that it was no worse for Czolgosz to have murdered the president than for the state to execute him, and that Theodore Roosevelt, who succeeded McKinley to the White House, was responsible. The police rescued her from an irate mob.

The last act was played at Auburn Prison when the assassin was put to death in the electric chair.

The automobile was readily accepted in Central New York. To prove it, by 1900 the only six owners in the area had formed the Automobile Club of Syracuse, one of the first groups of its kind in the world. It was one of the nine founding clubs of the American Automobile Association when the AAA was instituted in 1902.

Marcellus had been used to power-driven machinery since the 1860s and to early steam tractors. The role of the "Cradle of Industry" engineers in the development of the bicycle transmission and their ways with machinery of all sorts made the Syracuse area a natural as an active participant in the automobile revolution.

The Franklin Car Company, with its unique air-cooled engine, turned out its first vehicle in 1901, and before long the firm, with John Wilkinson playing a major role, was producing cars capable of establishing national speed records.

The New York State Fair track was supposed to be the site of a one-mile speed exhibition by David Wolfe Bishop in 1901. He was one of fifty-five drivers racing their cars from New York City to Buffalo in a five-hundred-mile endurance run—a bone-jarring, spring-cracking jaunt over rutted dirt roads. But steady rains and

poor conditions of the track precluded the effort. Instead, the racers spent the night at the Yates Hotel in downtown Syracuse, then took off for Rochester.

Author Lena P. Anguish recalls of early touring, "George Lewis used to get dressed up for the trip in a long duster, cap, goggles and elbow length gloves. Then we would sit there and go along about twelve miles an hour. You couldn't see anything for dust if the wind blew."

The cars of the day were either open or covered with a tonneau (a removable canvas top), with isinglass windows. Leaky roofs were par. And tires seldom lasted the whole journey, regardless how short. Name automobiles like the Rambler Gasoline Car and the Waverly Electric were exhibited at auto shows.

There was another side to motoring: the races, which were first held at the state fair in 1902. The Syracuse Automobile Club sponsored the initial events, with Barney Oldfield, already the most recognized name in auto racing, invited (he was a no-show). Coming, however, was Jules Sinchille of Paris, France, driving a Darracq Racer which was capable of a steady sixty miles an hour over long road races.

The crowd was delighted by the show, which included the setting of a new world's record for five miles for cars under twelve hundred pounds, set by Dan Wurgis of Cleveland, Ohio, in an Oldsmobile which included only a chassis, an engine and a seat for the driver. The previous record in the class had been set by John Wilkinson in a Franklin car at the Empire City track in Yonkers, near New York City (now Yonkers Raceway). Later in the day at the fairgrounds, Wilkinson, driving from the scratch position, won a five-mile handicap run for road cars from Central New York. He passed two cars on the backstretch to win.

The Wright Brothers' flight and subsequent trials of flimsy homemade aircraft had whetted Central New York's appetite for more. Glen Curtiss, an inventor and motorcycle racer from Hammondsport, at the south end of Keuka Lake, built a successful seaplane, the forerunner of the Curtiss Aircraft Company. He also set new records for one- and two-mile flying starts on his speed bike at the state fair in 1905. That was the year Carl E. Myers

demonstrated his airship there, a gas-filled motor-driven balloon steered by a rudder.

J. A. D. McCurdy attracted a tremendous crowd in 1909 when he flew his Curtiss biplane three times over the track area at an altitude of two hundred feet. It was described by a fair official as "one of the greatest drawing cards ever."

As in canal days, the worst engineering ordeal in bringing in electricity from Niagara Falls was at the Montezuma swamp, where the seemingly bottomless mire left something to be desired for tower footings. Predictions were that the first strong wind would topple the entire line. The engineers persevered. Piles were sunk and reinforced concrete foundations were based on them; the problem was expensively solved. Fortunately another threat, that of fever, never materialized.

The interurban electric railways, building on the 1898 establishment of service to Fayetteville from downtown Syracuse, came into its own, introducing area farmers to outlying towns and new markets and city dwellers to the advantages of suburban living. The lines, in addition to commuter services, followed the pattern of the old streetcar line promotions, taking customers to company-owned amusement parks, baseball stadiums and beaches conveniently located at the ends of the lines.

The Syracuse and Eastern was the only line in the nation to have a "penitentiary" train which picked up prisoners at a siding next to the Onondaga County Courthouse and delivered them to the then-new Jamesville Penitentiary.

The Rochester, Syracuse and Eastern ran a line parallel to the New York Central tracks and routinely outran its bigger brother between the cities, even though the local line made frequent stops during the two-hour trip.

It was a time for new residential architectural designs, as well.

Ward Wellington Ward began his Upstate practice in 1908 and in the next two decades was to build more than two hundred private residences, many of them becoming period classics. A Chicago native, in 1900 he married Maude Moyer of Syracuse, the daughter of Harvey Moyer, the manufacturer of carriages and the

Well-dressed swimming and croquet were genteel summertime sports for young ladies in 1900. Courtesy of Onondaga County Historical Association

Moyer Automobile, and eventually relocated in Syracuse.

For a different clientele, Sears Roebuck opened the unique service of mail-order homes which came shipped in a box complete with plans, paint and nails.

Theatricals and circuses played major roles in Central New York at the turn of the century. It was the time of the Shubert Brothers Vaudeville and the storefront movie house in almost every neighborhood. The silent flicks, with piano accompaniment, often had a Central New York flavor, with many films produced in Ithaca. Others were products of Long Island City's studios and still others were made in Onondaga County.

The great San Francisco earthquake of 1906 had a minuscule counterpart in Central New York at 1:35 in the afternoon on February 10, 1914. Although the epicenter was in the northern Adirondack area, Syracuse and Albany were noticeably affected. People ran into Syracuse streets as the tremors hit, and heavy damage was reported at Grant School on Second North Street. At the William McKinley and Bellevue Heights Schools, windows were broken.

Natural phenomena occupied the front pages of American newspapers during the early years of the century. Central New York was no exception. Everyone focused attention on Halley's comet in 1910, with many anticipating the end of the world. The spectacular was not disappointing, with the comet and its tail said by some to cover half the sky in a great arc. It was every bit as exciting as the 1834 event, described by William Beauchamp, who said, "the tail of the comet, the head of which we never saw, was streaming halfway across the sky on a cold winter's night," both appearances were a great deal more interesting than the 1986 version, which was more noticeable on T-shirts than in the sky.

Medicine had progressed in the years since the smallpox epidemic of 1870, when Syracuse had been placed under virtual martial law, and by 1912 Crouse-Irving Hospital had joined St. Joseph's, Good Shepherd and Women's and Children's Hospitals in serving the needs of the sick. But even the best of contemporary medical care was insufficient to overcome the frightful toll and fears engendered by diptheria and infantile paralysis, which generally attacked children and those in the prime of life. The late summer was always a time of dread for parents. The paralysis would start, perhaps after a day at the beach or shopping for back-to-school clothes. Tiredness. A fever. The crisis. And then death, or paralysis, or recovery.

These were expected, and people learned to live with them, unlike the 1918 Spanish influenza. This disease appeared first regionally in the military installation at Devens, Massachusetts, then arrived at the army encampment at the state fairgrounds. The sickness came on suddenly. Within hours victims had high fevers, a general weakness and aches all over. Headaches, intestinal and stomach problems followed. In up to ten percent of the cases it progressed to massive pneumonia and death.

The epidemic was worldwide.

Efforts were made to relieve symptoms, but usually no relief occurred until the disease had run its course. Four thousand soldiers were stricken locally. Another eight thousand cases occurred among county residents. Other thousands suffered in Auburn, Cortland and Oswego. On October 19, two hundred fifty-three persons died in Syracuse alone. In addition, hundreds of soldiers had expired. The total for Central New York by the time the "Spanish Lady" left in early 1919 was close to two thousand and up to twenty million around the world.

Getting people to the hospital was always a problem. The fastest journey, especially in horse-and-wagon days, was not always the best for patients, even though better than the bone-jarring Indian-dragged litter journey of the wounded Samuel de Champlain in the seventeenth century.

In 1901 the city of Syracuse transferred the maintenance of its ambulance service to the hospitals of Syracuse, with one ambulance stationed at each institution. This required the addition of another intern to most staffs.

The locomotion for the early ambulances was, of course, horsepower. And one of the most beloved was Old Bullhead.

For twelve years until Christmas Day, 1915, when he was retired, Old Bullhead teamed with other horses, answering the alarms, making the quick descent from Prospect Avenue, then returning up the hill with their cargo.

Things were not made easier during Bullhead's last week. He had to make two round trips to carry victims from a streetcar wreck in Delaware Street.

Then there was the race up West Fayette Street with the big gray St. Joseph's wagon behind, as Old Bullhead and his partner beat another ambulance by a couple of blocks to the scene of a Solvay area industrial explosion.

By 1923 motorized ambulances were making more than fourteen hundred calls a year.

Not everyone went to the hospital. Central New Yorkers from the days of the Botanic Infirmary shared with other regions a trust, sometimes born out of desperation, in unusual care. Arlene LaRue, describes "the Rag Doctor" in her book, *All Our Yesterdays*. This doctor was Marianna Herbert, who was born in Bavaria, and who studied medicine in Germany before coming to this country. She eventually settled on the North Side, opening an office in Park Street. The waiting room was usually crowded with forty or fifty patients. She would tie a cloth around the patient's body. After wearing the cloth for a while, the patient would return, and Dr. Herbert would read the cloth, diagnosing the problem. Treatment was usually with medicines prepared from herbs she had brought from Germany. She took her secrets to the grave when she died in 1920.

When the Allies and Central Powers squared off in Europe in 1914, nobody believed the war could last long. The immense casualties and massive destruction meant it would be over soon. And, as Americans believed, the United States could certainly keep out of it. That did not mean people did not take sides. Local residents of English and Scottish descent supported the Allies. Those with German and Austrian blood were behind their countrymen. Some youths went overseas to serve as noncombatants in ambulance corps.

But mostly, Central New Yorkers had other matters on their minds—the educational system; the state of the fire department and the Roosevelt-Barnes libel trial.

But the progress toward war, spurred by the unlimited submarine warfare conducted by the Germans and the growing war materiel trade with the Allies by American industrialists came to a climax on April 6, 1917, when President Woodrow Wilson appeared before Congress to ask for a declaration of war. Within months thousands of Central New Yorkers were in uniform; the state fairgrounds was established as Camp Syracuse with six-hundred-acres of tent cities, and with firing ranges and parade fields extending several miles to the west.

The communities geared for war by establishing economic controls and ration boards. Every factory turned to war work. The state fair, which continued its annual show despite the encampment, featured war and production themes.

The home-town Twenty-seventh Division was in action at the Marne, Chateau Thierry, Soissons and in other positions along the Western Front before breaking through the Hindenburg Line in the closing days. The casualty lists had ominous messages for thousands of Central New York families. For example, Company C of the 108th Infantry, mustered at 255 strong when it moved up to the front for the Great Drive of September, 1918. After several days it had lost all of its officers. The decimated unit attached itself to Company D. By the time the combined unit was relieved, it was down to 42 men.

There were casualties at home. On July 3 Syracuse was shocked by a gigantic explosion. The munitions plant at Split Rock had disappeared. Fifty died. Then came the Spanish influenza.

Central New York was truly ready for the Armistice on November 11, 1918. The War to End Wars was finally over. Veterans returned home to parades and a period of readjustment. A lot of ideas had changed. The Suffragettes' time had come; women were about to gain the right to vote. Another great movement, the ratification of the Eighteenth Amendment, was about to usher in prohibition on New Year's Day in 1920. The manufacture and sale of alcoholic beverages were outlawed, except for special purposes, in the United States until 1933.

When the century had opened, three physical features were most noticeable by persons traveling through the city of Syracuse for the first time—the Erie Canal, the tracks through the streets and the decaying salt works along the northeastern shore of Onondaga Lake. But within twenty years the canal through the city was filled in; the salt wells sold and the land cleared, and the first meetings held to elevate the New York Central and DL & W tracks. Only Solvay would continue to turn out the products of Onondaga's salt fields.

An eleven-man bobsled with Carl Hotaling at the tiller was photographed in downtown Baldwinsville before the turn of the century. Others from left are Winsor Morris, John Sagar, Ed Crippen, a Mr. Elliott, James and Lance Cornwell, Ed Worley, Carl Sagar, Walter Betts and Harry Bigelow. Courtesy of the Town of Van Buren

Circus life attracted local people, too. George Satterlee, a rather colorful individual from Central New York with a flair for the dramatic, enlisted in the Civil War as a drummer boy because he was too young to serve otherwise. After the war he developed some magic tricks, learned ventriloquism and went on the road with what he called the Sig Sautelle Circus, headquartered in Syracuse. The roads were bad, so Satterlee switched for a number of years to a floating circus, then in 1888 reverted back to the highway, where his collection of educated dogs, ponies, ladder and trapeze performers, high-wire artists and clowns became one of the country's largest wagon circuses, specializing in appearances in the Hudson Valley and other sections of the northeast. His trademark was a huge diamond-studded pin set in the shape of a horse. When times were good, the circus man wore the emblem on his shirt front. When business was bad, it disappeared, probably to the pawn shop.

In February of 1899 Satterlee moved his headquarters to DeRuyter, next to a hotel he had bought. In May of that year DeRuyter had a great crowd come to see the opening performance. In the parade were forty wagons, one hundred and forty horses; twenty-five musicians and a cast of two hundred performers and employees.

The following year the headquarters were moved to Homer, and a couple of years later Satterlee had the octagonal training ring shown left built close to the Cortland-Homer Highway (Route 11). The circus then included an entourage requiring fifteen railroad cars. The troupe shown in the picture dates from this time, about 1900.

By 1904 twenty-three sixty-foot cars were needed to carry what was termed "The Greatest Show on Earth," complete with lions, elephants, kangaroos, hyenas, gorillas and snakes. The following year Satterlee sold the circus to Barnum and Bailey, who sent it to France, where it went broke. The promoter joined with Walter L. Main to form another troupe and, for the rest of his life, Satterlee was in show business. But nothing was ever to compare to his early twentieth-century exhibition. Courtesy of Cortland County Historical Society

The hermit of Owasco Lake caught the fancy of a photographer who turned the subject into a postcard in the early days of the century. Courtesy of Erie Canal Museum

The Hermit of Owasco Lake, Near Auburn, N.Y.

Four gentlemen found a pleasant way to relax in bygone years at Clift Park, Skaneateles, circa 1910. Courtesy of Erie Canal Museum

Main Street, Cortland, looking north from Court Street in 1900, was a busy place for bicycle riders of both sexes. Courtesy of Cortland County Historical Society

Willow baskets were "mass produced" at George's Basket Shop in Liverpool, shown here in 1901. The craft today has almost vanished. Courtesy of Onondaga County Historical Association

The Nestlé factory in Fulton at the turn of the century is viewed by the driver of a horseless carriage. The chocolate firm is still a leading Fulton manufacturer. Courtesy of Historical Society of Fulton

The Henri Nestlé factory at Fulton was opened in 1900 to produce Nestlé's Milk Food. In 1907 facilities were added to the Fulton plant for production of Swiss-formula milk chocolate under an agreement with

Peter Kohler Chocolate Suisse. The chocolate produced had less cocoa and more sugar, creating a sweeter-tasting variety of milk chocolate. Courtesy of Historical Society of Fulton

This can of condensed milk marketed by the Henri Nestlé Company was one of the first products from the Fulton plant in 1900. Courtesy of the Historical Society of Fulton

This was one of the condensers used in the production of condensed milk at the Henri Nestlé plant in Fulton circa 1900. Courtesy of the Historical Society of Fulton

SUNDAY EXCURSIONS
ON
SKANEATELES LAKE!

Commencing Sunday, August 4th, to and including September 8th, 1901, the

NEW STEAMER
CITY OF SYRACUSE
AND FAVORITE STEAMER
GLEN HAVEN!
(COMBINED CAPACITY 800 PEOPLE).

Will leave Skaneateles for Glen Haven and intermediate points, Sundays, as follows: Steamer "City of Syracuse," 10:10 A. M. Steamer "Glen Haven," 2:30 P. M., returning at 5:10 and 6:00 P. M., respectively.

The Steamer CITY OF SYRACUSE will connect with East-bound train arriving in Syracuse at 7:55 P. M. and New York at 7:00 A. M.

Steamer GLEN HAVEN will make close connection with trolley for Auburn.

AS A SUMMER RESORT SKANEATELES LAKE HAS FEW EQUALS!

Summer travel is now at its height, and the scenery never looked more beautiful along the shores of this charming lake than at present.

SKANEATELES LAKE PARK,

Ten miles from the village of Skaneateles, contains about forty acres of open and wooded land, eleven acres of which is a park admirably located for excursion parties. The grounds are provided with tables, a large pavilion and an abundance of pure spring water, making it a most desirable place for a day's outing for excursions of all kinds.

Skaneateles is reached in six and one-half hours from New York, fifty-five minutes from Syracuse, and from other cities on the line of the New York Central in equally quick time. It costs but 25c for a 32-mile ride over this picturesque lake. Picnic grounds free, and baggage transferred between trains and boats free of charge. The lake has daily communication with the New York Central Railroad, with six passenger trains each way over the Skaneateles Railroad, and telegraph and cable communications with all parts of the world.

For particulars, excursion rates, etc., apply to N. Y. C. passenger agents.

J. McNAMARA, Supt.

The Syracuse and Auburn interurban trolley line combined passenger and freight services. It also owned Lakeside Park on Owasco Lake and two passenger steamboats, the City of Auburn *and the* Nymph. *In Skaneateles the trolley firm operated the Skaneateles Lake Transportation Company, including a six hundred passenger boat, the* City of Syracuse, *shown here under way with a capacity crowd in the early twentieth century. Offered were searchlight cruises of the lake, accompanied by dance bands. Courtesy of Onondaga County Historical Association*

Vacationing passengers boarded the lake steamer Arundell *at the port of Oswego on August 15, 1906. Courtesy of Erie Canal Museum*

Leon Czolgosz, the killer of President McKinley in 1901, as he appeared in official mug shots at Auburn State Prison, where he was later executed. Courtesy of Cayuga County Historians' Office

THE WEATHER
Forecast for To-day: FAIR

THE POST-STANDARD.

16 PAGES

SEVENTY-EIGHTH YEAR. Whole No. SYRACUSE, N. Y., WEDNESDAY MORNING, DECEMBER 5, 1906. LATEST EDITION—PRICE TWO CENTS

CHESTER E. GILLETTE GUILTY OF MURDER IN FIRST DEGREE; VERDICT FOUND IN FIVE HOURS

PRISONER ON VERGE OF COLLAPSE AS HE ENTERS COURT ROOM

Pale and Almost Trembling, He Hears Doom from the Lips of the Twelve Jurymen.

QUICKLY RECOVERS HIMSELF AND SENDS A TELEGRAM TO FATHER

Jurors Ready With Their Finding at Eleven O'Clock. Left Court Room After Judge's Charge, a Few Minutes Before Six O'Clock.

COURT HOUSE, HERKIMER, Dec. 4.—Chester E. Gillette was declared guilty of murder in the first degree at 11:25 o'clock to-night.

The jury brought in this verdict after being out a few minutes over five hours.

Six ballots were necessary. Five of these six resulted in eleven of the jury voting for the verdict that was later made unanimous.

Gillette heard the awful announcement with blanched face, ashen lips and trembling hands. When he entered the court room to hear the decision he dropped his head, and as he sat down he staggered to one side and all but fell.

Immediately after Marshal Hatch announced the verdict Attorney Mills asked that the jury be polled. Each juror answered to his name and said that such was his verdict.

Attorney Mills then made a motion to set aside the verdict and moved for a new trial. Justice Devendorf stated that court would adjourn until Thursday at 10 o'clock when argument on the motion would be heard and sentence would be pronounced.

TELEGRAPHS TO HIS FATHER

As Attorney Mills spoke, Gillette leaned forward tore off a piece of paper from a pad and wrote the following telegram:

"Dear Father: I am convicted.

"CHESTER."

Immediately afterwards Gillette was shackled to Sheriff Klock and in custody of two other officers taken to the jail. The crowd in the court room was held behind closed doors until the prisoner was safe within the jail.

District-Attorney Ward went to Sheriff Richards and warned him that every precaution must be taken to guard against the prisoner doing himself any injury.

An officer had been detailed to take his station outside Gillette's cell from now until the time he is taken to Auburn.

READY AT 11 O'CLOCK

It was just 11 o'clock when a knocking from the jury room caused a death-like silence to spread over the crowd of 300 or more who had lingered the whole evening through in the hope of hearing the verdict.

In a moment word was passed that the jury had agreed upon its verdict.

CHESTER E. GILLETTE **GRACE BROWN**

(Young man who is defendant in celebrated case and his factory girl sweetheart, whom he is convicted of murdering at Big Moose lake last July.)

GILLETTE WRITHES AT WARD'S ADDRESS

District-Attorney, in Bitterest of Terms, Denounces Young Prisoner—Latter Divides Attention Between His Prosecutor and Jurymen.

SPECIAL TO THE POST-STANDARD.
COURT HOUSE, HERKIMER, Dec. 4.—

Dead Girl's Parents Satisfied When Extreme Penalty is Given

SPECIAL TO THE POST-STANDARD.
HERKIMER, Dec. 4.—When the verdict had been announced Frank Brown, father of the dead girl, said to a Post-Standard correspondent:

"Everything is perfectly satisfactory. My wife and myself would never have been satisfied if Gillette had not got the full extent of the law. If ever a man was guilty in God's world it was Gillette.

"My wife and myself and family are grateful for the treatment received since we have been in Herkimer. We are especially grateful to the Morrisons and all others about Big Moose lake who were so insistent in bringing about justice."

MESSAGE READ AMID APPLAUSE BY DEMOCRATS

Both Sides of House Join in Demonstration.

THE SENATE SOON ADJOURNS

Resolution on Japanese Situation Introduced by Rayner.

CANNON FILLS TWO VACANCIES

Cousins of Iowa Made Chairman of Foreign Affairs and Lowden is Named on the Same Committee.

Another Upstate crime, the murder of Grace Brown by Chester Gillette in Big Moose Lake on July 11, 1906, became a notorious event, translated by Theodore Dreiser into the classic An American Tragedy. *Both principals were residents of Cortland and employees of the Gillette Skirt Factory, where they met. The plant was owned by Chester's Uncle Horace.*

During the course of their relationship Grace became pregnant. Chester seemed particularly unconcerned, dating others. Finally the couple took a vacation trip to settle their differences. Meeting at the Taber House in DeRuyter, shown here, on the morning of July 9, they carefully concealed their movements from DeRuyter over the Lehigh Valley Railroad Station, shown above, to Canastota, where they changed trains to Utica and eventually to the Adirondacks.

While the couple were alone on Big Moose Lake, their rowboat somehow overturned. Chester made his way to land and continued his vacation as though nothing had happened. Only later was the missing boat and then the body recovered. The trial was one of the great events of Herkimer County history. Chester was found guilty of first-degree murder and sentenced to death.

At 10:18 on the morning of March 30, 1908, with Governor Charles Evans Hughes refusing to intervene, the sentence was carried out in the notorious Auburn chair. Courtesy of Ernest Baker and the Syracuse Newspapers

107

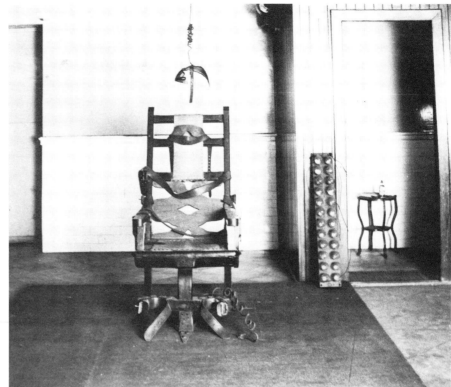

In this electric chair fifty-six convicted felons were executed at Auburn State Prison, among them Leon Czolgosz, assassin of President William McKinley, and Chester Gillette, convicted of the American Tragedy *murder of Grace Brown. Courtesy of Cayuga County Historian's Office*

President Theodore Roosevelt, right, during a trip to Syracuse in 1903 was accompanied by mounted troopers. Courtesy of Onondaga County Historical Association

A hazard of riverboating is evidenced by this excursion launch which hung perilously over the dam just west of Baldwinsville. No one was injured in the mishap, which occurred in the early 1900s. Courtesy of the Town of Lysander

This view of Canastota around 1900 shows the Hoist Bridge over the Erie Canal at Peterboro Street. Courtesy of Erie Canal Museum

On April 7, 1901 the bridge crossing the Oswego Canal at James Street collapsed under the weight of a trolley car. In the background, left, is Syracuse City Hall. Courtesy of Erie Canal Museum

The West Genesee Street bridge over the Erie Canal in Syracuse, circa 1900. The Botanical Infirmary building, now the location of a Denny's Restaurant, is at the right. Courtesy of Erie Canal Museum

The Iroquois *and the* Mohawk *were being built for Barge Canal travel at Baldwinsville in 1900. Courtesy of Erie Canal Museum*

This canal boat was being launched sidewise from a shipyard in Port Byron in 1900. Courtesy of Erie Canal Museum

The Lodi Lock of the Erie Canal, located at Lodi Street, Erie Boulevard, and Beech Street, Syracuse, was operated by lock-tenders O'Brien (left) and Jackson (first names unknown). The photo is believed to have been taken around 1905. Courtesy of Erie Canal Museum

Repair work on a canal or its navigation buoys required hard-hat diving equipment in the days before scuba diving. Hoses provided oxygen, while weighted belts kept divers on the bottom. The work shown in this photo was being conducted at Durhamville at the turn of the century. Courtesy of Erie Canal Museum

Burning proved the easiest way to rid the Erie Canal right-of-way of wrecks in downtown Syracuse following the break in the canal in July of 1907. Courtesy of Erie Canal Museum

No day in the history of the Erie Canal could have been more spectacular than July 30, 1907. It was a sultry afternoon with the usual crowd of hangers-on watching the activities along the canal. Then someone noted that the water seemed to be moving from east to west at an unusually fast pace. Canaleers sensed a problem and jumped to shore. The canal boats started to follow the flow, some breaking from their moorings. The drift carried them to where the canal crossed a viaduct over Onondaga Creek. From the west, water was flowing into a maw at the creek site. The boats plunged in. Seconds later the canalside walls of a mill gave way.

What had happened was the collapse of a keystone in the span. In minutes six miles of canal had poured through the resulting hole, causing the creek to suddenly flow upstream toward Onondaga Valley. Fortunately, no one was injured, but the future of Syracuse as the Venice of New York State was doomed.

This rare view looks east along the canal from near West Street, as the bottom dropped out. Niagara Mohawk's headquarters now occupies the site to the left. *Courtesy of Erie Canal Museum*

Workers' homes were a fixture in factory communities at the turn of the century. These houses were built for Solvay Process workers along Milton Avenue, Solvay, in the days when the electric railway provided suburban service. Courtesy of Solvay Public Library

The furnace chimney at Solvay Process Company underwent demolition in the early days of the century. Courtesy of Erie Canal Museum

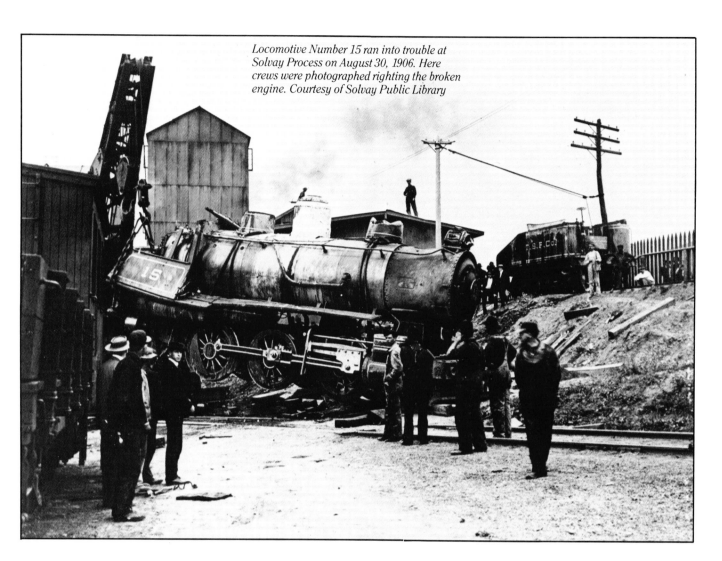

Locomotive Number 15 ran into trouble at Solvay Process on August 30, 1906. Here crews were photographed righting the broken engine. Courtesy of Solvay Public Library

In the days before a smoking factory chimney signaled trouble, Solvay Process was a major employer. This scene, looking west, was taken in 1911. Courtesy of Solvay Public Library

This was a trolley of the Auburn Interurban Electric Railroad Company prior to 1908. The company was later merged with the Auburn City Railway to form the Auburn & Syracuse Electric Railroad to provide high-speed transportation between the two cities. Courtesy of Cayuga Museum of History and Art

Suburban electric cars are shown arriving at a busy junction in DeWitt, around 1910. The Fayetteville-Manlius line ended at Suburban Park, which was owned by the trolley com-

pany. Another stop at Jamesville was the Fiddler's Green picnic grounds. Courtesy of Erie Canal Museum

Central New York motoring in the early days of the century. Courtesy of Automobile Club of Syracuse

The roads around Syracuse, especially the old turnpike routes, often left early motorists in awe. The automobile Blue Book warned drivers to beware of the Camillus hill (now Route 5), shown here as it descends past the Gates Variety Store. In the first transcontinental road race of 1909, a Ford driver in a testimony to his little car said, "On the heartbreaking Camillus Hill we actually beat the pace maker" (a larger, more powerful auto). The hill was an engine-testing site for the Franklin automobile and the Chase truck, both manufactured locally.

A Syracuse Herald reporter said of the Camillus highway, "Few Syracusans know much about Camillus except to know that it has two wonderful hills. They coast down one side into town, put on all speed (if they dare) through the center of town and dash madly up the hill on the other side in a hope, usually in vain, that they will be able to make the summit on high. It was a case of 'here it comes, there it goes!'" Courtesy of M. Jane Maxwell Estate

As Syracuse University became a national football power with the new century, it was recognized that the ramshackle wooden ball park on the quadrangle was not sufficient. Archbold Stadium, shown here, the first concrete athletic bowl in the United States, was built early in the century in a natural amphitheatre on the southwestern corner of the campus. The stadium originally had a roof covering the south stands, where tradition for many years seated the coeds. Male students were located in the north stand, resulting in the echo cheers for which Syracuse was famous. (The tradition died, along with the "frosh lids" as the campus grew spectacularly following World War II.) The roof over the south stands came down in a windstorm and was never replaced. Courtesy of the George Arents Research Library, Syracuse University

The Maypole Dance on Class Day in 1910 attracted a few watchers to Archbold Stadium at Syracuse University. Courtesy of the George Arents Research Library, Syracuse University

The Soldiers and Sailors Monument is shown as it was taking shape on Clinton Square in Syracuse. It was dedicated in 1910 as a memorial to those who served in the Civil War. Courtesy of Erie Canal Museum

Rain, dust and a lack of solid structures hampered the earliest local state fair events, and throughout the nineties county fairs competed fiercely, often at the same time as the Syracuse fair was being held. The state took steps through the new governor, Theodore Roosevelt, and a cooperative legislature, to take over the operation of the event from the Agricultural Society. This was the tent city of the state fair, with the grandstand in the background, circa 1905. At last the fair was on a sound and permanent footing. Courtesy of H. W. Schramm, from Empire Showcase

Under state tutelage the New York State Fair continued to expand, except at night when everyone went home. Syracuse businessmen saw the economic advantages of special events to keep visitors overnight. The Chamber of Commerce came up with the idea of an annual nighttime carnival just happening to coincide with the state fair dates. Similar in format to the New Orleans Mardi Gras, it was called the Ka-Noo-No Karnival, featuring parades, floats and a party atmosphere highlighted by dramatic electrical decorations throughout downtown.

The word Ka-Noo-No was believed to derive from the Mohawk word gannona, "a well-watered or guarded land"—especially appropriate to the Clinton Square area with its canal. Floats depicting Indian legends, fairy tales and romantic tributes to foreign lands were presided over by a king and queen, shown here. The Onondagas joined in the spirit of the event by adopting state and local public figures into the Iroquois Nation as blood brothers.

Harpers Weekly saluted Upstate: "Do not let them tell you that an American town cannot enter into the carnival spirit, and still preserve the graciousness and a certain underlying sense of decorum. Tell those scoffers to go to Syracuse during State Fair week."

The expansion of the state fair to include nighttime activities in the days just prior to the war was to lead to the gradual demise of the Karnival, but by then its purpose had been served. Courtesy of Erie Canal Museum

The Monster Mosquito was a popular float in the 1908 Ka-Noo-No Karnival parade. According to legend, the ancestor of all mosquitoes was said to live near the Onondagas. Whenever he was hungry, he would eat a few Indians, who sought help from the Holder of the Heavens, who came down and killed the insect. Courtesy of Erie Canal Museum

Steam tractors were engaged in stiff competition for business in 1907. Here a Case engine proved its hill-climbing ability before an appreciative audience of farmers and their womenfolk at the New York State Fair in Syracuse. Courtesy of Erie Canal Museum

Auto racing, as shown here with Ralph DePalma setting a mile record in 1910, continued to be a major fair attraction until 1911, when a blown tire threw a speeding race car driven by Lee Oldfield (no relation to Barney), into the crowd, killing eleven persons and injuring dozens of others in what was to be America's worst racing accident. The fairgrounds track from that time until the end of the decade was limited to horses—and airplanes. Courtesy of Onondaga County Historical Association

This early airplane called the fields adjacent to the Solvay Process Company home in the first decade of the twentieth century. Courtesy of Solvay Public Library

The biplane of J. A. McCurdy attracted a large crowd to the New York State Fair in Syracuse in 1910. Some people later learned that sitting on freshly painted benches could be a problem, as evidenced by the stripes on the man with the cane in the foreground. Courtesy of Henry W. Schramm, from Empire Showcase

An old foundry in Chittenango was photographed around 1910. Courtesy of Erie Canal Museum

President William Howard Taft greeted Central New Yorkers from the observation car of a New York Central train in 1911. He was in the area to attend the New York State Fair. Courtesy of Onondaga County Historical Association

A barbecue was (and still is) an important function at any fair. This photo is believed to have been taken before the turn of the century at a local county fair. Photo by John Clancy, courtesy of Onondaga County Historical Association

The first recorded tornado of significant size to hit a populated area in Central New York was the twister which struck down at Long Branch Park, then rampaged through Liverpool and Pitcher Hill on September 15, 1912. A trolley station and other buildings at the amusement park were destroyed, with several trolleys demolished, as these postcards show. Three persons were killed, the largest number to die in a tornado in the state. Courtesy of Erie Canal Museum

A freak episode of the tornado which struck in the Liverpool area on September 15, 1912, cut a swath through the door of a barn, removing the roof and leaving stacked hay intact. Courtesy of the George Arents Research Library, Syracuse University

The 1912 tornado twisted a tree into a pretzel shape around snapped-off trunks in the Long Branch Park area. Courtesy of the George Arents Research Library, Syracuse University

123

As usual, firemen were kept busy. The old Greenway Brewery, stretching an eighth of a mile between Franklin and West streets, lighted the sky on September 6, 1913, as it burned to the ground. That was the year when horse-drawn engines were first succeeded by motor-driven vehicles, an especially important step as Syracuse expanded. Courtesy of Onondaga County Historical Association

A local operating room theater circa 1910. Courtesy of the George Arents Research Library, Syracuse University

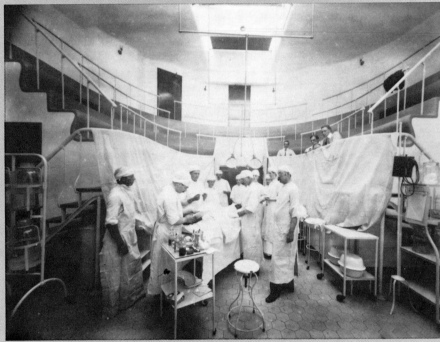

Indians at the Onondaga Reservation south of Syracuse demonstrate the game of lacrosse in a traditional woodland setting as it was played several centuries ago. The object is to get the ball past the defenders and into the goal. A lacrosse stick with a webbed pocket is used to throw and catch the ball. Courtesy of Onondaga County Historical Association

124

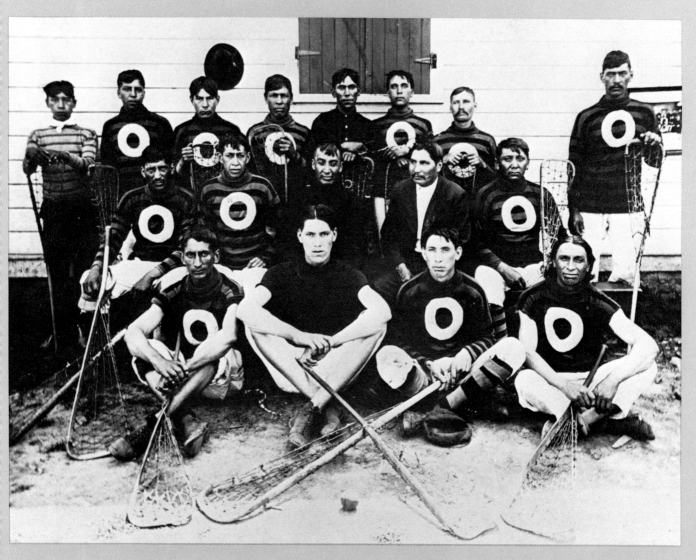

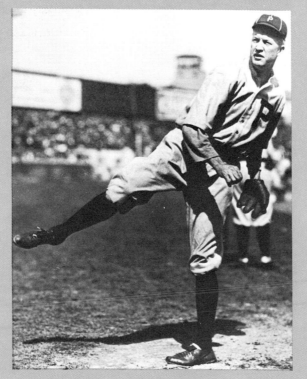

The Onondaga Indian lacrosse team has long been recognized as among the national leaders. This is the team more than a half-century ago. The sport, originating centuries ago, is said to have involved the men of entire Indian nations, participating in huge contests covering several miles.

Lacrosse is growing in popularity in schools and colleges throughout the northeast. Syracuse University and Hobart College in Geneva to the west are long-time superteams among collegians. Many Onondagas have played for the university, and the Onondaga Reservation's team is proficient in the fast, rough six-man game, which is played in a field the size of a hockey rink. Courtesy of Onondaga County Historical Association

Hall of Fame pitcher Grover Cleveland Alexander made a stop Upstate as pitcher for the Syracuse Stars in 1911, setting numerous records, including a final fling of fifty scoreless innings. The next year he was with the Philadelphia Phillies of the National League. Courtesy of the National Baseball Library

Architect Archimedes Russell designed some of his most enduring works, among them the new Onondaga County Court House, still in use on St. Mary's Circle, and Central High School, borrowing heavily from the sixteenth- and seventeenth-century Italian school of architecture. Here representatives of the Onondaga County Bar Association in a recent picture look at a wooden model of the court- house, originally used at the construction site to show passersby the finished building. Courtesy of Al Edison

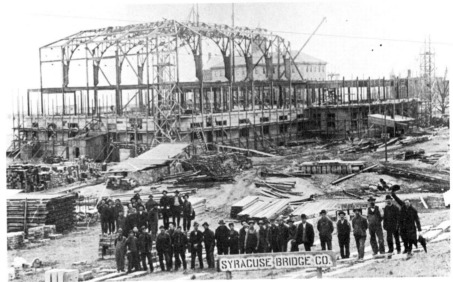

The work crew of the Syracuse Bridge Com- pany posed about 1903 in front of the frame skeleton for Archbold Gymnasium. The area under the arches at one time housed all Syracuse University basketball games plus an indoor running track. Courtesy of Onon- daga County Historical Association

Ward Wellington Ward's carefully detailed houses, some of stucco blending with brick and wood, were particularly designed to accommodate the integration of local arts and crafts. The buildings generally followed the English cottage style, often with carved wood finials and superbly designed porticos. Ward encouraged the owners of his houses to finish their homes with glazed porcelain creations of Adelaide Alsop Robineau, the furniture of Gustav Stickley, the tiles of Henry Chapman Mercer and the stained glass of Henry Keck, who apprenticed under Louis Comfort Tiffany. The Ward house shown here is located on DeWitt Street in Syracuse. Courtesy of Al Edison

About the time Ward Wellington Ward was beginning to design homes for well-to-do Central New Yorkers, Sears Roebuck was turning out something special for middle-class America—a catalog home, complete with everything but land, "cement, brick or plaster." Between 1908 and 1939, more than a hundred thousand Sears homes were sold throughout America.

One could buy a cottage for just $707 dollars—or go up to the "Magnolia," a top-of-the-line $5,140 home already cut "and fitted for a ten-room mansion," shown here in the 1500 block of James Street, Syracuse. Once the order was placed, Sears sent the new home owner plans and a complete kit including millwork, lumber, lath, shingles, porch ceiling, sizings, flooring, finishing lumber, building paper, eaves troughs; drain spouts, sash weights, hardware, nails, colonnade, roofing, painting material—even "mantle tile and grate."

If you did not have a contractor, or needed financial help, Sears was ready to provide these, too. Photo by Al Edison

A turn-of-the-century fisherman's paradise along Oneida Lake was the Anglers' Club at South Bay. The resort hotel boasted a shore front of five hundred feet. Courtesy of Erie Canal Museum

These were homes along Stage Hill on East Main Street, Morrisville, long before Route 20 was paved. Courtesy of Erie Canal Museum

The clubhouse at Onondaga Country Club at the turn of the century was then located closer to what is now Route 5 between DeWitt and Fayetteville. Courtesy of Erie Canal Museum

An organ grinder and his monkey attracted a gathering on a Syracuse street circa 1910. Courtesy of Onondaga County Historical Association

In 1912 an automobile made from a buggy, sporting a Robert Baker front, was ready to take to the road. Courtesy of Michael Plumpton and the Marcellus Historical Society

As people moved into suburban areas, new developments sprang up in former rural areas. In the early 1900s real estate developers in Auburn prepared the Hoopes Avenue area, shown here before the construction began and after the tract of homes was complete, in 1912. Courtesy of Cayuga County Historian's Office

This cell block was typical at Auburn State Prison a half-century ago. Courtesy of Cayuga County Historian's Office

Prisoners at Auburn State Prison are shown in lock-step formation while wearing the traditional striped uniforms which were later abolished. Courtesy of Cayuga Museum of History and Art

Sanderson Brothers Steel Works on Magnolia Street in Syracuse was the forerunner of Crucible Steel in Solvay, a producer of high-quality steel. The original plant above, later became the Sanderson-Halcomb Works of Crucible Steel Company of America. The firm, now locally acquired, is a survivor in a period of plant closings and mergers, and is now known as Crucible Specialty Metals. Courtesy of Crucible Specialty Metals, a Division of Crucible Materials Corporation

A Graves-Etchelle furnace is shown in operation at Crucible Steel in Solvay during the days of World War I. Courtesy of Crucible Specialty Metals, a Division of Crucible Materials Corporation

A photo of a picnic table around 1912 shows that straw hats were popular with both men and women. Courtesy of the George Arents Research Library, Syracuse University

Hopper's Glen offered cool seclusion. The picnic and hiking area south of West Seneca Turnpike was destroyed during the widening of the turnpike hill in the 1960s. Courtesy of the George Arents Research Library, Syracuse University

The Cardiff Giant en route to an unknown destination in 1913 was loaded aboard one of the Brockway Motor Company's new Cortland-produced trucks. Courtesy of George Snyder

The south side of Syracuse was the scene for a circus performance in 1911. Circus parades, replete with elephants, shown here along an unpaved street en route to the circus grounds, were always popular with youngsters. Courtesy of Onondaga County Historical Association

In the years before the flood dam along Onondaga Creek was erected, flooding was common on Syracuse's south side. This view is along South Salina Street, with a patient youngster waiting for the waters to go down. Courtesy of the George Arents Research Library, Syracuse University

The Cortland County fair, held in Cortland, attracted thousands, who arrived by street-car, as this photo of the main entrance taken in 1912 indicates. Note that visitors came in their Sunday best. Courtesy of Cortland County Historical Society

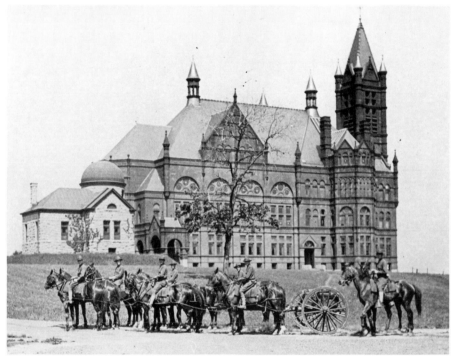

A reserve officers' field artillery training unit is shown at Syracuse University at the June 1914 graduation. Crouse College is the building in the background. Courtesy of the George Arents Research Library, Syracuse University

Guardsmen at the Life Saving Station at Oswego, shown above about 1900, performed superbly in rescuing ships approaching the treacherous entrance to the heavily trafficked Port Oswego. Today the Coast Guard bears this responsibility. Courtesy of Erie Canal Museum

Within the school system, students at Central High School in Syracuse went on a week-long strike in 1911 against a proposed school session change from the two short periods—8:30 a.m. to 12:45 p.m. and 1:15 p.m. to 4:40 p.m.—to a single 8:45 a.m. to 2:45 p.m. session. Parents who encouraged their children to work supported the pupils. Others pointed out that students would no longer have three warm meals at home.

The one-session day won out, with the disclosure that studies of Regents examination results proved the single session best.

Further, some cafeteria prices at the time indicate that schools were able to provide nourishing food at low prices: bananas or apples, two cents; sandwiches, two, three or five cents; cupcake or bun, one cent; dinner (meat, creamed potatoes, melba salad, bread and butter), ten cents.

The lunch scene shown above was photographed in an unidentified Syracuse school, apparently on a special occasion, as the chalkboards in the background indicate a classroom rather than a cafeteria. Courtesy of Onondaga County Historical Association

These were the officers quarters at Fort Ontario around 1910. The base served French, British and then United States troops in eight wars, including World War II. It is now part of the state parks system. Courtesy of Erie Canal Museum

This is the interior of the Billy Sunday Tabernacle in Syracuse. Tens of thousands jammed the wooden structure during the evangelist's visit in 1915. Courtesy of Erie Canal Museum

Crowds lined up outside the Syracuse Tabernacle to attend Billy Sunday's appearance in November 1915. Courtesy of Onondaga County Historical Association

Billy Sunday, third from left, gave the devil the boot as he and his wife arrived for a Syracuse spiritual crusade. He appeared in Syracuse several times, in 1915 and again in 1923. Courtesy of Onondaga County Historical Association

137

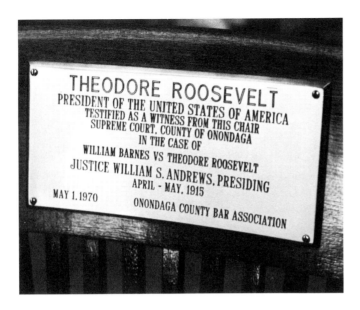

About the time the torpedoing and sinking of the British ship Lusitania, was making headlines, local attention was focused on one of the great trials of the century—the Barnes-Roosevelt libel action which opened in the Onondaga County Court House on April 19, 1915. William Barnes of Albany, a state Republican leader, was suing former President Theodore Roosevelt for remarks Roosevelt had made in a campaign speech the previous year. Roosevelt had linked Barnes with boss rule, leading to what Roosevelt called a state government "rotten throughout in nearly all its departments."

Roosevelt asked for a change of venue from Albany to Onondaga County. Spectators filled the courtroom to watch the parade of prominent witnesses pass in review and to hear the colorful ex-president, who was on the stand for nine days. As one reporter said, "The audience learned a lot about the charge up San Juan Hill."

The jury deliberated forty-two hours to reach a verdict for Roosevelt. But both men were tarred by the testimony. Barnes died shortly afterward.

The witness chair used by Roosevelt and Barnes is now on exhibit in the New York State Supreme Court Room in Onondaga County Court House, Syracuse. Photo by Al Edison

Theodore Roosevelt is shown here on the witness stand during the 1915 libel trial. In the background is presiding State Supreme Court Justice William Andrews. Courtesy of Onondaga County Historical Association

Soldiers at Camp Syracuse and those on troop trains passing through benefited from Red Cross Canteen services during World War I. Courtesy of the Syracuse and Onondaga County Chapter, American Red Cross

The community's War Chest was established in Syracuse in 1917 as a consortium of war-related charities. It was the forerunner of the Community Chest, and eventually the United Way, concept in Central New York. Courtesy of Syracuse and Onondaga County Chapter, American Red Cross

Of the twelve thousand area men serving in World War I, ninety percent went overseas, with the Syracuse University Ambulance Unit, formed early in 1917, the first to reach France. Troop D of the First Cavalry, New York Guard, traded in horses for machine guns and fought at Ypres and in the drive across the St. Quentin Canal. In this picture, troops of the New York Twenty-seventh Infantry Division go over the top at St. Mihiel in September 1918. Courtesy of U.S. Army

The Packwood Hotel, Skaneateles, now the Sherwood Inn, was a temporary hospital for flu victims during the 1918 influenza outbreak. Courtesy of the Syracuse and Onondaga County Chapter, American Red Cross

Not all of the 1918 casualties were limited to the front or the flu epidemic. The early evening of July 2 was a typically lazy summer day—a time to enjoy supper and plan a relaxing few hours on the front porch. People at Taunton and Howlett Hill just west of Syracuse could look toward Split Rock and its forested hills. There was no warning.

Initially a flash spread across the horizon, momentarily blotting out the landscape. The sound took longer—eight, ten or fifteen seconds, before it rolled into downtown, spread across Solvay and swept toward Camillus. No one questioned what it was. The trinitrotoluene plant at the Semet-Solvay works, located on a thousand-acre site at the old Split Rock quarries, had blown. The explosives produced there were shipped to munitions plants and Allied forces around the world.

Investigations pieced together the causes. An overheated gear in a grinding unit set afire a wooden building. Firefighters sought to control the flames—until water pressure failed.

In an instant fifty men were blown up; another hundred were rushed to area hospitals. But this was wartime. The shattered buildings, production lines and transport facilities were immediately replaced, as were the workers. The shipment of munitions continued as before. Courtesy of Onondaga County Historical Association

Rail birds get a good look at the finish of a trotting race at a Cortland County Fair circa 1930. Trotting events were part of the local tradition in the Homer-Cortland area. Courtesy of Cortland County Historical Society

CHAPTER SIX

Triumphs and Trials 1920-1945

Mostly, people were looking toward the twenties as the time when they could reap the rewards for their sacrifices during the war years. Factories returned to producing peacetime goods. The Wilsonian Democrats were swept from office in 1920. America withdrew from foreign affairs. The Senate refused to ratify American membership in the League of Nations. The whole Allied scheme to intervene in Russia's Communist revolution in order to stabilize the giant land into a constitutional democracy died through lack of perseverance on the part of the United States, Britain and France.

On January 1, 1920, the Volstead Act became the law of the land. And America's lifestyles changed overnight.

The great event began quietly enough. Beer signs came down. Brewery doors were boarded. Federal agents joined local people as enforcers of the prohibition laws.

It was not long, however, before enterprising individuals were doing their best to meet a demand. The proximity to the Canadian border made Central New York an underground railroad in reverse. Cargoes of contraband liquor by truck or auto trunk slipped over the St. Lawrence and into northern New York, then south to Syracuse and Cortland via Route 12. Some of it of course, stayed for local imbibers. The rest of the shipments went to the Southern Tier and Pennsylvania.

The transporters were known by agents as "flyers" because they took a shipment and "flew" with it. Usually they were young men looking for fast, easy money and a bit of high-speed adventure. At times they came to grief because they sampled the product while driving along. The border agents did their best to get the boats as they crossed the river, thus avoiding high-speed auto chases. But only about one boat in fifty could be overtaken.

The turbulent years of the twenties led to dramatic busts of stills and speakeasies. But public opinion shifted, and by 1933 the Volstead Act and prohibition were history.

Although the postwar period commenced with a recession, the economy of the 1920s was marked by a general exhilaration. The automobile industry was in its ascendancy. The Franklin Automobile Company employed five thousand workers in its Geddes Street plant, giving the consumer one of the finest mass-produced cars in the world. In Cortland the Brockway Truck Company, no longer a fledgling, was turning out custom-designed trucks, buses and fire engines.

The growth of the automobile and the emergence of the airplane as something more than just a rich man's toy or a war weapon meant new worlds for the oil industry. The value of petroleum stocks went through the roof. Other industries were reaping the benefits of consumer demand, new products and new buildings. The stock market kept going up. Everyone had a tip. Buying on margin at a fraction of the cost of a share and then selling as it went up was a sure way to a fortune—if the stocks did not go down, requiring the buyer to pay the whole cost. Everyone was sure that stocks could only go up.

The great old stores were the centers of downtown Syracuse: E. W. Edwards, Dey Brothers, the Lincoln Store, Chappell's and Witherill's made a trip to the city a special treat. Improved trolley and interurban railway service, newly paved roads and cars which no longer required a mechanic-in-residence to operate made a trip to town much easier.

Restaurants and tearooms—Schrafft's, Childs', and other fine restaurant chains offered luncheon treats.

The movies, with live vaudeville—skits, circus acts and song and dance routines—offered a full afternoon's entertainment after a morning of shopping and then lunch.

The greats of the day appeared in Central New York in the twenties and thirties, with the Upstate cities regular stops on the vaudeville circuits. Eddie Cantor, George Burns and Gracie Allen and Jack Benny were all veterans of the local vaudeville stage, appearing at one or more of the dozen Central New York movie palaces. They were to be followed in the thirties by the big bands of the period, the Dorseys, Jimmy and Tommy; Glen Miller, Benny Goodman and Abe Lyman, all of whom appeared in one-night stands at college campuses, at amusement parks and for hotel engagements at the Persian Terrace in Syracuse.

The flying machine was bolstered by the return of the war flyers who often bought surplus planes and then barnstormed the country offering rides and lessons. Often they gathered a crowd by performing stunts over a village. One of the aviators would leave the cockpit and walk on the wing. Sometimes the spontaneous show would end with the walker leaping into space, depending upon his or her parachute for a safe landing. Any fairly level pasture could become an aerodrome for a day.

Thousands of residents would visit the municipal field in Amboy on weekends to watch the daring flyers of the late twenties

The mass destruction occurring in the 1929 Auburn Prison break was evidenced in this early use of aerial photography by the Syracuse Herald *in capturing a fast-breaking news story. Courtesy of Cayuga County Historian's Office*

ply their trade. Charles Lindbergh was one of them, landing the *Spirit of St. Louis* there in 1927 following his flight to Paris earlier that spring. It was also the terminus for several unsuccessful endurance flights in 1928.

In the early thirties Syracuse was a regular stop for American Airways flights to New York and Chicago, and for Colonial planes en route from Canada south to Philadelphia and Washington.

The rudimentary wireless contraption which enabled people to communicate without wires over long distances via a series of dots and dashes achieved broadcast capability by the early twenties, so that on September 15, 1922, Clive Meredith of Cazenovia was able to broadcast from his home. The first listeners heard Melville Clarke of Syracuse, a nationally prominent harpist, play from the Meredith home via the newly designated station WMAC. Central New Yorkers affiliated with the amateur radio operators of America were contacting their colleagues throughout the world. In 1927, Charles Heiser of Auburn was the chief transmission point in sending and receiving news by radio for the *New York Times* from the Schooner Morrissey in Baffin Bay on a polar expedition. He was later in constant touch with Admiral Richard Byrd in Antarctica.

The story of Auburn Prison, which had become world famous since its opening in 1816 because of its dramatic electrocutions (the electric chair was introduced there in 1890 when William Kemmler of Buffalo was executed for murdering his wife), achieved new heights of raw drama in 1929 with a riot that was not to be surpassed until the Attica Prison uprising more than four decades later.

The prison itself was a place of terror in its early days. Beatings and the use of the cat-o-nine tails were standard. Captain

Elam Lynds introduced new ideas of brutality during his stay as warden, including the lockup of a third of the prison population into continuous silent solitary confinement without even the solace of labor. Within a year five inmates had died; one became insane and another threw himself from a gallery landing onto the courtyard below. The captain also reintroduced the lockstep and devised the punitive shower and other unique practices. During Auburn's earliest days, convicts were marched two hundred miles across the state to help build Sing Sing State Prison in the lower Hudson Valley, then marched back.

The use of electricity as an execution tool was frowned upon by the electric companies who feared a backlash again their generators (which did not happen). But before all state executions were transferred to Sing Sing in 1916, electrocutions in Auburn totaled fifty-seven, including Leon Czolgosz, Chester Gillette and Mary Farmer, the first woman to be electrocuted in the state.

Then shortly after noon on July 28, 1929, the prisoners revolted. By nightfall, when an uneasy peace had been established, four convicts were found to have gone over the wall, two were dead and five guards and six city firemen were shot or otherwise wounded. But that was only the start. Six months later, on December 11, a group of prisoners, mostly with life or long-term sentences, killed Principal Keeper George Dunford and grabbed Warden Edward S. Jennings as hostage.

The convicts were enticed into a hall with their captives. Police, state troopers and guards leveled a barrage of tear gas. The armed convicts returned fire and retreated to the cell blocks, where they were shot down in a final standoff. Eight prisoners were killed, and nine persons, including two convicts, were wounded. Three convicts, Claude Udwin, William Force and Jesse Thomas,

This is the hall at Auburn Prison where the warden and other prison officers were held captive during the bloody 1929 riot. Courtesy of Cayuga Museum of History and Art

were electrocuted at Sing Sing for their roles in the riot.

Immediately afterward, a major remodeling of the prison began, continuing for five more years.

The second outbreak had occurred less than two months after the stock market crash of October 29 and six days after C. Harry Sanford, a Syracuse banker, spoke over WFBL Radio to share with Central New Yorkers his opinion that there would be no serious long-range effects from problems on Wall Street.

The stock market was not the only problem. People were overspent. They could not meet their bank obligations. Companies laid off workers who then could not afford to buy even necessities. Banks were over their heads in repossessed homes and factories. Farmers could not sell their produce. International trade went into hiatus behind a facade of protective tariffs. The world economy was coming apart at the seams.

Smaller banks failed; then larger ones, hard-pressed to meet depositors' demands for return of their cash, closed their doors. It was before the days of deposit insurance, and many people were lucky to get ten cents on their dollar.

Despite public work projects and a variety of legislative bandaids, the depression continued, becoming worse. Governments toppled. Franklin Delano Roosevelt replaced Herbert Hoover in the White House, pulled America off the gold standard and closed the banks for a day. Some never reopened. In Germany, Adolph Hitler took over the Wiemar Republic.

The depression, despite a brief easing, continued until 1941, when the lend-lease of supplies and equipment to the Allies and war production began to sponge up surplus goods and production space. The newly established draft and hiring competition meant almost one hundred percent employment.

The depression meant an end to many firms in the luxury car field. The Franklin Motor Car Company struggled to keep up, but it could not compete with Fords or Chevrolets at five hundred dollars. Layoffs and cutbacks followed one after another. Then, on April 3, 1934, the last Franklin came off the Geddes Street assembly line. It went to Syracuse University Chancellor Wesley Flint.

Syracuse needed a replacement industry. Local banks and businesses got together. Carrier Corporation, a Newark, New

Jersey, company headed by Dr. Willis Carrier, who had found a way to cool the air, was looking for a new home. The Chamber of Commerce served as the marriage broker for the Geddes Street site. And Central New York found another major employer.

The depression offered several other positives for Central New York. Works projects resulted in the development of a number of major works, including the Onondaga Lake Parkway, the Salt Museum and the French Fort along the northern shoreline of Onondaga Lake.

And at least prices were down, unlike prices in Germany in the mid-twenties, when a wheelbarrow full of marks was needed to buy a loaf of bread.

On February 1, 1935, the A&P offered a two-pound can of pork and beans for nine cents; a Birdseye fish dinner of one pound of fillet of sole, a box of washed spinach and a box of fresh strawberries for seventy-five cents; rolls of Waldorf paper were at six for twenty-five cents; while a carton of cigarettes was $1.20. Coffee—Eight O'Clock brand, was nineteen cents a pound. Veal went for eleven cents a pound at Kreischer's Market, with lamb at eighteen cents and roast beef at nineteen cents.

Carl J. Ballweg advertised funerals at $89, with complete quality service at $195.

A new Pontiac Standard Six went for $615 and a suit or overcoat at Howard Clothes sold for $19.75, alterations included.

For amusement, a Sunday excursion round trip from Syracuse to Niagara Falls was two dollars.

Prices had not changed much by 1936. On May 1 Wells & Coverly was advertising suits at $25, while the Addis Company was offering dresses for $10.95 and $16.95 and Roy's was listing a seventeen-piece living room set, including rug, for $55, with $1 down.

On the football field, Syracuse University had developed a national reputation. Several games stood out. The "Battle of the Plains" at West Point in 1926 degenerated into a riot, with the game called very suddenly in the fourth quarter following a Cadet score and an Army 27 to 21 win. The officials were escorted off the field by armed military policemen. Ribs Baysinger (later to coach the Syracuse Orange), was thrown out of the game and barred for the season for flattening referee Victor Schwartz after a questionable call. Syracuse fullback Ray Barbuti was last seen at the game in full pursuit of Schwartz, being slowed down somewhat by a cluster of his teammates.

Syracuse did not play Army again until 1955.

Two other highlights of the prewar years both occurred in 1938 at Archbold Stadium. Grantland Rice, the legendary sports journalist, called the October Syracuse-Cornell game the most exciting college game he had ever seen.

Until late in the fourth quarter, though, it was not much for Orange supporters. Cornell was leading 10 to 0. Then Syracuse quarterback Sidat-Singh threw for a touchdown, making the score 10 to 6. Cornell ran the kickoff back for ninety-four yards. Score, 17 to 6. Sidat-Singh ran the kick off back into Cornell territory. Two successive passes to Harold "Babe" Ruth, and it was Cornell 17, Syracuse 12 with three minutes to go. Cornell tried to run out the clock, but a Cornell backfield man threw a lateral—to a Syracuse player. On the next play, Sidat-Singh threw his last pass of the day—to Phil Allen for the winning touchdown.

Several weeks later Syracuse defeated Colgate, 7 to 0, for the first time in fifteen years, setting off wild demonstrations on campus and downtown.

The state fair building program continued in the postwar

years, with the Coliseum dedicated in 1923 by Governor Al Smith as a "million-dollar mile of cows" paraded passed attendees at the World Dairy Congress. Visitors from Japan, the Netherlands and South America were joined by five thousand dairy farmers, area officials and family members who arrived in a fleet of a thousand automobiles from Cortland and a trainload of dairy enthusiasts from Philadelphia.

Three years later the Hambletonian, America's premier harness race, (the equivalent of the Kentucky Derby for trotting horses) was inaugurated at the state fair with a purse of $73,600. Guy McKinney, a bay colt owned by Henry B. Rea of Pittsburgh, was the winner. After several years the race was moved to Goshen, New York. It has never returned, being presently located in the New Jersey Meadowland complex.

During the depression the fair provided both farm families and city dwellers with the best entertainment for the dollar.

By the mid-1930s, Syracusans were enjoying baseball at newly built Municipal Stadium, with the Syracuse Chiefs once again International League contenders. Long Branch and Suburban Parks in Manlius and Auburn's Emerson Park offered amusements and a way to forget the still-persistent depression.

The trains no longer ran through city streets. After many years of debate, legislation and land acquisition, both the New York Central and DL & W were elevated in 1936.

Two years later there were no railed vehicles running on any streets. Buses replaced the last of the electric trolleys, and the interurban system had also become another casualty of the automobile age.

The third decade of the twentieth century had its share of uncertainties. The depression, huge carnage on the highways, and the constant threats of infantile paralysis were commonplace concerns. Art-deco architecture startled the sensibilities of many, while talking movies and an ever-expanding network of radio stations vied with swing music and jitterbugging as ways to while away the time. To the east, there was an ominous sense of uncertainty, where Europe was in turmoil. By 1940, the Luftwaffe was prevailing over British skies. U-boats were decimating Allied shipping and leaving heavy deposits of bunker oil along America's beaches even while American destroyers escorted British convoys across the Atlantic. Hitler moved into Russia, threatening to overcome the Soviets in a few months. To the west, the Japanese were increasing pressure on China, and its relationship with the United States was at an all-time low.

Still, on December 7, 1941, a grey, snowy Sunday in Central New York, no one really expected anything significant to happen. Few even knew where Pearl Harbor was.

The shock and inaction lasted less than twenty-four hours. By the next day, volunteers were in line at the recruiting offices; civil defense systems were forming, and war was declared.

In Central New York the community geared for war in an incredibly short time. Civilian products took back seats to military needs. Carrier air conditioners were needed more for submarines and aircraft carriers than for suburban theaters. Lipe Rollway was building gun-turret bearings; other plants produced land mines and parts for carbines. Alco's locomotives were needed to muscle the railroads here and abroad; Brockway was producing military trucks. Auburn Penitentiary's cargo nets were used as ship-side ladders for debarking troops on dozens of invasion beaches.

With the National Guard called up, the Jefferson Street State Armory was used as a draft reception center and headquarters for the hastily organized state guard, a home-defense unit devised to serve in event of emergency or invasion. Fortunately, its service was mostly passive.

As male students went into the military or war work, college campuses were populated mainly by coeds, army or navy units for special training, or scientists engaged in military research.

There was no local college football in 1943. Baseball continued in the former Municipal Stadium, now renamed for General Douglas MacArthur. But nearby facilities, instead of Florida, were the sites of spring training.

Travel was an ordeal. Trains and buses were jammed. Reservations—available only on a priority basis—were required for air travel.

Casualties, far heavier than in World War I (the only comparison was with the Civil War), were carried in daily newspaper columns.

Civilians were earning big money, but had no place to spend it other than on War Bonds or black market items. New cars were not even being made.

A thirty-five hundred acre plot of ground north of the Syracuse city limits was marked off by government surveyors. The land, flat and with few nearby hills, had the perfect configuration for an airport—a large airport—to handle the biggest planes yet created.

Syracuse and Auburn became liberty ports for sailors from the new naval boot camp at Sampson on the eastern shore of Seneca Lake fifty miles to the west.

The Cavalier Room at Hotel Syracuse was transformed into an officers' club while the lower level of the former Third National Bank Building at James and Salina streets became the home of the USO (United Services Organization).

Central New Yorkers were fighting on every front. General Jonathan Wainwright, a former Skaneateles resident, was captured by the Japanese at Corregidor, in the Philippines. Many were in the Aleutians. Others trekked across the Pacific with General Douglas MacArthur's forces or with the Marines on their invasions of Japanese outposts from Tarawa and Kwajalein to Guam and Iwo Jima in early 1945. A few months later the war in Europe was over. Soldiers were placed on transports, headed toward the Pacific and told they would be in at the final chapter—the dreaded invasion of the Japanese homeland.

Then, on August 7, came the dawn of the atomic age, with the bombing of Hiroshima.

By December, tens of thousands of soldiers and sailors were on their way home to Central New York. The war industries were producing only surplus, and began to ring down the production lines. Wartime workers stepped aside for returning veterans. And colleges and universities were trying to decide how they could participate in the government's new G.I. bill educational program. There were twelve million veterans, a substantial number interested in getting an education. Colleges did what they could, providing housing and classrooms in Quonset huts, trailers, and prefabs. Nighttime classes and trisemester years were augmented by the establishment of new campus locations, and even new colleges, at former bases such as Plattsburgh and Sampson.

During Prohibition, a lot of liquor came from stills in Puerto Rico, shown in these photos spirited home by a former Prohibition agent from Syracuse. Near beer, a legal product, was laced with alcohol to give it a buzz. Pure alcohol, cut several times and mixed with flavors and coloring, was bottled, often behind counterfeit labels.

Any old barn or out-of-the-way loft building could be converted into a still, brewery or bottling plant. Any old ingredients might be used also, with less than healthy results. One concoction called for mixing radiator alcohol, motor oil and sulfuric acid. Supposedly this lethal mixture could be conjured into a safe drink by straining it through a felt hat—but in fact the concoction would remain potentially deadly.

The results of all this industry made Al Capone and his cohorts multi-multimillionaires. The Mafia had found a true niche in the New World. Courtesy of Onondaga County Historical Association

The delivery system of illegal liquor was not complete until places to dispense the liquor were opened. By 1921 there were two hundred such spots in Syracuse—all behind locked and guarded doors. Some were fashionable homes; others, upstairs apartments. Still others were in cellars or behind curtained storefronts.

The police were effective. They would periodically raid the places, dump the liquor and leave. The bootleggers were also effective. The proprietor would have his, or her, wrist slapped. The bail bondsmen would be at the jail, often before the paddy wagon arrived, and in a few days everyone would be back in business.

Bootlegger counteraction was through the efforts of government agents like Elliott Ness in the Midwest and Charles Kress and Lowell R. Smith, who arrived in Central New York in 1930 with a team of twenty agents setting up headquarters in Syracuse for Prohibition enforcement in eastern New York.

Shown here is a raid circa 1926 when the Strand Cafe at 521 South Salina Street was stormed by, from left, agents Jacob Ehrlich, Fred Hazeltine, James Kehoe and Robert Weddington.

One of the biggest raids against a wildcat brewery was the attack by Captain Kress and his units on the home of Conrad J. Kitsz. A complete brewery, capable of turning out 1,750 gallons of beer a shift, was seized. The owner's wife, however, was not happy. She threatened to unloose two attack dogs on the raiders. The agents forced their way in, taking charge of twenty-one barrels of beer, a thousand bottles and the still, then valued at seventeen hundred dollars. Courtesy of Onondaga County Historical Association

147

By the early 1930s a groundswell of public opinion to repeal the Eighteenth Amendment was demonstrated locally by a massive anti-Prohibition parade in the spring of 1932. Franklin Roosevelt used repeal as an effective plank in his successful run for the presidency that fall. Courtesy of Onondaga County Historical Association

General John J. Pershing, leader of the American Expeditionary Forces in Europe during World War I, is shown here speaking to the 1922 New York State American Legion convention delegates in Syracuse. Second to his right, with white hair, is Baseball Commissioner Judge Kenesaw Mountain Landis, with Army Chief of Staff George C. Marshall next to him. Courtesy of Onondaga County Historical Association

148

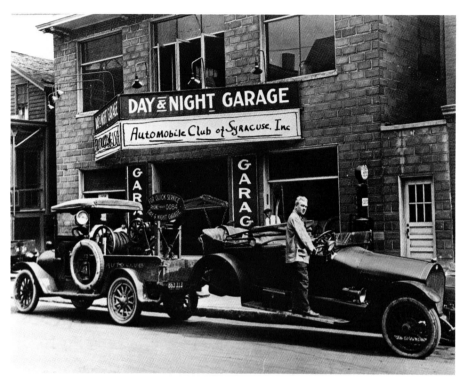

The early AAA towing service provided by Day & Night Garage was a big selling point for Automobile Club membership in the days when almost every motor trip could mean mechanical or tire trouble. Courtesy of Automobile Club of Syracuse

Clinton Square, Syracuse, became a temporary parking lot in the early 1920s as the Erie Canal was filled in. The work on the Canal is visible in the upper middle section of the photo where the old canal bed and the Warren Street bridge can still be seen between Syracuse Savings Bank and the Gridley Building. Courtesy of Erie Canal Museum

Publicity photos are not all that new. Here is a 1922 picture of the Truax Hotel being moved across Harrison Street by a woman-powered winch. The purpose of the move was to make room for the Hotel Syracuse, which still remains on the site. *Courtesy of Erie Canal Museum*

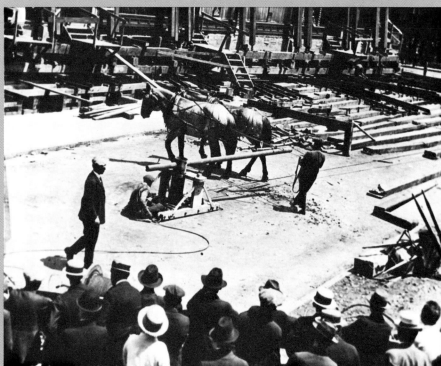

After the publicity photo was taken, a team of horses took over the work of turning the windlass which moved the Hotel Truax across Harrison Street while scores of spectators watched the unusual transfer of the four-story brick building. *Courtesy of Erie Canal Museum*

The movers of Hotel Truax managed to pull the building across Harrison Street without disrupting electric and water service for the hotel residents, although presumably no one took the ride. *Courtesy of Erie Canal Museum*

This was an opening day in the twenties at the old Star Park on the west side of Syracuse near Genesee Street. In the background is the Onondaga Pottery Works, leveled in the 1960s. The playing field had previously been a dumping ground for broken pottery and players would often dig out pieces in the outfield during lulls in play. Courtesy of Onondaga County Historical Association

Schrafft's, which opened in Syracuse in 1906, was the brainchild of a relocated Brooklyn candymaker, Frank G. Shattuck. The restaurant, shown in its South Salina Street days, soon captivated the imagination and taste buds of Central New Yorkers. Schrafft's closed on January 5, 1965, as a result of changes in both downtown and in lifestyles. A few recipes from the menu demonstrate its attraction in an era of high calories.

Hot Fudge Sauce
One stick of butter
Three ounces unsweetened chocolate
One cup sugar
Pinch of salt
One cup heavy cream

Melt butter, chocolate and sugar over hot water in double boilers. Add other ingredients. Let cook for two hours. Just before serving, add one teaspoon vanilla. Makes about a pint of sauce.

Chicken À La King
One-half cup butter
One-half cup flour
Dash of paprika

Melt butter, add flour and paprika. Blend.

Add slowly, stirring constantly:
Two cups hot chicken stock
One-half cup heavy cream
One-quarter cup milk, scalded

Heat and cook five minutes on low heat. Remove from stove and add:

Two slightly beaten egg yolks
Two cups cooked chicken, cut in strips
One cup mushrooms, sauteed in butter
One-half teaspoon salt
One-half cup pimento strips

Use on toast or in patty shells.

Courtesy of Onondaga County Historical Association

Director Harry Harvey (with megaphone), appears here driving the camera crew during the shooting of the silent movie Sitting Bull, *which was filmed on the Onondaga Reservation in the early 1920s. Courtesy of Onondaga County Historical Association*

The movie, by the 1920s no longer a novelty, gave new interest to the lives of many. Rudolph Valentino, the star of The Sheik *and other romantic films, is shown here during a visit to Syracuse. In a short but dramatic career before his death in 1926, Valentino set a new style for screen romance, as did Mary Pickford and Douglas Fairbanks. Courtesy of Onondaga County Historical Association*

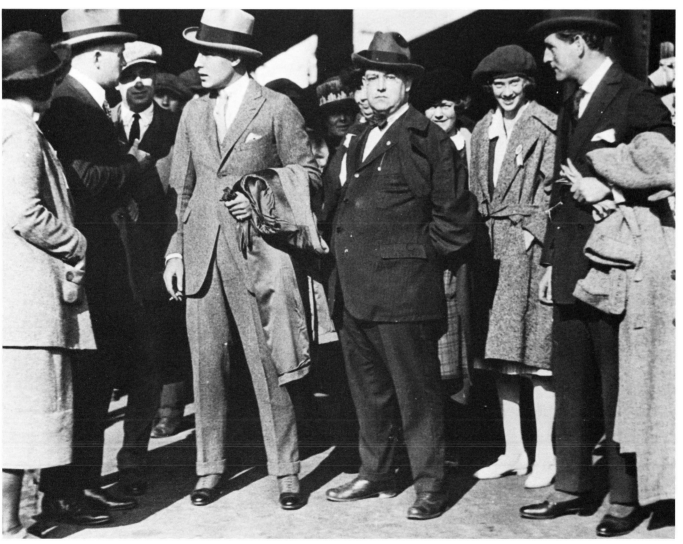

One major film, A Clouded Name *starring Norma Shearer, was filmed on location in Syracuse around 1923, with the Calthrop Estate (now part of Route 81), Chittenango Falls, the Hotel Syracuse and the New York State Fair among the familiar backgrounds. Shown here is the cast on location and a scene from the film. Courtesy of Onondaga County Historical Association*

The Strand Theater at Harrison and South Salina streets was an important stage and movie house in Syracuse until the late 1950s, when it was leveled to make room for a parking garage. This scene is from the early 1920s. Courtesy of Erie Canal Museum

The popular Long Branch Amusement Park along the western end of Onondaga Lake was reached by both steamer and trolley in the days before World War II. Courtesy of Erie Canal Museum

An early airliner was photographed nose-down in Bethke Field, where Brace-Mueller-Huntley is now located in East Syracuse. No one was injured in the 1920s accident. Courtesy of Onondaga County Historical Association

Central New Yorkers were eager to greet Charles Lindbergh when he arrived at Amboy Airport with the Spirit of St. Louis *on July 28, 1927, during his tour of the United States following his solo flight to Paris. Courtesy of Onondaga County Historical Association*

Charles A. Lindbergh, the first person to fly solo across the Atlantic, was escorted by a Syracuse motorcycle patrolman on his arrival at Amboy Airport in 1927. Courtesy of Onondaga County Historical Association

News of the exploits of aviation pioneers was front-page copy, as were the all-too-common crashes. The Zeppelins, which were as long as a couple of football fields end to end, were fascinating sights as they roared majestically across the sky. The first Zeppelin to come to Central New York was the Shenandoah; then came the USS Los Angeles. Thousands of residents stayed up all night in 1928 awaiting a flyover by the Graf Zeppelin as it completed its round-the-world journey, but they were to be disappointed when the ship changed course to avoid thundershowers. Courtesy of Onondaga County Historical Association

The produce market at North Salina Street near Pearl Street preceded the present regional market on outer Park Street. The Salina Street market closed in the early 1930s. Courtesy of Erie Canal Museum

The partially completed statue of Columbus is shown around 1930 on St. Mary's Circle in Syracuse. Hotel Onondaga, demolished in the early 1960s, can be seen between the Cathedral of the Immaculate Conception, left, and the Towers of the combined First Baptist Church and Mizpah Hotel Building, which is now being sold. Courtesy of Erie and Canal Museum

Fine arts students at Syracuse University found the old Yates Castle shown on facing page a suitable subject for romantic art. The gothic fantasy was built by Cornelius Tyler Longstreet in the mid-1850s on Irving Avenue just below the present site of Crouse College on the Syracuse University campus. It was then bought by Alonzo Yates. Later the home of a teachers' college and then the journalism school, it evoked speculations of secret passageways behind a main entrance hall mirror and a reported waiting room on the Underground Railroad capable of accom-

modating a hundred persons. Yates was known as an abolitionist sympathizer, so the rumor may have been more than mere supposition.

In 1950, however, expansion was in the works for the Upstate Medical Center. The Yates Castle, despite the generations of talented writers and publicists who studied there and who offered their help in saving the structure, was doomed. A last social ball in 1953 beat the wrecking ball by a few days. Courtesy of Syracuse University

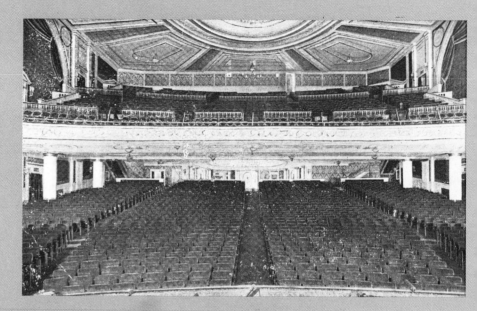

B. F. Keith's movie theater on South Salina Street in Syracuse, shown here in a view from the stage, was one of the grand motion-picture theaters of the twenties. It was razed to make room for Sibley's Department Store in the 1960s. Keith's management called it "the most magnificent theater in all the universe. Come when you will, there's a welcome to greet you, a handclasp to thrill, and a true smile to meet you."

A converted storefront or ballroom was suitable in early movie days for presenting the latest from Hollywood, but it was soon recognized by promoters that ambience and an exotic setting with comfortable seats strengthened the moviegoer's sense of getting away from it all. In the years just prior to the Great Depression, a chain of remarkable specialty theaters, utilizing Spanish-Moorish architectural motifs in opulent crimson and gold, carpeting and dramatic lighting effects, were built across the country. In Syracuse, Loew's, the Strand, the Paramount and Keith's all provided luxurious surroundings for enjoying an imaginative interlude. All except Loew's were demolished in the 1960s. Courtesy of Erie Canal Museum and Onondaga County Historical Association

The State Tower Building in Syracuse had been recently completed when this photo was taken circa 1927. Note the electric trolley lines overhead. Courtesy of Erie Canal Museum

The great movie palaces of the prewar years survived until the mid-1950s, when the growing impacts of television, urban renewal and a deteriorating downtown environment led to the closing of most central-city houses. In Syracuse only Loew's on facing page survived, although its doors were closed for several years until it was rescued by historical preservationists using a mix of private contributions and government funding. Even now, however, it is used only for special films, stage presentations and concerts; but the splendidly ornate lobby, balcony, box seats and stage accoutrements remain intact and in good repair. Only the massive organ is missing; some believe it was removed to a West Coast pizza parlor. Photo by James Scherzi Photography

The Chimes Building looms along West Onondaga Street, Syracuse. To the left is the Fourth Presbyterian Church, subsequently razed to make way for a parking lot and eventually the expansion of Hotel Syracuse. The sketch was by Louise Shrimpton on March 5, 1931. Courtesy of Onondaga County Historical Association

The Cafe DeWitt, at the intersection of Erie Boulevard East, Water and South State streets offered Syracuse a unique art-deco style during the twenties. It did not survive the depression. Courtesy of Erie Canal Museum

Skyscrapers reached the Upstate area in the mid-twenties with the incentives for big investment returns leading to the financing of the State Tower Building on the site of the old Bastable Block in 1927. At the other end of downtown Syracuse, the Chimes Building was erected at Salina and Onondaga streets.

A few years later art deco entered into local architectural thinking, with the Niagara Mohawk headquarters on Erie Boulevard, West going up in 1932. Created by the Bley & Lyman firm of Buffalo, the gleaming steel and glass building with its 114-foot illuminated tower was adorned by the Spirit of Light, *a massive stainless steel sculpture, shown here in closeup and in its final position on the building.*

The new building was in keeping with the dominant Chrysler Building in New York City, Radio City Music Hall, the interior of the French superliner, the Normandie, *and the New York Central's streamlined* Twentieth Century Limited. *Courtesy of Niagara Mohawk Power Corporation*

Miss Tiby's class at Elmwood School in Syracuse is shown in June of 1930. Teachers in training are standing along the farther walls. Courtesy of Onondaga County Historical Association

Miniature golf drew thousands of enthusiasts when the craze hit in 1930. This course was located in Syracuse. Courtesy of Onondaga County Historical Association

"The Greatest Show on Earth" drew a capacity crowd to the big top in the Syracuse Valley area in the mid-thirties. More adults than youngsters seem to be working their way forward. Courtesy of Onondaga County Historical Association

The scourge of polio was treated in cumbersome iron lungs during the 1930s. These patients were at City Hospital for communicable diseases located on Renwick Avenue, Syracuse, to the southwest of Crouse-Irving Memorial Hospital. Polio victims often had to live in the machines, some for the remainder of their lives. Courtesy of Henry W. Schramm

President Franklin D. Roosevelt, right, applied the trowel at the cornerstone laying for the new School of Medicine building at Syracuse University on September 30, 1936, while Vice Chancellor William P. Graham looked on. Courtesy of the George Arents Research Library, Syracuse University

An alphabet soup of government economic palliatives as passed by Congress and signed into law—the NRA (National Recovery Act), with its blue eagle symbol shown above; the WPA, (Works Project Administration); the CCC (Civil Conservation Corps); SS (Social Security) and the AAA (American Agricultural Act). The AAA commenced a system of farm subsidies that continues to this day, paying farmers for not producing, or buying surplus produce, thus preventing prices from going below a pre-set level. Courtesy of Onondaga County Historical Association

165

One of America's first depression-bred federal housing projects was the $4.5 million Pioneer Homes development in Syracuse, which provided low-cost housing for more than seven hundred families in an eastside area cleared of blighted homes in the mid-1930s. The development is still operational. Courtesy of Henry W. Schramm

Dr. Willis Carrier, the developer of the air conditioner, is shown with the Onondaga Pottery centrifugal refrigeration machine in the Smithsonian Institution, Washington, D.C. Carrier moved to Syracuse from New Jersey after a community-wide recruiting effort to attract industry in the later part of the 1930s. He took over the abandoned Franklin Motor Car plant on South Geddes Street. Courtesy of Henry W. Schramm, from They Built a City

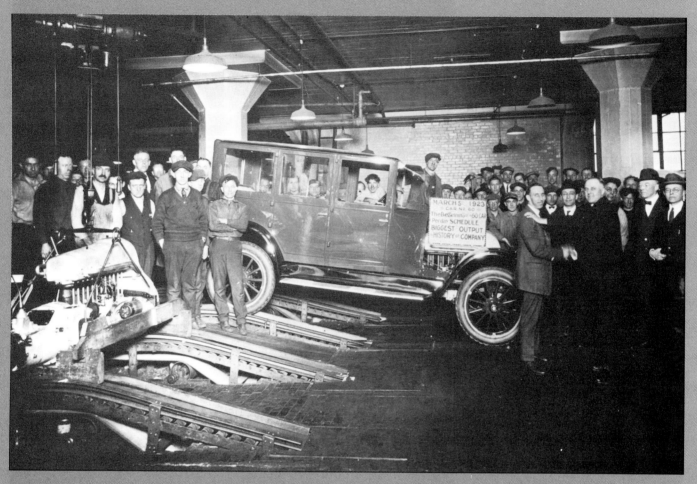

Sixty quality cars a day rolled off the South Geddes Street assembly line at the Franklin Automobile Company in Syracuse in 1923, the greatest output in the firm's history. The auto plant, taken over by Carrier Corporation after Franklin closed in 1935, was later a General Electric factory before being leveled to make way for Fowler High School. Courtesy of Onondaga County Historical Association

This was a trainload of community pride. A New York Central steam engine on East Washington Street stopped in front of the University Building, at left, with freight cars taking thirty-two Franklin cars to market in the early twenties. Proud Franklin car owners formed a guard of honor along the street. Courtesy of Onondaga County Historical Association

A uniquely Syracusan scene, as a New York Central passenger train shared city streets with motor cars. This is a view along elm-lined East Washington Street before the tracks were elevated in September 1936. Courtesy of Onondaga County Historical Association

On a rainy September afternoon in 1936, the westbound Empire State Express ran along Washington Street, through Vanderbilt Square and then to the West Street Station. It was the last train on the street tracks of Syracuse. The next train stopped at the new Erie Boulevard East depot at the base of Crouse Avenue, then continued over the elevated section of track west of the city past Solvay. Finally people in downtown offices could leave their windows open on summer days without inviting drastic rings around the collar. Courtesy of Onondaga County Historical Association

The westbound Empire State Express, *at right,* was the last train through Syracuse city streets on September 24, 1936. The locomotive is shown approaching the West Street Station for the last time. World War I dough boys squeezed into their uniforms for a last hurrah on a special float saluting the new station at Erie Boulevard East (now a bus terminal). The first steam engine crew over the elevated tracks were, from left, Norm Lynch of Utica, R. E. Barrett, Buffalo, and George Forsythe, Syracuse. The lucky engine was Number 5278. Courtesy of Onondaga County Historical Association

Former President Herbert Hoover, right, with Chancellor and Mrs. William P. Graham of Syracuse University, attended the dedication of the Maxwell School of Citizenship on November 12, 1937. Courtesy of the George Arents Research Library, Syracuse University

This was the scorecard for the August 8, 1938, baseball game in Truxton between the New York Giants and the Truxton Giants. The game was played as a salute to the late John McGraw, a Truxton native and Hall of Fame manager of the Giants. Courtesy of Cortland County Historical Society

John J. McGraw, born in Truxton in 1873, went on to become the manager of the New York Giants from 1902 to 1932. He died in 1934. Courtesy of Cortland County Historical Society

Truxton celebrated its Sesquicentennial in 1958 at the mid-village monument to native son John J. McGraw, baseball Hall-of-Famer and former manager of the New York Giants. At the ceremony at left is Jack McGraw, descendant of the ballplayer; Bernard Potter, partially hidden, and Albert Kenney. Courtesy of Cortland County Historical Society

A Central New York blizzard had left these train passengers among the missing in the mid-1930s. Happy to be found, they eagerly greeted photographer Art Cornelius of the Herald-Journal. *Courtesy of Onondaga County Historical Association*

Wrong-Way Corrigan was besieged by fans during his August 18, 1938, visit to Amboy Airport in Syracuse. Corrigan filed flight plans in New York for a trip to California, then showed surprise to airport officials in Ireland when he landed there instead. *Courtesy of Onondaga County Historical Association*

A trio of Syracuse University greats coached Bill Orange in the late 1920s. From left are Roy Simmons, Sr., head coach; Victor Hanson, who was All-American in both football and basketball; and Lewis P. Andreas, who became athletic director. *Courtesy of the George Arents Research Library, Syracuse University*

Wilmeth Sidat-Singh was a black player on the Syracuse University football team in 1938. But in an era when neither colleges nor professional sports teams accepted black athletes, he was billed as a Hindu. In one game at College Park, Maryland, he sat in his hotel room because Maryland refused to play with a black on the Syracuse squad. The hero of the 1938 Syracuse-Cornell football game, Sidat-Singh is shown here participating in his second-best sport, basketball. Courtesy of Athletic Department, Syracuse University

More than thirty-five-thousand spectators at the 1938 Syracuse-Colgate clash on November 5 watched as John Long, (number sixty) Colgate's half-back, just missed a pass. The Syracuse defense was up for the game. Colgate's was almost as good. Phil Allen ran around Colgate's left end for fourteen yards and a touchdown early in the third quarter for the only score in the game. With the extra point it was Syracuse 7 to 0.

Syracuse—the university and the city— celebrated. Streetcars were lifted off the tracks. Downtown hotels were ransacked. Thousands jammed the streets. Traffic came to a halt. It was the biggest celebration since Armistice Day, almost twenty years before. Courtesy of the George Arents Research Library, Syracuse University

Changing times reflected in this late 1930s photo in which buses moved side by side with trolleys along Salina Street in Syracuse. The tracks were soon replaced by macadam, as the next photo shows the work in progress. Courtesy of Henry W. Schramm

Guests on the last streetcar in service in the city of Syracuse wore this badge for the 9:30 p.m. ride on January 4, 1941. Buses took over from the electric trolleys, which had entered service in 1888. Courtesy of Onondaga County Historical Association

GUEST

LAST
STREET CAR RIDE

JANUARY 4. 1941

1888

1941

SYRACUSE, N. Y.

One of the most disastrous fires in Syracuse was the Collins Block blaze of 1939. Here the photographer caught the moment that the building collapsed into East Genesee Street, *entombing nine city firemen, while office workers watched from windows in the adjacent State Tower Building, left. Courtesy of Key Bank of Central New York*

Radio meant news, sports and entertainment. Edgar Bergen and Charlie McCarthy, Fireside Chats, Lowell Thomas and the news and Joe Louis fights joined the shower of noise and voices. And a successful Herald-Journal newspaper editor, E. R. Vadeboncoeur, above, switched from print to join the staff of WSYR as a news commentator on August 24, 1939—a few days before the German invasion of Poland opened World War II. Within two years Vadeboncoeur was to be covering the war as a foreign correspondent, a contemporary of Edward H. Murrow, H. V. Kaltenborn and Walter Cronkite. Courtesy of the Syracuse Newspapers

One of the local men stationed at Pearl Harbor was Sgt. Howard Keller, a Syracusan who was serving with the army in Hawaii. He was writing a letter home when he began to hear shellfire from Pearl Harbor three miles away—a little unusual for a Sunday morning. Going outside, he saw plumes of thick black smoke. An officer came by, and said, "We're at war with the Japanese." Keller soon found his .45 automatic was of little use against aircraft.

Keller never forgot the lesson. "I don't think there's been a day in my life since Pearl Harbor that I haven't thought about it," the sergeant said. Invalided out of service for wounds received in Guadalcanal shortly afterward, Keller was a frequent speaker for preparedness until his death in 1986. The war scene shown here was taken during the attack on Pearl Harbor. Courtesy of U.S. Department of Defense

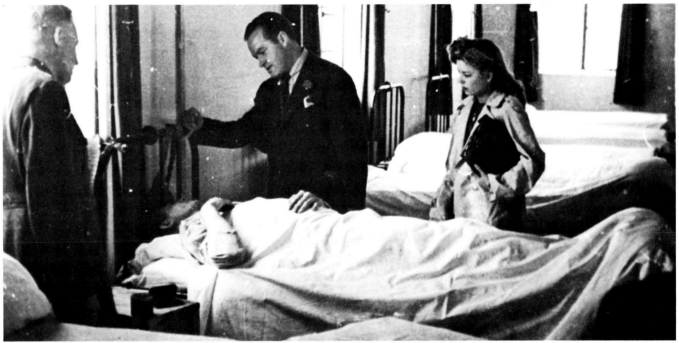

The Fifty-Second General Hospital unit, organized by the Syracuse University College of Medicine with a skeleton group of medical officers early in 1941, was activated in 1942 and trained at Camp Livingston, Louisiana, and Camp Kilmer, New Jersey, before undertaking a January crossing of the Atlantic. In England the unit established a hospital of seventeen hundred beds in Woverly, in Britain's Midlands, in just over ninety days, receiving its first patient on April 15, 1942.

The hospital staff found themselves caring for some unusual ailments. The American nose did not do well in the English climate, and respiratory ailments were common. Then there were patients from a detachment stationed in Iceland for two years; some were psychotic.

The battle casualties did not really start to arrive until the invasion of Normandy on June 6, 1944—or more accurately, five days later, on June 11, with the arrival of the first hospital trains from the British Channel ports. With the winter weather came the great influx of the soldier's curse, trench foot.

During its stay in England, the Fifty-second handled twenty-five thousand hospital bed patients, plus huge numbers of outpatients. During this entire period through June 1945, it experienced only five battle casualty deaths, and a few others from accident or disease.

Col. Walter Perry, commander of the Fifty-second General Hospital unit, Maj. John Marsellus, Adjutant, in the background, and Col. Richard S. Farr, who was later to command the unit, are shown here during an inspection of the grounds, with British civilians looking on from the periphery.

Patients at the Fifty-second General Hospital were sometimes visited by concerned celebrities; in the photo above, Bob Hope and Frances Langford were taking time for a wounded soldier at the facility.
Photos courtesy of Maria Farr

Scrap metal was needed for the war effort, so relic cannons of bygone years, even an ancient steam fire engine, found their ways to the scrap heap. Courtesy of Onondaga County Historical Association

The New York state fairgrounds became an army depot in World War II, not a training camp as in the first World War. A series of storms destroyed the race track grandstand. As shown here, a break in the Solvay wastebed dike on November 26, 1943, flooded part of the grounds, State Fair Boulevard and nearby homes with sludge. Courtesy of Erie Canal Museum

Wartime aviation at the Amboy Airport often meant something a little unusual. On December 16, 1944, a snowstorm left travelers with no choice but horsepower to get to their American Airlines DC-3. Courtesy of Onondaga County Historical Association

Everything during the war was in tight supply. Sugar, cigarettes, coffee, gasoline, tires, meats, and butter were hard to get. Ration cards or stamps were needed—although there was no guarantee the goods would be available. A thriving black market persisted in many products. Even golf balls were hard to come by, costing three or four dollars apiece. Pricing gouging was a way of life. *Courtesy of Onondaga County Historical Association*

Production of weapons at an Onondaga County plant during World War II was taken over by women. *Courtesy of Onondaga County Historical Association*

Packages for troops were prepared by young women during World War II. Courtesy of Onondaga County Historical Association

On August 30, 1942, the first B-17 arrived. It was the forerunner of hundreds of giant aircraft which used the Syracuse bomber base as a stepping-stone to Europe. A hut city sprang up south of the runways to house thousands of maintenance troops, guards and transient aircrews. Courtesy of Richard Palmer

Army Air Corps men from the Syracuse bomber field and their dates enjoyed skating at the Drumlins Country Club. Courtesy of Richard Palmer

The Syracuse bomber base provided a storage area for hundreds of hooded B-17 and B-24 bombers at the conclusion of World War II. Courtesy of Richard Palmer

Lt. Gen. Jonathan Wainwright, a former Skaneateles resident, broadcast the announcement of the surrender of Corregidor Island in the Philippines in 1942. The picture is from captured Japanese files. Courtesy of the Defense Department

A headdress for Lt. Gen. Jonathan Wainwright, following his return to Skaneateles from a Japanese prison camp, is delivered by a relay of local boy scouts. The tribal headdress was a gift of the Onondagas. Photo by Robert W. Johnston, courtesy of Onondaga County Historical Association

Lt. Gen. Jonathan Wainwright was greeted by Gen. Douglas MacArthur after Wainwright was released from Japanese prison camp in 1945. He was honored with a giant parade in September 1945 upon his return to Skaneateles. Courtesy of Onondaga County Historical Association

Chief John Big Tree of the Onondagas, whose profile appeared on the Indian Head five-cent piece, was photographed years later, in 1955, in an expressive study by Edison. The nickel had a buffalo on the reverse side. Courtesy of Al Edison

C·H·A·P·T·E·R S·E·V·E·N

The Postwar Era
1945-1987

Again, within two generations, the nation returned from war into a world of technology with expectations and desires reshaped into unusual patterns. The last desperate Nazi efforts brought about rocket development and ended global distance as a way to survival, leading instead to a delivery system for the atomic bomb and space travel. Advancements in radio technology, radar and aircraft construction evolved into a worldwide network of airlines. New materials and technologies opened ways as diversified as treating illness and the perfection of television. The entire package was cemented into place by advances in computer technology.

The universal availability of education for millions of veterans expanded their visions of a different future for themselves and their families. The baby boomer generation was born. There was to be an end to poverty. A start was made by leveling the neighborhoods of the inner-city poor.

Jobs were there for the taking. Carrier Corporation, Crouse-Hinds, L. C. Smith (which was to be merged into the Marchant Corporation, with the major manufacturing operations being moved to Cortland), Lipe-Rollway, New Process Gear, Crucible Steel, Allied Chemical, Brown-Lipe-Chapin, Rockwell and Columbia Rope had all benefited from war work. The economic future for Central New York was bright as industry turned to consumer goods.

Unfinished business from World War II and two previous wars rose to haunt successive generations. The Civil War's reconstruction opened its second century with a fierce flow of civil violence. The communist threat, abetted by new technology, moved out of the limited Soviet orbit into areas of Eastern Europe, Africa, China, southeastern Asia and Central America. Central New York was to have a major role in all of it.

When the troops returned from World War II there was a difference. Unlike the triumphant return of the Civil War and World War I veterans, there were no victory columns; main streets were not festooned with bunting. Companies, battalions and divisions did not return as units. Rather, the men as they were mustered out came singly or in pairs by bus and trains.

A few years later, in June of 1950, men were again called to the colors. The draft offices at the Chimes Building served as the rallying place for new recruits. Reservists and draftees were once more hustled through training as a small cadre of regulars held the line in Korea. The war, technically a police action, ended in stalemate. Again, the soldiers, sailors and airmen came home quietly.

Vietnam was the first war to be fought in Central New York's living rooms, with the network news bringing the front home in living color. The result was an internal conflict that divided the nation. Campus unrest soon created a reservoir of discontent, with both Syracuse and LeMoyne marked by protest, teach-ins, sit-ins and splits within the student bodies of those who supported and those who opposed the war.

David J. Miller, LeMoyne, Class of 1965, became the first of many Americans to burn his draft card, this at an antiwar demonstration in New York City that October. Peace vigils and protest meetings during 1968 were exacerbated by the assassination of Dr. Martin Luther King, Jr., and Senator Robert F. Kennedy, the riots at the Democratic Convention in Chicago, and the high casualties suffered on the Vietnamese front.

The Kent State shootings, student disapproval of college administrative authority and other instances of unrest were to leave scars still traceable today.

Another "police action" concluded with Americans retreating under fire, leaving behind their Vietnam allies. Soldiers and marines returned unhonored except by their loved ones.

Probably no invention in history has had more impact on society, including Central New York, than television. It started off blandly enough, with Melville Clarke performing with his harp from a hastily constructed studio in lower Court Street at 7 p.m. Wednesday, December 1, 1948. It was the same Melville Clarke who had appeared on the first radio show in 1922. WHEN-TV was on the air.

From these beginnings the community sampled a smorgasbord of local, national and worldwide politics, warfare, civil strife, accidents and disasters. People could see a tornado happening in Texas; rescue crews trying to pry people from train wrecks; the latest in fashion, music and the stage from New York and Hollywood. Sports happened in the living room. People in Auburn watched as golfer Lew Worsham holed a shot from mid-fairway to win a title in Chicago. Cortland residents saw Syracuse University dump the Penn State football team in 1959. The assassination of John F. Kennedy was a television event, as was the on-the-air shooting of Lee Harvey Oswald, his assassin, by Jack Ruby.

The Big Eye became the babysitter for the younger generation, with all of the moral and ethical implications this involved. The photogenic politician was in. Surface news coverage replaced in-depth reporting. Owners of baseball parks and movie houses had to change their tunes to bring back their audiences. And much of the equipment—the tubes and first color sets—came off General Electric's Electronics Park assembly line.

The thirty-year dream of Jerome Rusterholtz, a Syracuse auto dealer, came true in 1955 when Governor Thomas E. Dewey ceremonially opened the initial link in the new Thruway just outside Syracuse. The Thruway was to be joined by the rest of the Rusterholtz vision in the 1960s when the Penn-Can Highway, Route 81, was built connecting the Southern Tier and points south with the St. Lawrence and Canadian markets. Communities along the old canal route east and west and the north-south wagon trails were now linked by high-speed, limited-access roads. Arterial expressways relieved traffic problems in cities across the state, including Auburn, Syracuse, Homer-Cortland and Rome-Utica.

The new emphasis on auto travel changed the configuration of cities to what educators and community planners called the doughnut concept—a core city of business, industry and retailing surrounded by residential suburbs, with the periphery including a number of independent and centralized school districts. Manufacturing firms and offices were relocated in the periphery where taxes and congestion were more moderate. Physical deterioration soon turned sections of the inner cities into crisis areas. Crime and social problems found fertile soil. It would almost seem that bureaucrats in many communities greatly admired the devastated areas of bombed-out London, Hiroshima or Amsterdam.

Urban renewal to clean up substandard housing and business zones often left rubble-strewn no-man's-lands, with inadequate public housing for the dispossessed and no plans for appropriate commercial usage. The disadvantaged moved to the adjacent neighborhoods. It was one more factor in the poor-versus-middle-class theme and racial mistrust which led to open conflicts. The cast was set for the civil disturbances of the 1960s.

The end of World War II also significantly altered the life of Upstate's black communities. The blacks who had gravitated to the Fifteenth Ward in the near east side of Syracuse found themselves displaced by urban renewal while they were being joined by thousands of newcomers from the south who had arrived to work in defense industries and then stayed on. The black population grew 120 percent from 1940 to 1950. In the 1950s, the increase was 144 percent, while between 1960 and 1970, another doubling occurred. The trend continues.

Unlike New York City and other regional centers, Central New York was fortunate in the 1960s. Although there were campus demonstrations and some disturbances resulting from the civil rights movement, untoward violence did not occur. A relatively minor flareup in Syracuse's east side was responsibly handled by police and local officials in cooperation with black leaders.

After two hundred years, some elements of the conflict between member nations of the Iroquois Confederacy and the Continentals during the Revolution continue to rise up. The courts are still considering claims by the Oneidas for millions of acres of land in Jefferson, Lewis, Oneida, Madison, Cortland, Chenango and Broome Counties, which they say were illegally bought by the state of New York in the 1780s, and claims by the Cayugas to the west, for other territory.

In an area bounded by lakes, streams and rivers, the shortage of water was at one time unthinkable. But by 1960 industrial expansion and population growth set a group of Central New

The entrance to Fort Ontario in Oswego is shown in this painting by an unknown artist who was among the liberated refugees from Europe who were at the fort from August 1944 until July 1946. They included seventeen nationalities and were mostly Jewish. Courtesy of Fort Ontario State Park

Yorkers to thinking about water needs into the next century. Alexander F. "Casey" Jones, a tough-minded editor of the Herald-Journal, was named to chair the committee. The outcome was a monumental plan by the Onondaga Water Authority to tap Lake Ontario as an unlimited source of fresh water. A spirited publicity campaign featuring a cartoon drop of water helped convince voters to approve a referendum.

Growth meant greater demand for gas and electricity, too. With hydroelectric plants along the rivers reaching limits, the webbing of shared power lines continued to encroach on new areas. New generations of oil and nuclear-powered generators were built, with Niagara Mohawk the major Central New York provider of power.

New York State Gas and Electric, meanwhile, was expanding its facilities and linkages to assure power to its Central New York and Southern Tier customers, while the little independent Solvay Power Company continued to churn out enough electricity to meet the needs of Solvay Process, business in the town of Geddes and area residents.

The great energy crisis of the seventies was enough to encourage drilling in the Auburn area to tap resources of natural gas, a process which provided gas in commercial quantities by the late 1970s.

Henry Schliemann uncovered seven levels of the ancient city of Troy, indicating that the city was built and rebuilt over earlier ruins for a period covering many centuries. Central New York has moved a lot faster. It is common to find blocks in downtown areas where in just one hundred fifty years four or even five buildings have existed on the same site. Major fires gutted many; others merely outlived their economic usefulness.

The elite James Street of Syracuse may as well have been hit by a series of buzz bombs. The gorgeous elms, some already stricken with Dutch elm disease, came down to make way for a wider street. More than a dozen elegant mansions, built in the late nineteenth century by wealthy industrialists and merchants and

Syracusan Jerome Rusterholtz for years had lobbied for a superhighway from New York to Chicago without a red light—an idea sparked by a talk in 1920 by a General Motors executive, given long before the German Autobahn was built during the Third Reich. Participating in ground breaking for the Thruway in Liverpool on July 11, 1946, are, from left, Syracuse Mayor Frank Costello, Liverpool Mayor Michael Heid, Governor Thomas E. Dewey, for whom the superhighway was eventually named, and Jerome B. Rusterholtz, the "father" of the Thruway. Courtesy of Automobile Club of Syracuse

tended by staffs of retainers, could no longer be adequately maintained. Heirs sold the properties to developers, making way for sprawling one- and two-story offices and a few high-rise apartment buildings.

The loss of the elms, however, was part of a catastrophe which affected the entire state, although Syracuse was particularly hard-hit because of its identity as the City of Trees. Now efforts are being made not only to provide a mix of shade trees in Upstate counties, but to develop a disease-resistant elm as well. Already ten such elms are growing at the headquarters of the Syracuse Parks and Recreation Department.

Education was undergoing changes, as well—both physically and philosophically. LeMoyne College came on the scene in 1942, continuing to expand from its original four hundred fifty students at a downtown building to a large campus east of the city and a student population of close to two thousand.

Still, this was not enough to accommodate the hundreds of thousands of Upstaters seeking a college education. Syracuse University branched out into Utica and Endicott (Harpur College). In the nineteen sixties the State University of New York came into its own under Governor Nelson Rockefeller, with vast infusions of state money and effort eventually making SUNY one of the world's largest universities.

The roles of corporate and governmental research on campus were evidenced at Syracuse as the university's corporate research share grew, since 1980, from one percent to twenty-six percent of its total research budget. Software technology got a boost from the establishment of CASE (Computer Application and Software Engineering), the computer software center at the school. The SUNY College of Environmental Science and Forestry and Upstate Medical College are deep into highly sophisticated studies unheard of a decade earlier.

The schools at Cortland and Oswego, formed originally as teachers' colleges (or normal schools), expanded their curricula and physical plants, offering liberal arts and business administration courses and specialization in social studies as well as teaching.

Two-year community colleges were created in the nineteen-sixties in Onondaga and Cayuga Counties to provide a higher educational experience for students who otherwise could not afford or qualify academically for four-year schooling. Courses were geared to meet community business and industrial needs. Eventually the limited schools improved their stance to gain acceptance of their credits at the bigger institutions.

SUNY at Morrisville expanded its agricultural school as well. Colgate University, a men's four-year college in Hamilton, and Cazenovia Junior College, previously a girls' school, both became coeducational institutions.

The medical profession has experienced unparalleled growth since World War II and the discovery of penicillin, the sulfa drugs and new uses for whole blood and blood derivatives. Doctors remember that in the mid-1930s a person surviving to age sixty-three was said to have lived a long life. Pneumonia, often fatal, was beaten down by sulfanilamide. Office visits cost two dollars; home visits, three to five dollars. It was not until the 1950s that measles, mumps and polio could be counteracted by immunization.

Blood banks did not come into general service until World War II, with the various refinements in processing and component production through the Red Cross's Central New York Blood program coming even more recently. Hospital or medical insurance came into general usage following the war. Previously a charge of eighteen to twenty dollars a day was not unusual for a private hospital room; and with fewer tests, equipment and special procedures, other costs were also far less. Of course, fewer people lived as long as they do today.

Dr. J. G. Fred Hiss is believed to have been the first doctor in Syracuse to have used penicillin. A local woman suffering from a blood infection was the patient, with Crouse-Irving Hospital the scene. The woman fully recovered.

It has been only within the past few years that Central New Yorkers have undergone successful heart transplants. A Brewerton resident who in the spring of 1985 could not walk across his lawn is one typical example of this new technique. A year later, following the receipt of a new heart at a Boston hospital, he was playing golf, mowing instead of walking across the lawn, and riding a bike several miles a day. Others, a Syracusan and a Canastota resident, also underwent successful transplants—an operation deemed impossible twenty years ago.

Hospitals evolved from local, specialized institutions to great medical centers offering broad services to growing numbers of expectant mothers as the baby boom materialized, and to treatment of the chronic diseases of the elderly, as life expectancy continued to rise and communicable diseases lessened. City Hospital (for infectious diseases) Syracuse and Onondaga Generals, St. Mary's Maternity Hospital, People's Hospital, Canastota Hospital and Auburn's Mercy Hospital (converted to Mercy Rehabilitation Center) all closed their doors. Crouse-Irving and

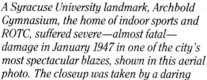

A Syracuse University landmark, Archbold Gymnasium, the home of indoor sports and ROTC, suffered severe—almost fatal—damage in January 1947 in one of the city's most spectacular blazes, shown in this aerial photo. The closeup was taken by a daring

Daily Orange *photographer who risked his neck crawling along an icy ledge on the nearby library building. Although rebuilt, the stadium was never quite the same. Courtesy of Syracuse University*

Syracuse Memorial joined to form Crouse-Irving Memorial. St. Joseph's filled up Prospect Hill. The University Hospital of the Good Shepherd became Upstate Medical Center, establishing a major off-campus complex, and Community General came into being on the crest of Onondaga Hill.

Faced with a dilapidated municipal airport which was a site highly desired by Solvay Process as an extension of its wastebed, the community decided that the former Syracuse bomber base, with thirty-five hundred acres of cleared land, runways, revetments and a control tower, would be ideal for a commercial field. In 1949 the first airliner landed at the former bomber base now called Hancock International Airport. In that first year, around a hundred thousand passengers enplaned or debarked. By 1986 the yearly total was 2,852,615. More than 161,000 planes took off or landed.

But it was just the start of a remarkable success story. Enlarged several times to its present east-west runway length of eight thousand feet, the airport is by far the best in Upstate New York, able to accommodate the largest airplanes.

The military aspects of the base continued at full tilt during the 1950s and 1960s when the Northeastern NORAD (North American Air Defense Command) headquarters was established in a massive reinforced-concrete blockhouse installed with electronic air control and combat readiness equipment. The unit was phased out in the early 1980s, following budget cuts in federal spending and new advances in technology which made it redundant.

The state fair itself nearly didn't survive the peace. Central New York had been without a major agricultural and industrial exhibition for six years. The premises were rundown. Other uses for money were being considered, and some people were looking to locations in other parts of the state. Governor Dewey turned down one suggestion that the fair be transferred to Oneida County. Then a temporary commission recommended a $52 million state expenditure for a year-round world's fair or exposition at the former bomber base in Mattydale.

Local political pressure enabled a limited fair to be mounted

in 1948. Basically a dairy exhibition with a horse show and rodeo as spectator attractions, the five-day event drew a total of twenty-five thousand persons, including exhibitors—less than a poor one-day showing in previous years. Yet it proved that the equipment still existed at the old grounds and that repairs could make it functional—even the mile track.

By 1949 the fair was ready to stage a full-scale comeback. And comeback it was, traffic jams and all. On Labor Day 103,000 people flocked to the grounds, many walking the final mile from abandoned cars and buses gridlocked along State Fair Boulevard. Many others caught in the crush never got to the fair at all.

Changes were in the works. A network of highways was eventually developed connecting the fair to the new Thruway, to Route 81 and to the center of downtown Syracuse. The Solvay Process wastebeds to the north became parking lots to absorb tens of thousands of cars. The fair had survived its greatest crisis.

As Central New York developed into an educational center and as industrialists and entrepreneurs found the time to travel abroad, the region's artistic sense developed. The performing and visual arts required showcases for display.

Although local artists had attained fame in New York and Europe, there was no real fine arts museum until an upper floor of the Onondaga Savings Bank Building in Syracuse was made available in 1900 for a tight little exhibit hall for paintings and sculpture. This was followed in 1906 by an "attic" museum at the new Carnegie Library on St. Mary's Circle. It was not until 1937, when the old Lynch homestead at North State and James streets was donated as a museum, that art shows finally made the ground floor.

Even so, much was lacking in exhibit space, parking, and facilities for teaching. It took almost three decades and settlement of a complex legal dispute before the Syracuse Museum of Fine Art actually became the Everson Museum, in its new I. M. Pei creation at Harrison and South State streets.

The region's performing arts programs, on hold since the

early 1930s, when the depression and overspending wiped out a promising future for a local symphony orchestra, came on strong in the nineteen sixties with the formation of the Syracuse Symphony under Karl Kritz.

With Christopher Keene's retention as conductor, and with the establishment of a new home for the performing arts in the Civic Center providing an acoustically superior hall of twenty-two hundred seats, the Syracuse Symphony advanced to perform in New York City's Carnegie Hall in April 1978. The Symphony has since positioned itself as a major orchestra.

Syracuse Stage, a professional acting ensemble, has located just off the Syracuse University campus, joining the Salt City Playhouse and the Pompeian Players, two amateur stage organizations, to carry on the traditions of the Shuberts and the early stock and traveling companies which visited the Wieting Opera House and the Bastable Building.

The movies, as well as many of downtown's retail establishments, have moved into neighboring shopping malls, a shift which commenced in the early 1950s when Shoppingtown in DeWitt became the first suburban retailing center in Central New York. It has been followed by several dozen malls and plazas of all sizes and shapes throughout the region, including the newly established Finger Lakes Mall west of Auburn.

Some major stores such as Syracuse's Witherill's and Edwards have gone out of business locally, unable to cope with discounters. But others, including Chappell's and Dey Brothers, both old-line local establishments, have successfully moved into shopping mall circles.

Thousands of children lamented the closing of Edwards in 1974 because it meant as well the passing of the monorail at Christmastime in the Annex Store on Clinton Street. After a visit to Santa, who sat at the foot of a seemingly endless stairway to the sky, a youngster would rush to the top where, for ten cents, he or she could jump into one of a series of dangling cars. A man would come by, closing car doors. A few seconds later, the train was moving, passing over the countless fascinating toys in the departments below, then on to the mysterious storage rooms. As it returned to the toy department, a youngster could spot Mother's anxious face in the crowd below.

One Edwards tradition remained alive into the 1980s. The Edwards Tea Room featured each week for years a special luncheon of creamed salt pork, which was especially appreciated by men on cold winter days. The Tea Room survived for a number of years in Syracuse Mall, built on the old Weiting site, until the entire building was renovated for office space.

The sports scene in Central New York took on the aspects of a kaleidoscope in the postwar era. In addition to a resurgence of college sports, pro basketball came with the National Basketball Association establishing a major league franchise in Syracuse in 1946.

The construction of the Onondaga County War Memorial enabled the area to attract top boxing talent, with televised championship events a frequent occurrence.

Hockey of the American League variety came to Syracuse, in 1951, then left, to reappear again, then leave as other professional leagues vied for attendance. Now there are none.

College basketball, for years a popular sport, with the university fielding on-campus teams since 1900, reached its nadir in the 1950s, unable to compete with the Nats. However, when the big leaguers, seeking a larger market, moved on to Philadelphia after the 1962 season, Syracuse University cagers took on new life. The newly constructed Manley Field House provided a suitable arena during the build-up stage, as Bill Orange commenced to appear from time to time in the nation's Top Ten listings. When the Carrier Dome opened in September, 1980, as a football-basketball

Although the growth of Syracuse University was truly spectacular—a three-fold increase in student population in just two years—other local colleges were also registering students in unprecedented numbers.

LeMoyne, a new Jesuit college named after the explorer-priest of the 1600s, was founded in Syracuse, with a freshman class of 450 beginning their college careers on September 22, 1942, in church quarters renamed

LeMoyne Hall, at 245 East Onondaga Street. Ground was broken for the present LeMoyne campus on the heights east of the city in May of 1946. Aerial photo by Al Edison, courtesy of LeMoyne College

crowd replacement for Archbold, which had been allowed to crumble away, plans had been made for a basketball seating arrangement for thirty thousand or more viewers. Then, in 1987 the team climbed to the top, reaching the finals of the NCAA championship, losing by one point to Indiana in a last-second shot, 74 to 73. The nationally televised game was attended by more than sixty-five thousand persons in New Orleans. It took a week for Central New York to recover.

Football, long the premier Central New York entertainment attraction, picked up at Syracuse University after a series of false starts immediately after the war, with the retention of Floyd Schwartzwalder as head coach in 1949. By 1952 Syracuse was bowl-bound—its first ever. But Alabama was in another league, and Syracuse underwent a trouncing of 61 to 7 in the Orange Bowl before a national television audience. Then came the Jim Brown-Ernie Davis-Floyd Little-Jim Nance-Larry Czonka years, with Bill Orange rising to Number one national ranking in 1959, with an 11 to 0 record, topped off by a 23 to 14 victory over Texas in the Cotton Bowl on New Year's Day, 1960.

The racial tensions of the 1960s led to team difficulties, followed a few years later by Schwartzwalder's retirement. Archbold began to crumble physically and teams under coach Bill Maloney just did not jell when facing powerhouses like Penn State or Pittsburgh.

The weatherproof Carrier Dome, with fifty thousand football seats, was just what was needed to get Syracuse back on track. Standing-room-only crowds have come out to see many games, even though the team has not yet measured up to the National Championship Squad of 1959.

International League baseball, which survived the war, had its greatest years in the Hank Sauer era of 1946 through 1948, and then fell on hard times. By 1956 the team had been sold to Miami, and except for a short period as an Eastern League city, Syracuse had no baseball until 1961, when a makeshift community-owned team again entered the International League. After a last-place appearance the first year, the team got even worse as the newly

formed New York Mets established its farm team in Syracuse. A few years later, however, Detroit became the parent club and the Syracuse Chiefs began to climb. In 1970, with the Yankees as franchise-holder, the Syracuse squad won the Little World Series, the nation's top minor league honor.

In Auburn the New York-Penn League continues to thrive, with the city witnessing the first game umpired by a woman, and the appearances of Pete Rose and of Ed Kranepool of the New York Mets at Auburn's Falcon Park in their rookie years.

The region's college campuses, transportation, sports sites and hotel-motel accommodations resulted in the selection of Syracuse as the site for the 1981 National Sports Festival and for a half dozen Empire State Games. In addition, special olympics for the handicapped and junior olympic activities have found homes here.

An old standby, auto racing, once again returned to the state fairgrounds in 1949, with more than eighty thousand people surrounding the track and jamming the infield to watch Indianapolis cars and drivers in a hundred mile AAA championship won by Johnny Parsons. It was the start of a continuing series of annual races which today features the richest dirt track events in the world, with the Miller 300 offering $300,000 in awards, with $75,000 going to the winner. In 1985 Sammy Swindell set a new world record for a dirt mile of 137.2631 miles an hour.

Water sports on Onondaga Lake took a major leap forward when the Intercollegiate Rowing Regatta, previously run on the Hudson River at Poughkeepsie, settled in for the annual national championships, a traditional event bringing in the best eight-man crews from across America for a series of two-thousand-meter races. The race site, near the location where Hiawatha is said to have met with the Iroquois chiefs to form the Iroquois Confederacy, is also the scene of unlimited hydroplane racing, the largest category of speedboats, featuring jet and turbine-powered craft capable of two-hundred miles an hour. A new world's record for a two-mile oval course was established in August of 1987 by Jim Kropfeld in his *Miss Budweiser* thunderboat at 145.6 mph.

Golf, always a local favorite since its inception before the turn

It was move-in time as parents helped newly arrived freshmen move into their LeMoyne College dormitories during orientation week in the fall of 1982. Courtesy of LeMoyne College

of the century, got a shot in the arm through postwar development and the enlargement of several local clubs. In addition, the stimulus resulting from the selection of Oak Hill in Rochester for the 1967 national open and the development of the B. C. Open as a regular annual Professional Golfers Association tour stop in Endicott seventy miles south of Syracuse, led to the establishment of Syracuse as the site for an annual PGA Seniors tournament.

The mid-1960s can boast of one incident residents can share with their grandchildren in much the same way the Blizzard of Eighty-eight was a mystic event for those who lived through it. This was the Blizzard of Sixty-six.

But Syracuse, with only 42 inches, could not compare with Oswego, known for its rough winters. Residents there measured up to 102 inches—several years' supply for many eastern metropolises.

Cortland's greatest storm? That occurred in 1961, when it was hit with 40 inches in one storm. The effects of lake-effect snowfall can best be seen when long-term annual records are compared. Auburn and Cortland, just off the direct flow of lake-effect activity, accumulate about 90 inches annually. Syracuse receives 110 and Oswego, 128 inches each year. Syracuse itself has had more than 650 official feet of snow since records were first kept by the Weather Bureau there in 1902.

It's been almost two hundred years since the military tracts were established, providing the necessary incentive to populate and develop the region known as Central New York. The interim changes have been astounding. The Industrial Revolution, wars and cultural shock all have interplayed. The past is past, a nice place to visit, but no one can stay there. This is a place of economic and social change. Old-line industries such as Columbia Rope and Solvay Process have departed. New industries are coming into focus. Much of the subject matter taught at the colleges and universities may well be obsolete by the turn of the century. Present medical knowledge may not be current even that long. The makeup of population—the average age, the ethnic backgrounds—are far different from just a half century ago. Even more changes lie ahead.

Except for one thing—Central New York weather!

Former Secretary of State Alexander Haig, left, had a brotherly chat with the Very Reverend Frank Haig, president of LeMoyne College, on March 3, 1987, at the testimonial dinner honoring the outgoing college head. Photo by Ron Trinca, courtesy of LeMoyne College

Fire Controlman William Francher, left, and an unidentified shipmate operated equipment controlling heavy battery fire aboard the Battleship New Jersey *off the North Korean coast during the Korean War. Courtesy of William Francher*

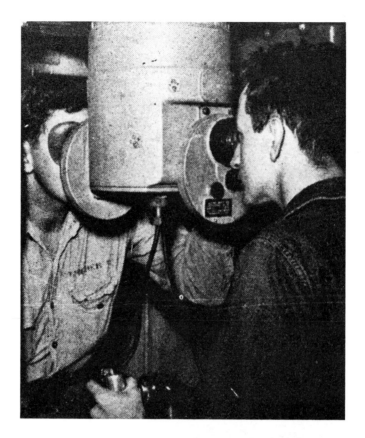

The Battleship New Jersey's *Turret One fired into the beach at Kosong, despite heavy rain and nighttime conditions in this episode during the Korean War. Courtesy of William Francher*

Taking shape in the closing days of World War II were manufacturing and research structures at General Electric's Electronics Park in Liverpool. It has been a center for high-technology research and production of military materiel and television and electronic goods. Other GE facilities in Auburn and Utica added significantly to the massive firm's Upstate presence. Courtesy of General Electric

Dr. W. R. G. Baker, left, head of General Electric's Electronics Park, greeted a celebrity television salesman for G. E. products—Ronald Reagan during a Syracuse stop in the 1950s. Courtesy of General Electric

Chancellor William P. Tolley of Syracuse University was photographed with former President Harry Truman during the chief executive's visit to the campus during the mid-1950s. Courtesy of the George Arents Research Library, Syracuse University

Mel Corp is shown winding the Marcellus Methodist Church clock in 1952. The clock, with its six-foot-wide face, was operated by a 145-pound running weight with an 800-pound sticking weight. It was installed in 1909, a gift of Mr. and Mrs. George Case. The mechanism was wound twice weekly until 1962, when it was electrified. Courtesy of Michael Plumpton and the Marcellus Historical Society

The exploits of the boxing DeJohn family of Syracuse were overshadowed by Carmen Basilio (at right), an ex-marine from Canastota who held both the world welterweight and middleweight championships in the mid-1950s. He is shown here regaining his welterweight title from Johnny Saxton. Eventually Basilio's nephew, Billy Backus, would go on to be the welterweight champion. Courtesy of Onondaga County Historical Association

The Syracuse Nats were on the march against the Philadelphia Warriors of the National Basketball Association, as Dolph Schayes (number four) is about to sink a layup in this 1950s game. Courtesy of Al Edison

This view of the jam-packed house was taken from the Onondaga County War Memorial stage in 1956 as the Syracuse Nats went against Fort Wayne for the National Basketball Association championship. The Nats won in the last minute of the seventh game. The Nats were to prosper for a decade, appearing in several final rounds against the Boston Celtics, in addition to their championship win in 1956. All-time great players such as Dolph Schayes, Johnny Kerr, Paul Seymour and Larry Costello played for owner Danny Biasone, the man who invented the 24-second clock to speed up the game and make it a truly popular big-league sport. Courtesy of Al Edison

The National Championship Syracuse football team in 1959 was congratulated by Dean Frank Piskor, at left, with head coach Floyd Schwartzwalder in center and team captain Gerhard Schwedes, after defeating Texas in the Cotton Bowl. Courtesy of George Arents Research Library, Syracuse University

One of the most spectacular fires in Syracuse history was the 1956 blaze which destroyed the First Methodist Church and Wesleyan Methodist Publishing Company at South State and East Onondaga streets. It broke out during the evening rush hour on a subzero day and left fire apparatus trapped for days under tons of ice. Courtesy of Onondaga County Historical Association

During the late 1950s this Brockway fire engine traveled well in excess of ten thousand miles across South America from Argentina to arrive in Cortland as a turn-in. The firemen were away from home for almost a year as they visited fire stations throughout the South and Central America. Here they were in New York City, just 250 miles short of their goal. *Courtesy of George Snyder*

The G. Lee Trimm mural at the Veterans Memorial Hall at the Onondaga County War Memorial was viewed by former President Dwight D. Eisenhower and Tully Congressman R. Walter Riehlman during a 1962 dinner at the auditorium. *Courtesy of Al Edison*

John F. Kennedy, at the time a senator, was in Central New York to meet with farm representatives. *Courtesy of Al Edison*

Charles P. LeMieux, a Syracuse Red Cross Chapter executive, helped to manage delivery of medical supplies to Havana, Cuba, in April 1963 for prisoners taken in the Bay of Pigs operation. Anna DiNatale of Syracuse's Nursing Services was also sent to Cuba and served aboard one of nine ships carrying refugees. Courtesy of the Syracuse and Onondaga County Chapter, American Red Cross

Richard M. Nixon was met by Congressman R. Walter Riehlman of Tully, left, during his October 1964 visit to Hancock International Airport. New York Secretary of State John P. Lomenzo is at right. Nixon was in town to speak on behalf of Republican presidential candidate Barry Goldwater. Courtesy of Onondaga County Historical Association

The nearby Canadian border became a haven for those opting to avoid the draft with their feet after President Lyndon Johnson announced his Gulf of Tonkin Resolution on the Syracuse University campus on August 5, 1964. The occasion was the dedication of the Samuel I. Newhouse Communications Center. In 1968 President Johnson found the heat in office too great as guns and Great Society spending proved not to mix. Richard Nixon moved in. Courtesy of the George Arents Research Library, Syracuse University

Jesse Devendorf was a Chittenango resident and an old-time steam packet operator on the Erie Canal; the photo was taken during his retirement, in 1964. Courtesy of Onondaga County Historical Association

The rural roads of Pompey are noted for snow. In this scene the plow is cutting through fifteen-foot drifts on March 29, 1948. Courtesy of Onondaga County Historical Association

Alley Oop, Dinny and their sculptors pose during a Syracuse University winter weekend. The year was in the early 1950s. Courtesy of Onondaga County Historical Association

The storm started on January 29, 1966, moving north along the East Coast and picking up moisture from the Atlantic. The center traveled up the Hudson Valley and then stalled over Montreal. The rotation of the storm caused northwest winds to run the length of Lake Ontario, leading to the well-known lake-effect snowfall—the phenomenon of water drawn up from the lake dropping as snow over the land.

On January 20, seventeen inches fell in Syracuse; another twenty-two inches on the 31st and three more inches on February 1. Combined with winds reaching fifty-five miles an hour and whiteouts, giant drifts of hard-packed snow closed everything. Well over a thousand motorists were marooned for several days at the Mohawk rest stop of the Thruway east of Herkimer; travel in Central New York was possible only by helicopter or snowmobile. Television crews camped in their stations. All businesses, stores, industry and schools were at standstills. *Courtesy of Al Edison*

Niagara Mohawk Power Corporation (NIMO), founded through the merger of a multitude of smaller utilities in 1940, built a gigantic oil-powered generator station at Oswego, shown above. The station was crowned by a 750-foot smokestack erected in 1974 and visible to Lake Ontario shipping for thirty miles. It was not long before this plant and the massive hydroelectric plant along the St. Lawrence at Massena were just not enough for Upstate and its downstate linkage. Nuclear power came to Oswego when the

Nine Mile Point Plant Number One opened in 1969. Almost before it was on line, plans were under way for an even greater unit, Nine Mile Two—a new design which had the misfortune of being constructed when anti-nuclear activities, new layers of regulatory bureaucracy and such experiences as Three Mile Island and Chernobyl led to extensive delays and multibillion-dollar cost overruns. Courtesy of Niagara Mohawk Power Corporation

A hard-hat diver here works below the water in the spent fuel pool at the Nine Mile Point Plant Number One, which has been in service since 1969. Courtesy of Niagara Mohawk Power Corporation

By 1967 the Ontario water system was completed, and in ten years had been enlarged to furnish five million gallons a day. The system provided the region with one of its four strongest advantages to encourage business and industry to settle in the area—skilled labor, surplus energy, proximity to markets and unlimited water. Miller Brewing settled in Fulton and Budweiser in Baldwinsville, establishing as well several satellite industries, including a major bottle-making plant near Auburn. Here, Thomas W. Smith, president of the Water Authority, throws the switch to start the flow in 1967 while County Executive John Mulroy, Ephraim Shapiro, chairman of the Board of Supervisors, and Syracuse Mayor William Walsh look on. Courtesy of Onondaga County Executive

203

Construction on Routes 81 and 690 took place in downtown Syracuse during the late 1960s. The present Syracuse industrial park was still serving as a busy railroad yard, upper center, while the Primex Parking garage, the white circular structure at right center, and the Yates Hotel, several blocks toward the center, still stood. The MONY Center, at far left, had just one tower and no nearby garage. Photo by Al Edison

Whole blocks came tumbling down in both the near east side and the downtown of Syracuse, as well as in Auburn and Oswego in the 1960s. Some blocks went by fire, but most were leveled to clear the rights-of-way for Route 81 in Syracuse and for arterial roadways, to remove eyesores and fire traps, and to make way for new downtown construction including the MONY (Mutual of New York) Center which served both as an employment anchor for downtown Syracuse and the beginning of local emphasis on service and financial industry. In this photo the Durston Building makes way for a parking lot at James and Warren streets. The Nettleton Company, a victim of foreign imports, closed, with the building renovated into office and residential space. The new Route 81 stands between the wrecking crews and the Nettleton Shoe Company plant. Courtesy of Erie Canal Museum

Poolo's, shown above, was one of Auburn's (and Central New York's) last ice cream parlors. It was noted for the marble counter, unique stools, tables and candy display case and the tantalizing odors of icy cold vanilla, and of heated chocolate. The building was demolished for urban renewal in the early 1980s. Courtesy of Cayuga County Historian's Office

This nineteenth-century gothic cottage, Bob-O-Link, at 7 Albany Street was saved from demolition in 1964 and is now a part of the charm of Cazenovia, where it serves as a town office building. Courtesy of Cazenovia Library

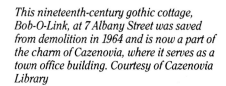

A firm foundation for downtown Syracuse took place in 1964 when a base for the twin 19-story towers of MONY Center was poured. The arrival of Mutual of New York and its data processing center was symbolically to mark the turnaround of the primarily manufacturing economy of the Syracuse region to high technology and service industries. The weather star was placed on top of MONY Center's weather tower more than 350 feet above street level in a final spectacular step of the construction. Photo by Al Edison

419 James St. Syracuse, N.Y.

Two views of the same intersection epitomize the changes of the past eighty years. Circa 1910 James Street, Syracuse, looking east at State Street, shows a sparse mixture of horse-drawn and motorized vehicles. A railroad crossing is visible, and trolley tracks lead off through a tunnel of elm trees.

Nearly eighty years later, the same intersection is bustling with cars and trucks moving by electric traffic signal; the road is wider and the buildings are denser. All tracks are gone, as are the elms. The Snowden apartments to the right remain, although in a less grand condition. Courtesy of Erie Canal Museum and Al Edison

The Syracuse Chiefs' all-time old-timers' game on August 26, 1963, brought in, from left, pitchers Charles "Red" Barrett and Teddy Kleinhaus; catcher Louis "Doc" Legett; right fielder Albert "Dutch" Mele; Goody Rosen, center field; Hank Sauer, left field; Jimmy Outlaw, third base; Claude Corbitt, shortstop; George "Specs" Torporcer, second base, and Frank McCormick, first base. Courtesy of the Syracuse Chiefs

Here MacArthur Stadium is packed for a Key Bank Night game. The park, considered one of the finest in the minors, was in danger of demolition in 1969 following a midseason fire which almost demolished the grandstand. Today the Syracuse Chiefs of the International League are affiliates of the Toronto Blue Jays. Photo by Al Edison

Karl Kritz, left, founded the Syracuse Symphony Orchestra in 1961. He died while conducting the orchestra in concert on December 17, 1969. Here he is shown discussing a score with musician Louis Krashner. Courtesy of Syracuse Symphony Orchestra

Kazuyashi Akiyama was named to succeed Christopher Keene at the podium of the Syracuse Symphony in 1985. Here he is with his wife Keiko. Courtesy of Syracuse Symphony Orchestra

Christopher Keene led the Syracuse Symphony Orchestra in a triumphant concert at Carnegie Hall in April 1978 and to national recognition as a major orchestra. Here he is shown during a rehearsal. He succeeded Karl Kritz as conductor. Courtesy of Syracuse Symphony Orchestra

The "attic" Museum of Fine Arts was located for many years on the upper floor of the Carnegie Library on Columbus Circle in Syracuse. This is as it appeared circa 1918. Courtesy of the Everson Museum of Art

The unique configuration of the Everson Museum at State and Harrison streets, Syracuse, is displayed in 1968 during construction of the building created by the noted architect, I. M. Pei. Courtesy of the Everson Museum of Art

Following some colorful but controversial exhibitions in its early days, the Everson Museum of Art has settled in under the more recent directorship of Ronald Kuchta. Among art acquisitions are a Stuart George Washington and Edward Hick's The Peaceable Kingdom, shown above, painted in the mid-1800s and purchased by the museum after a vigorous public fund-raising effort. In recent years there has been a move to return the International Ceramics Exhibition to Syracuse, building further on the area's recognition as a prominent manufacturer of quality china. Courtesy of the Everson Museum of Art

Hopper's Gorge, the former picnic and recreation area off Seneca Turnpike, was rendered in oil in this painting by Levi Wells Prentice, circa 1870, now at the Everson Museum in Syracuse. Courtesy of the Everson Museum of Art

The 1978 Syracuse varsity crew completes a heat race en route to its victory in the regatta on Onondaga Lake, the first national rowing championship for the Orange in more than fifty years. Courtesy of the George Arents Research Library, Syracuse University

Syracuse University football's finest hour in the present decade was on September 29, 1984. After three games, the Syracuse eleven was apparently not going far, after losing 19 to 0 to Rutgers the previous week. Coming into town was Nebraska, the Nation's number one team, in a game to be on national television. Aside from forty-five thousand Syracuse faithful who were expecting a trouncing, the Cornhuskers imported several thousand of their own fans to watch them continue their undefeated streak of twenty-three straight games. The previous year Syracuse had lost 63 to 7 at Nebraska's home in Lincoln. Oddsmakers said Syracuse would lose by twenty-five points. And that's the way the game seemed to be starting. On its second try, Nebraska scored its touchdown. Two possessions later, the Cornhuskers were on Syracuse's fourteen-yard line. But then the Orange's All American Tim Green rushed in to cause a fumble. Syracuse marched eighty-three yards, then scored a field goal. At half-time the score was 7 to 3. Then the Syracuse defense began to unravel the Nebraska squad. What happened next is described by Dana Cooke in the November 1984 Syracuse University Magazine. "With the ball on Nebraska's 40, SU quarterback Todd Norley stepped straight back and, defying more conservative strategies, lofted toward the roof a high, floating pass seemingly destined for catastrophe.

"As it floated through the soft, synthetic stratosphere of the Dome, onlookers all but closed their eyes. Those that didn't were fortunate: Wide receiver Mike Siano and two Nebraska defenders, converging at the goal

line, leaped to meet the ball. It disappeared among their six outstretched arms and, as if the ball had exploded, Siano and his adversaries parted in three separate directions. Siano was the one blown into the end zone, and Siano was the one with the ball. It was a

Syracuse touchdown."

Here Coach Dick MacPherson displays an uncharacteristic loss of cool as his team goes on to beat the Number One Nebraska Cornhuskers. Courtesy of Syracuse University Magazine

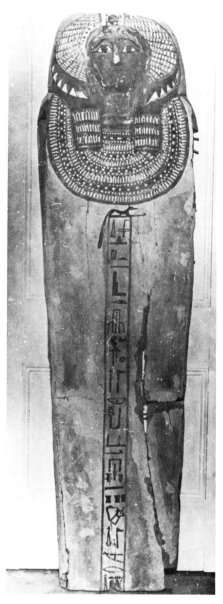

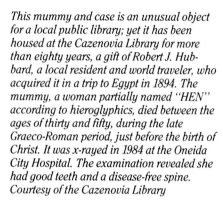

This mummy and case is an unusual object for a local public library; yet it has been housed at the Cazenovia Library for more than eighty years, a gift of Robert J. Hubbard, a local resident and world traveler, who acquired it in a trip to Egypt in 1894. The mummy, a woman partially named "HEN" according to hieroglyphics, died between the ages of thirty and fifty, during the late Graeco-Roman period, just before the birth of Christ. It was x-rayed in 1984 at the Oneida City Hospital. The examination revealed she had good teeth and a disease-free spine. Courtesy of the Cazenovia Library

In a celebrated incident, Dennis Banks, a co-founder of the American Indian Movement, sought sanctuary on the Onondaga Reservation from federal authorities following charges involving him with riots in South Dakota ten years earlier.

The FBI was not certain whether to storm the reservation and to arrest Banks by force if necessary, or to seek other means. Then the Justice Department ruled that the government agents had no jurisdiction on Indian land, which represented territory of a sovereign nation. Governor Mario Cuomo refused to allow New York State Police to interfere.

However, Banks was at liberty only on the reservation. If he stepped off, he could be picked up. On October 8, 1984, eighteen months later, he agreed to surrender to authorities and eventually served a fourteen-month prison sentence in South Dakota.

Now free, Banks is an adult drug counselor at the Loneman School on the Pine Ridge Reservation in South Dakota, is involved in business, and enjoys coaching long-distance runners, recalling fondly his time among the Onondagas. Courtesy of the Syracuse Newspapers

The future Galleries of Syracuse site along the west side of the 400 block of South Warren Street in Syracuse on July 30, 1985, is shown prior to the demolition of old buildings on the site. Photo by Mike Greenlar, courtesy of the Syracuse Newspapers

Downtown landmarks disappeared on a Sunday morning, October 13, 1985, as the W. T. Grant department store and the Daniels Building were imploded. The event was to clear the way for the new $48.3 million Galleries of Syracuse development and was staged by Controlled Demolition of Phoenix, Maryland. Series photos by David Lassman, courtesy of the Syracuse Newspapers

The new Galleries of Syracuse development took shape along South Warren Street, as it readied for opening in late 1987. Photo by Al Edison

The new altar at Syracuse's Roman Catholic Cathedral of the Immaculate Conception is consecrated by Bishop Frank Harrison on the occasion of the rededication of the cathedral on January 11, 1987. To his right is Wesley Brush, deacon. Courtesy of the Catholic Diocese of Syracuse

An earlier sanctuary by Archimedes Russell was installed in 1903 to 1904 in the cathedral on Columbus Circle in Syracuse. The sanctuary displays Russell's skill as an architect in the use of gothic design. Courtesy of the Catholic Diocese of Syracuse

Falcon Park, home of Auburn's minor league baseball teams for many years, has served as a stage for such baseball greats as Pete Rose and Ed Kranepool. The quaint stands are typical of the ball parks of sixty or more years ago. Courtesy of Cayuga County Historian's Office

Competitive cycling and hot-air ballooning are a bit of the nineteenth century updated for present-day Central New Yorkers, with international stars and Olympic bicycle competitors in action at Syracuse's Upper Onondaga Park course in 1980. Courtesy of Key Bank of Central New York

The uniquely profiled Concorde arrives at Hancock International Airport on September 28, 1986, with Captain Colin Morris at the controls. Some thirty thousand people crowded area roads to watch the plane come in. Photo by Rob Randall, courtesy of the Syracuse Newspapers

The late J. Leonard Gorman, editor emeritus at the Post-Standard and one of the last of the Central New York newsmen who bridged the prewar years with the present, was photographed as he reminisced over World War II headlines at his retirement in the early 1980s. Photo by Dick Blume, courtesy of the Syracuse Newspapers

Joe Miller, right, a marine, and Dave Hollihan, an army airborne veteran raised the flag above the Onondaga County Korea-Vietnam War Memorial as the monument at Warren and East Onondaga streets, Syracuse, was dedicated on November 11, 1984. Photo by C. W. McKeen, courtesy of the Syracuse Newspapers

Burnet Park Zoo's antiquated animal house, shown here in 1980, was replaced in 1986. Photo by David Lassman, courtesy of the Syracuse Newspapers

An aerial view shows the new Burnet Park Zoo under construction in August of 1984. Photo courtesy of the Syracuse Newspapers

The gigantic opening-day crowd at Burnet Park Zoo in Syracuse on August 2, 1986, was greeted by a gigantic arrival, as an elephant tripped through the ceremonial ribbon. Photo by Dick Blume, courtesy of the Syracuse Newspapers

Many were openly dubious—thirty thousand coming out for basketball on a Central New York winter's night? Yet that is exactly what happened. With the advent of a Big East Conference bringing to Syracuse such teams as Georgetown and St. Johns, a strong basketball thrust and the unveiling of such stars as Duane Washington, Syracuse was soon setting national records for on-campus game attendance. The team continued to improve. In 1987 it went to the National Collegiate Athletic Association (NCAA) Final Four in New Orleans, losing to Indiana in the last three seconds of the final game. Courtesy of Athletic Department, Syracuse University

After a quarter of a century in office as head of Onondaga County, John H. Mulroy, the longest-serving county executive in the nation, prepared to retire on January 1, 1988. Announcing his plans to leave office during an April 1987 press conference, he was flanked by, from left, his wife, Virginia; County Court Judge Kevin Mulroy, his son; Emily Manfredi, his granddaughter, and his daughter, Martha Manfredi. Photo by Toren Beasley, courtesy of the County Executive's Office and the Syracuse Newspapers

Syracuse Mayor Thomas Young, shown here with his family and well-wishers on election night, was elected in 1985, succeeding Lee Alexander, who had served in the post for sixteen years. Young, a Democrat, was a former New York State Fair director. Courtesy of Office of the Mayor

The world's largest polar bear, a thirty-foot-high ice sculpture by Pat Galbraith, was viewed in February 1987 by visitors to Syracuse's Clinton Square. Photo by Al Edison

Miss Seven-Eleven, *an Unlimited hydroplane out of Kent, Washington, is at speed on Onondaga Lake. The only contacts with water are via the skid fin and the propeller blade as the boat, driven by Steve Reynolds, is going close to 150 miles an hour. The 2,650-horsepower boat is turbo-powered. Courtesy of Al Edison*

For more than fifty years Cayuga County residents have "enjoyed" a dip each New Year's Day in frigid Owasco Lake. Courtesy of Cayuga Museum of History and Art

The New York State Fairgrounds track still maintains its reputation as the world's fastest dirt mile with a sprint car driven by Sammy Swindell timed at 137 miles an hour for the distance. The events are run under the auspices of DIRT (Drivers Independent Race Tracks), an eastern states sanctioning body developed by Glenn Donnelly, a Weedsport promoter, which now ranks second only to NASCAR as the nation's largest auto-racing organization. Courtesy of DIRT

Ace Lane, Jr. Photo

Modified stock cars, some of them valued at more than fifty thousand dollars, moved into the home stretch of the New York State Fairgrounds track during the Miller 200, the world's richest dirt race, with a 1987 purse of more than three hundred thousand dollars. Photo by Al Edison

A half dozen other auto tracks draw well, including the five-eighths of a mile paved oval in Oswego, which annually draws a hundred thousand spectators to weekly races and to view the world championship race for unlimited short-track race cars. Among its alumni are Gordon Johncock, a two-time Indianapolis winner and Geoff Bodine, who won the 1986 Daytona 500. This photo shows the start of the 1981 Classic. Courtesy of Oswego Speedway

Elizabeth "Libba" Cotton, the legendary folksinger and songwriter who became Syracuse's first "Living Treasure" in 1983, is shown here in concert in February 1984 in the city's Martin Luther King School. The composer of "Freight Train" and a recipient of a Grammy Award, Cotton came to Syracuse in 1978 to be with her daughter but continued to appear nationally. She celebrated her ninetieth birthday at a 1982 concert in her honor at the Smithsonian Institution and in 1984 was named a National Heritage Fellow.

Other songs by Cotton include, among many others, "Shake, Sugaree" and "Oh, Babe, It Ain't No Lie." She wrote "Freight Train" when she was eleven; she and her brother would play near the railroad tracks and made up songs about the trains.

Cotton died in Syracuse on June 29, 1987, at the age of ninety-five. Courtesy of Syracuse Newspapers

Syracusan Alice King was the 1986 recipient of the Woman of Achievement Award for Government Service presented by the Post-Standard. King has served as Commissioner of Parks and Recreation for the city of Syracuse and is currently director of the city's Division of Housing and Neighborhood Revitalization.

Since 1949 the Woman of Achievement Awards have honored hundreds of Central New York women in all areas of endeavor, including business, government, education, arts, volunteer leadership and community service. In 1953 the Post-Standard was joined by the Syracuse Federation of Women's Clubs in joint sponsorship. Photo by C. W. McKeen, courtesy of Syracuse Newspapers

Billy Graham, then thirty-four years of age, brought his crusade to the War Memorial in Syracuse for four weeks in August 1953, attracting more than a hundred thousand persons, including four thousand for the first service, above. Shown during conference with local church leaders are, seated from left, Jerry Beavan, executive secretary, Billy Graham team; E. J. Willett, crusade chairman; the Reverend Graham; the Rev. L. T. Hosie, executive secretary of the Syracuse Council of Churches and Clinton H. Tasker, vice chairman of the crusade. Standing are, left, the Rev. Cliff Barrows, song director, and the Rev. Grady Wilson, associate evangelist. Billy Graham is scheduled to return to Syracuse in 1989 when he and his team will appear in the Carrier Dome. Courtesy of Syracuse Newspapers

This pastel study of Martin Luther King, Jr., by a convict artist at Auburn Correctional Institute was presented by Parke W. Wicks, right, president of First Trust & Deposit Company, to pupils and faculty of the Martin Luther King School in Syracuse during the observances of King's birthday in 1977. Photo by Al Edison

Bibliography

Alexander, E. P. *Iron Horses: American Locomotives 1829-1900.* New York: Bonanza Books, 1941.

Alumni Association of State University College of Forestry, Alumni Newsletter, vol. 55, no. 1, (1955).

Andrist, Ralph K. *The Erie Canal.* New York: American Heritage Publishing Co., 1964.

Anguish, Lena Putnam. *History of Fayetteville-Manlius Area.* Fayetteville, N.Y.: Fayetteville-Manlius Central School District, 1966.

Architecture Worth Saving in Onondaga County. Syracuse: New York State Council on the Arts and Syracuse University School of Architecture, 1964.

Armstrong, George. *Forestry College: Essays on the Growth and Development of the New York State's College of Forestry.* Syracuse: Alumni Association of State University College of Forestry at Syracuse University, 1961.

Baker, Anne Kathleen. *A History of Old Syracuse, 1654-1899.* Fayetteville, N.Y.: Manlius Publishing Co., 1937.

Barclay, Katherine J. *Brewerton, New York, U.S.A.* Syracuse: Privately printed, 1973.

Beauchamp, William M. *Notes of Other Days in Skaneateles.* Onondaga Historical Association Annual. Syracuse: Dehler Press, 1914.

_____. *Past and Present of Syracuse and Onondaga County.* Vols. 1 & 2. Syracuse: S. J. Clarke Publishing Co., 1908.

Beveridge, William. *Influenza: The Last Great Plague.* New York: Prodist, 1977.

Bicentennial History of Springport and Union Springs, New York, With Illustrations. Ovid, N.Y.: W. E. Morrison & Co., 1976.

Blizzard of '66. Syracuse: Scotsman Press, 1966.

Bogdan, Robert. "Sing for Your Supper, Part I." *Syracuse Metropolitan Review,* September 1971, pp. 10-13.

Brewster, Arthur Judson. *Memories of Clinton Square and Other Tales of Syracuse.* Syracuse: Syracuse University Press, 1951.

Brownell, Joseph W. and Wawrzasaek, Patricia A. *Adirondack Tragedy: The Gillette Murder Case of 1906.* Interlaken, N.Y.: Heart of the Lakes Publishing, 1986.

Bruce, Dwight H. *Memorial History of Syracuse.* Syracuse: H. P. Smith and Co., 1881.

Bulletin, Onondaga County Medical Society, July 1976.

Cantor, George. *The Great Lakes Guidebook: Lakes Ontario and Erie.* Ann Arbor: University of Michigan Press, 1978.

Carrington, Henry B. *Battles of the American Revolution, 1775-1781.* New York: Promontory Press, 1877.

The Castle Story. Syracuse: Journalism Alumni Association, 1953.

Chard, Eleanor C. and Grills, Russell. *Cazenovia: The Story of an Upland Community.* Cazenovia, N.Y.: Cazenovia Preservation Foundation, 1977.

Chase, Franklin H. *Syracuse and Its Environs.* Vols. 1-3. Chicago: Lewis Historical Publishing Co., 1924.

Clark, Olga. *Oswego Illustrated.* Oswego: Heritage Press, 1976.

Clayton, W. H. *History of Onondaga County.* Syracuse: D. Mason & Co., 1878.

Collier, Richard. *Plague of the Spanish Lady.* New York: The Antheneum, 1974.

Cooley, Miriam. *The First 100 Years: A History of the Syracuse Chapter of the American Red Cross.* Fayetteville, N. Y.: Manlius Publishing Corp., 1981.

Cooper, Charles B. *The Story of the Steamboats on Skaneateles Lake.* Skaneateles, N. Y.: Privately printed, 1980.

Cortland County Sesquicentennial Celebration. Cortland: Cortland County Historical Society, 1958.

Crane, Stephen, Cady, Edwin H., Fryckstedt, Olov, Sutton, Walter E., Wells, Lester G., Williams, Ames W., and Zara, Louis. *Great Bugs in Onondaga.* Syracuse: Syracuse University Library Associates, 1964.

Crosby, Alfred W., Jr. *Epidemic and Peace 1918.* Westport, Conn.: Greenwood Press, 1976.

Cummings, Jack. *The Primitive Paintings of Ruth Reed Cummings.* Syracuse: Visual Arts Publications, 1975.

Drago, Harry Sinclair. *Canal Days in America: The History and Romance of Old Towpaths and Waterways.* New York: Bramhall House, 1972.

Durso, Joseph. *The Days of Mr. McGraw.* Englewood Cliffs, N.J.: Prentice-Hall, 1969.

DuVall, John. *Years of Our Youth.* Unpublished manuscript in possession of Sarah DuVall.

Ellis, David M., Frost, James A., Syrett, Harold C., and Carmen, Harry J. *A Short History of New York State.* Ithaca, N.Y.: Cornell University Press, 1957.

Estey, Emily. *Papa Was Positive.* Sherburne, N.Y.: Heritage Press, 1966.

Fairs, U.S.A.: New York State. Ithaca, N.Y.: Image Digest, 1970.

Fellows, Byron F., Jr., and Roseboom, William F. *The Road to Yesterday.* Fayetteville, N.Y.: Manlius Publishing Corp., 1948.

Finley, Howard J. *Weedsport-Brutus: A Brief History.* Weedsport, N.Y.: Weedsport Bicentennial Committee, 1976.

Foley, Jasena R. *The Night the Rock Blew Up.* Syracuse: Privately printed, 1973.

Fowler, George W. *The First 120 Years.* Syracuse: Syracuse City School District, 1969.

Gabriel, Cleota Ree. *The Arts and Crafts Ideal: The Ward House.* Syracuse: Institute for the Development of Evolutive Architecture, 1978.

Galpin, W. Freeman. *Central New York: An Inland Empire.* Vol. 1-2. Chicago: Lewis Publishing Co., 1941.

Geology of New York: A Short Account. Albany: University of the State of New York, 1966.

Hambrick, Charles. *The Dry Years in the Salt City.* Unpublished manuscript. Onondaga Historical Association, 1965.

Hamilton, Ellis C. *The Love of the Train.* New York: Grossett & Dunlap, 1971.

Hamilton, New York. Hamilton, N.Y.: Colgate Printing, 1983.

Hand, H. C. *Syracuse From a Forest to a City.* Syracuse: Master & Stone, 1889.

Hanson, Lee, and Hsu, Dick Ping. *Casemates and Cannonballs: Archeological Investigations at Fort Stanwix, Rome, New York,* Washington: U.S. Department of the Interior, National Park Service, 1975.

Hardin, Evamaria. *Archimedes Russell: Upstate Architect.* Syracuse: Syracuse University Press, 1980.

Hedinger, Bud. *Weather Guide.* Syracuse: WIXT, 1979.

Hoehling, Adolph. *The Great Epidemic.* Boston: Little Brown, 1961.

Horseman, Reginald. *The War of 1812.* New York: Alfred A. Knopf, 1969.

Howe, John B. *The New York State Fair: Its Genesis and Its History.* Syracuse: Hall & McChesney, 1917.

Kenney, James E. *History of LeMoyne College: The First 25 Years.* Syracuse: Brown Printing Co., 1973.

Langdon, John W. *Against the Sky: The First Forty Years of LeMoyne College.* Syracuse: LeMoyne College, 1986.

LaRue, Arlene. *All Our Yesterdays.* Fayetteville, N.Y.: Manlius Publishing Corp., 1977.

Luke, Marion L. *History-thon: A Walk Through Historic Syracuse.* Syracuse: The Consortium, 1976.

Luzader, John F., Torres, Louis, and Carroll, Orville W., *Fort Stanwix: Construction and Military History, Historic Furnishing Study, Historic Structure Report.* Washington: U.S. Department of the Interior, National Park Service, 1976.

MacDonald, Rod. *Syracuse Basketball 1900-1975.* Syracuse: Syracuse University Press, 1975.

Madison County Historical Society, *Madison County Heritage,* no. 13 (1983).

Maxwell, Mary Ellis. *Among the Hills of Camillus.* Camillus, N.Y.: Privately printed, 1976.

McKinley, J. W. *Assassinations in America.* New York: Harper & Row, 1975.

Melone, Harry R. *History of Central New York.* Vol. 1-2. Indianapolis: Historical Publishing Co., 1932.

Melvin, Crandall, Sr. *A History of the Merchants National Bank and Trust Company.* Syracuse: Syracuse University Press, 1969.

Merrill, John. *Handbook of Geology Field Trips in Onondaga County.* Paper prepared at Syracuse University [1970?].

Munson, Lilian Stelle. *Syracuse: The City That Salt Built.* New York: Pageant Press International, 1969.

Mystique Krewe Program 1905, 1906, 1907, 1908, 1909, 1910. Syracuse: Mystique Krewe Committee, Syracuse Chamber of Commerce, 1905-1910.

New York: A Guide to the Empire State. American Guide Series. New York: Oxford University Press, 1962.

O'Brian, William. *Forty Years on the Force.* Syracuse: Syracuse Herald, 1926.

O'Connor, Lois. "A Giant Discovery." *New York Alive,* 1986, pp. 30-32.

Onondaga County Medical Society 1906-1956. Syracuse: Onondaga County Medical Society, 1956.

Onondaga County War Memorial, The. Syracuse: Midstate Offset Printing Corp., 1951.

Onondaga Landmarks. Syracuse: Cultural Resources Council of Syracuse and Onondaga County, 1975.

Palmer, Richard R. *The Old Line Mail.* Lakemont, N.Y.: North Country Books, 1977.

Profile of Central New York. Syracuse: Syracuse Governmental Research Bureau, and Metropolitan Development Association, 1975.

Quigley, John P. *A Century of Fire Fighting.* Syracuse: The Syracuse Herald, 1946.

Rappoport, Ken. *The Syracuse Football Story.* Huntsville, Ala.: Strade Publishers, 1975.

Roseboom, William F., and Schramm, Henry W. *They Built a City.* Fayetteville, N.Y.: Manlius Publishing Corp., 1976.

Rusterholtz, Wallace P. *The Swiss Family Rusterholtz in America.* Erie, Pa.: The A.K.-D. Printing Co., 1972.

St. Joseph's Hospital Centennial. Syracuse: St. Joseph's Hospital, 1969.

"Salina: A Business History." Special supplement in *Syracuse Business,* 1980.

Schmitz, Marian K. *The Hollow and the Hill.* Parsons, W. Va.: McClain Printing Co., 1983.

Schramm, Henry W. *The City Built on a Pillar of Salt.* Unpublished manuscript. Syracuse, 1955.

_____. *Community of Promise.* Woodland Hills, Cal.: Windsor Publications, 1980.

_____. *Empire Showcase: A History of the New York State Fair.* Utica: North Country Books, 1985.

_____. "We Can Save Our Elms." *Kiwanis Magazine,* March 1955, pp. 10-13.

_____. and Roseboom, William F. *Syracuse: From Salt to Satellite.* Woodland Hills, Cal.: Windsor Publications, 1979.

Schwartz, Mrs. Max H. *1910: Onondaga County in the War of the Rebellion.* Syracuse: Pinzer-Union Publishing Co., 1910.

The Seward House. Auburn: The Foundation Historical Association, 1955.

Seymour, Harold. *Baseball: The Early Years.* New York: Oxford University Press, 1960.

Smith, Edward. *History of Schools of Syracuse.* Syracuse: C. W. Bardeen, 1893.

Solvay Process Company, 1881-1902. Syracuse: Solvay Process Co., 1902.

Spaulding, A. G. *America's National Game.* New York: American Sports Publishing Co., 1911.

Sperry, Earl E. *The Jerry Rescue.* Syracuse: Onondaga County Historical Association, 1920.

Spritz, Kenneth. *Theatrical Evolution: 1776-1976.* Yonkers: The Hudson River Museum at Yonkers, 1976.

Storey, Mike. *Heartland: A Natural History of Onondaga County, New York.* Syracuse: Onondaga Audubon Society, 1977.

Strong, Gurney S. *Early Landmarks of Syracuse.* Syracuse: The Times Publishing Co., 1894.

The Syracuse New Times. *Syracuse Guidebook '76.* Syracuse: Kasco Media, 1975.

Teall, Sarah Sumner. *Onondaga's Part in the Civil War.* Syracuse: Onondaga County Historical Association, 1915.

Turkin, Hy, and Thompson, S. C. *The Official Encyclopedia of*

Baseball. 2d rev. ed. New York: A. S. Barnes and Company, 1959.

Two Faces of Janus. Syracuse: Carrier Corp. [1974?]

University of Rochester Library Bulletin 31, no. 1 (1978).

Volunteer Fire Services of Onondaga County. Syracuse: Onondaga County Volunteer Firemen's Association, 1976.

Von Engeln, O. D. *The Finger Lakes Region: Its Origin and Nature.* Ithaca: Cornell University Press, 1961.

Walker, Dale M. "The Medal and Doctor Walker." *The Retired Officer,* February 1984, pp. 32-37.

Watson, Elkanah. *New York State Agriculture: The Rise, Progress and Existing State of Modern Agricultural Societies of the Berkshire System.* Albany: D. Steele, 1820.

Williams, Howard D. *A History of Colgate University 1819-1969.* New York: Van Nostrand Reinhold Co., 1969.

Witcher, Marcia. *Early History of the Negro in Syracuse and Onondaga County.* Syracuse: Syracuse City School Districts, 1968.

Wyld, Lionel D., ed. *40' x 28' x 4': The Erie Canal—150 Years.* Rome, N.Y.: Oneida County Erie Canal Commemoration Commission, 1967.

Index

A

Abolitionist movement, 36, 37
Akiyama, Kazuyashi, 208
Alaska Treaty, 54, 55
Albany, 19
Alco, 97
Alexander, Grover Cleveland, 125
Alexander, Tsar, 30
Algonquins, 5, 6
Alhambra, 78
Allen, Phil, 145
Amboy Airport, 143, 144, 156, 172, 178
Ambulance Service, 99
American Airlines, 178
American Airways, 146
American Red Cross, 72, 139, 187, 199
AME Zion Church, 37
Andreas, Lewis P., 172
Andrews, Justice William, 138
Anglers' Club, 127
anti-tobacco movement, 74
Archaeological Society of Central New York, 7
Archbold Gymnasium, 188
Archbold Stadium, 118, 145
Archbold Stadium Maypole, 118
Army Air Corps, 181
Army Football, 145
Arundell, 106
Auburn, 5, 19, 20, 21, 22, 55, 190
Auburn-Cayuga National Bank and Trust Co., 33
Auburn Real Estate, 129
Auburn State Fair, 37, 40
Auburn State Prison, 41, 66, 130, 146
Auburn State Prison riot, 144, 145
Auburn-Syracuse Railroad, 34
Auburn Whig Convention of 1853, 37
Aurora, 33
Automobile Club of Syracuse, 97

B

B-17, 180, 181
Backus, Billy, 194
Baker, Dr. W. R. G., 193
Baldwinsville, 109
Baldwinsville Boat Yard, 111
Balloonist, 45
Ballwe, Carl J., 145
Bank of Salina, 33
Banks, Dennis, 213
Barbuti, Ray, 145
Barnes-Roosevelt Libel Trial, 138
Barnes, William, 138
Barnum, P. T., 9
Barrow, John D., 83
Barrow Art Gallery, 83
Barton, Clara, 72
Basilio, Carmen, 194
Battle Island, 6
Battle of the Plains, 145
Baum, Frank L., 61, 83
Baysinger, Ribs, 145
Beauchamp, William M., 7, 10
Beebe, Joseph, 21
Berkshire Agricultural Society, 40
Beth Israel, 36
Bethke Field, 156
Biasone, Danny, 195
bicycle racing, 90, 216
Big Tree, Chief John, 184
Billy Sunday Tabernacle, 137
Birge, Gen. J. Ward, 35
black communities, 186
Bley and Lyman, 163
Blizzard of Sixty-six, 191, 201
Bob-O-Link, 205
Bogardus Corners, 23, 26
Borgoyne, Gen., 14
Botanical Infirmary, 38, 43, 110
Brant, Joseph, 6, 7, 13, 20

Brewerton, 5, 21
Brinkerhoff Point, 21
Brockway Carriage Works, 71
Brockway Fire Engine, 198
Brockway Motor Truck Company, 71, 134
Brown, Alexander, 56
Brown, Grace, murder of, 107
Brown, Jim, 190
Brown, John, 36
Brown-Lipe-Chapin, 56
Brule, Stephen, 6
Buckley, Christopher, 35
Buffalo, 22
Burnet, Governor, 6
Burnet, Moses D., 34
Burnet Park Zoo, 219
Burr, Aaron, 20
Burroughs, William Seward, 56
Butler, Capt. John G., 62
Butler, Col. John, 7

C

Cafe Dewitt, 162
Camillus, 37, 66, 86
Camillus Hill, 117
Cammerhoff, Bishop John Frederic Christoph, 6
Camp Black, 62
Camp Onondaga, 38
Canadian Laurentians, 5
Canajoharie, 7
Canal Act, 22
Canal Commission, 21
Canandaigua, 20
Canastota, 22
Canastota Hoist Bridge, 109
Canastota Hospital, 187
Canastota onion fields, 95
Cardiff Giant, 6, 9, 134
Cardiff, Village of, 9

Carheil, Stephen de, 11
Carnegie Hall, 189
Carnegie Library, 188, 210
Carpenter, Francis Bicknell, 44
Carrier, Dr. Willis, 145, 166
Carrier Corporation, 145, 146,
    166, 167, 185
Carrier Dome, 189, 190
CASE Center, 187
Case steam engine, 120
Cathedral of the Immaculate
    Conception, 215
Cayuga County, 20, 30, 33, 34
Cayuga County Fair, 60
Cayuga County Poorhouse, 34
Cayuga Lake, 6, 9
Cayuga Nation, 5, 6, 7, 11
Cazenove, Pheolius de, 21
Cazenovia, 10, 20, 21, 22, 94, 95, 205, 213
Cazenovia Junior College, 187
Cazenovia Lake, 23
Cazenovia Seminary, 65
Central Baptist Church collapse, 67
Central High School, 136
Champlain, Samuel de, 6, 10
Chapin, H. Winfield, 56
Chase, Salmon, 48
Chaumornot, Joseph, 11
Cheney, George N., 39
Cheney, Timothy S., 7
Cherry Valley Massacre, 7
Cherry Valley Turnpike, 20
Chimes Building, 162, 185
Chittenango, 20, 23
Church of the Messiah, 36
Cicero, 7, 32
cigar manufacturing, 74
Citizen, 35
City Hospital, 187
City of Auburn, 105
City of Syracuse, 105
Civil War, 39
Civil War, Battle of Bull Run, 39
Civil War, Battle of Gettysburg, 39, 50,
    51, 52, 53
Civil War, military routine, 39

Civil War, Onondaga County involvement,
    39
Civil War, Oswego County involvement,
    39
Clark Reservation, 4, 5, 6
Clarke, Melville, 144, 185
Clay, Henry, 37
Cleveland, Grover, 72
Cleveland, Philo, 10
Clinton, Dewitt, 21, 22, 23
Clinton Square, 81, 118, 149
Clinton Square monument, 50
Clinton Square, Syracuse, 41
Colgate University, 39, 187
Colgate University Football, 145, 173
Collins Block Fire, 175
Colonial Airline, 144
Columbia Rope Company, 97, 185
Columbia Circle, 158
Community General Hospital, 188
Concorde, 217
Congressional Medal of Honor, 52
Connoisseurs, The, 44
Continental Number Three, 55
Corinth, 23
Cornell, Ezra, 33
Cornell University, 59
Cornell University Football, 145, 173
Cornplanter, Chief, 7
Corp, Mel, 194
Corregidor, 146, 182
Corrigan, Wrong Way, 172
Cortland, 5, 19, 20, 103
Cortland County Fair, 135, 142
Cortland Normal School, 64
Cortland snowfall, 191
Cortland Standard, 35
Cossitt's Corners, 23
Costello, Larry, 195
Costello, Mayor Frank, 187
Cotton, Elizabeth "Libba," 223
Cotton Bowl, 196
Crane, Stephen, 61, 82
Crosby, Miss Fanny, 94
Crouse College, Syracuse University, 80
Crouse-Hinds Company, 185

Crouse-Irving Memorial Hospital, 99,
    187, 188
Crucible Steel Workers, 131, 185
Curtiss, Glen, 98
Czolgosz, Leon, 97, 106, 146
Czonka, Larry, 190

D
Danforth, Asa, 19, 20
Davendorf, Jesse, 200
Davenport, J., 36, 37
David Harum Tavern, 92
Davis, Ernie, 190
DeChaumont, James LeRay, 37
Delaware and Lackawanna, 146
DePalma, Ralph, 120
DeRuyter, Admiral Michiel, 22
DeRuyter, Village of, 22, 23
Dewey, Gov. Thomas E., 186, 187
DeWitt, Moses, 19
DeWitt Clinton, 38
Dey Brothers Department Store, 87, 189
Dickens, Charles, 60, 61
DIRT, 222
Donnelly, Glenn, 222
downtown renewal, 204
Drumlins Country Club, 181
Dunford, George, 144
Dunford, H. W., 33
Dutch elm disease, 186, 187, 189

E
Edwards, E. W., 143, 189
early medicine, 38
Eighteenth Amendment, 100
Eighty-sixth New York Volunteers, 39
Eisenhower, Dwight D., 198
electric chair, Auburn Prison, 108
electric power, 57
Electronics Park, 186, 193
Elliott, Charles Loring, 44
Ellis, Gen. John, 36
Elmira, 39
Elmwood School, 164
Emmett, J. K., 60, 61
Empire State Express, 168, 169

Engine 999, 84
Erie Canal, 21, 22, 23, 26, 27, 28, 29, 33, 56, 86, 100, 149, 200
Erie Canal bottom collapse, 113
Erie Canal Lodi Lock, 112
Erie Canal repair, 112
Everson Museum of Art, 188, 210
Explosion of 1841, 37

F
Falcon Park, 190, 215
Fargo, C. D., 33
Farmer, Mary, 144
Farmers Museum, 9
Farr, Col. Richard S., 177
Fayetteville, 21, 23
Fifty-second General Hospital, 177
Fillmore, Millard, 33, 37
Finger Lakes Mall, 189
First Baptist Church, 35
First Methodist Church fire, 197
First National Bank of Syracuse, 48
Fitzsimmons, Robert, 86
Flint, Chancellor Wesley, 145
Force, William, 144
Ford, Henry, 56
Forman, Joshua, 21, 23, 27, 36
Fort Brewerton, 7
Fort Herkimer, 7
Fort Hill, 5
Fort Ontario, 6, 12, 20, 25, 136, 186
Fort Stanwix, 7, 13, 14, 19, 27
Fort Wayne Pistons, 195
Fourth Presbyterian Church, 162
Fowler High School, 167
Francher, William, 192
Franklin, Benjamin, 27
Franklin, Herbert H., 56
Franklin Automobile Co., 97, 143, 145, 167
Franklin Car, 56, 98
Free Soil party, 37
Freemasons, 6
French powder, 23
Frontenac, Count Robert de, 6
Fulton, 6, 11, 25, 62, 91

G
Galbraith, Pat, 221
Galleries of Syracuse, 214
Garrison, William Lloyd, 36
Gazette, 35
Geddes, James, 19, 21, 23, 36, 60
Genesee Trail, 20
Geneva, 57
Geneva College, 57
German Musical Machine, 35
Gibbud, Henry Burton, 59, 76
Gillette, Chester, 107, 144
Good Shepherd Hospital, 57, 58, 99, 188
Gorman, J. Leonard, 217
Goshen, New York, 146
Graf Zeppelin, 157
Graham, Billy, 224
Graham, Chancellor William P., 165, 170
Granger, Gen. Amos P., 37
Granger, Henry Ward, 44
Grant, Ullysses S., 55
Greenway Brewery, 124
Graves-Etchelle Furnace, 131
Greeley, Horace, 37
Green Bay, Wisconsin, 7

H
Haig, Alexander, 191
Haig, Very Rev. Frank, 191
Halley's comet, 99
Hambletonian, 146
Hamilton Institute, 39
Hancock International Airport, 188, 217
Hanson, Victor, 172
Hardenbergh, Capt. John L., 19, 21
Hargin, Mrs. Caroline, 36
Harrison, Bishop Frank, 215
Harum, David, 61, 92
Harvey, Harry, 153
Hathaway, Judge Joshua, 27
Hazard, Rowland, 55
Heid, Mayor Michael, 187
Heiser, Charles, 144
Herbert, Dr. Marianne, 99
Herkimer, Gen. Nicholas, 13
Hiawatha, 5, 8

Hiawatha Boulevard, 10
Hier and Leighton Cigar Factory, Inc. fire, 18, 91, 60
Higgins, Col. Benjamin L., 39
Higgins, Jane, 39
Higgins, Robert, 62
Hiss, Dr. J. G. Fred, 187
Holland Land Co., 21
Homer, Village of, 21
Hoover, Herbert, 145, 170
Hoppers' Glen, 32, 211
horsecars, 34
Hoyt, Dr. Hiram, 66
Huntington, Bishop Frederick D., 57
Huron Nation, 5, 6

I
immigration, 58
Indian Hill, 6, 8
infantile paralysis, 99, 165
Intercollegiate Rowing Regatta, 190
iron plough, 30
Iroquois Confederacy, 5, 6, 7, 8, 15
Iroquois Nation, 7

J
Jackson, Andrew, 33
Jacob Amos and Sons Mill, 64
James Street, 206
Jamesville, 5
Jay Treaty, 20
Jefferson, Thomas, 21, 30
Jefferson Street Armory, 146
Jennings, Warden Edward S., 144
Jerry Rescue, 36, 46
Jesuits, 6, 11
John Butler's Zouaves, 39
Johns, Aunt Dinah, 73
Johnson, Lyndon B., 199
Johnson, Sir John, 20
Johnson, Sir William, 6
Jones, Alexander F. "Casey," 186
Jones, 22
Judson, Edward, 48

K

KaNoo-No Karnival, 119
Keaton House, Cortland, 73
Keck, Henry, 126
Keene, Christopher, 189, 208, 209
Keith's Theater, 160
Keller, Sgt. Howard, 176
Kemmler, William, 144
Kennedy, John F., 198
Kerr, John, 195
King, Alice, 223
King, Martin Luther, Jr., 224
Kingsford and Son Starch Factory, 63
Kinne, Cyrus, 21
Kirk, William, 35
Kirk Park, 78, 90
Kirkpatrick, William, 21
Kitsz, Conrad J., 147
Kolbe, Trooper Gustave A., 62
Korean-Vietnam War Memorial, 218
Korean War, 185
Kress, Agent Charles, 147, 148
Kritz, Karl, 189, 208
Kropfeld, Jim, 190
Kuchta, Ronald, 211

L

L. C. Smith Typewriter Co., 185
LaCrosse, 124, 125
LaFrance, Ferdinand, 5
Lake Ontario, 4, 8, 21, 22
Lamb, Col. Joseph, 16
Lamoka Lake, 5
Landis, Judge Kenesaw Mountain, 11, 18
Lee, Ned, 59, 76
Leland Hotel, Inc., 60
LeMieux, Charles P., 199
LeMoyne, Simon, 6, 11
LeMoyne College, 185, 187, 190, 191
Liberty Party State Convention, 46
Life Guards at Oswego, 135
Lilly, Color Sgt. William C., 50
Lima, 57
Limestone Creek, 4
Lincklean, John, 21, 22
Lincoln Store, 143

Lindbergh, Charles A., 144, 156
Lipe, Charles E., 56
Little, Floyd, 190
Little Falls, 27
little red schoolhouse, 20
Loew's Theater, 160, 161
Long Branch Park, 123, 155
longhouse, 8
Longstreet, Cornelius Tyler, 158
Loguen, Jermain Wesley, 37
Lorenzo, 23
Louis XV, 12
Los Angeles, 157
Loyalists, 7
Lynds, Capt. Elam, 144

M

Mabie, Elisba, 65
MacArthur, Gen. Douglas, 146, 183
McCarthy, Thomas, 35
McCormick, Patrick Henry, 62, 68
McCurdy, J. A., 121
McGraw, John, 62, 68, 170, 171
McIntosh, James G., 55
McKinley, William, 99
McKinney, Guy, 146
MacPherson, Dick, 212
Madison University, 39
Magnolia home, 127
Magoon, Dr. Isaac, 43
malaria, 23
Manley Field House, 189
Manlius, 20, 22
Marcellus, 23, 88
Marcellus Road, 79
Marsellus, Maj. John, 177
Marshall, Gen. George C., 148
Martin Luther King School, 224
May, Samuel J., 36
Menard, Rene, 11
Mercer, Henry Chapman, 126
Mercy Hospital, 187
Meredith, Clive, 144
Mickles, Nicholas, 24
military tract, 16
Miller, David J., 185

Miller Stock Car Race, 190, 222
miniature golf, 164
Miss Budweiser, 190
Mohawk, 22
Mohawk River, 4, 5, 19
Mohawk Nation, 5, 7
Monster mosquito, 119
Montcalm, Louis Joseph, 6
Montezuma Swamp, 23
Montezuma, 22
MONY Center, 204, 205
Moody, Dwight L., 58
Moravia, 32
Moravians, 6
Morris Centrifugal Pump Works, 49
Morris, Gouverneur, 21
Morrisville, 127
Mound Builders, 5
Moyer, Harvey, 98
Mulroy, County Executive John H., 203, 220
Munroe, David Allen, 37
Myers Block, 64
Myers, Carl E., 98

N

National Bank Act, 33
National Recovery Act, 165
NCAA Final Four, 220
Nebraska University Football, 212
Needham, William, 19
Nelson, 20
Nestle Factory, 104
New Jersey, USS, 192
New Orleans, The, 22
New Process Gear, 185
New York Central Railroad, 34, 146, 168
New York Central Railroad flood, 151
New York Giants, 170, 171
New York State Agricultural Society, 37
New York State Barge Canal, 97
New York State Fair, 37, 60, 97, 98, 118, 145, 146, 178, 188
New York State Fair Coliseum, 146
New York State Gas and Electric, 186
Newburgh, 7

Newell, William, 9
Niagara Falls, 7, 57
Niagara Falls Power Company, 98
Niagara Mohawk Power Corp., 163, 186, 202, 203
Niagara Mohawk Power Corp. Headquarters, 163
Niagara Presbyterian Church, 35
Nichols Pond, 10
Nine Mile Point, 203
Nixon, Richard M., 199
NORAD, 188
North Syracuse, 32
Nott, Joel, 37

O
Old Bullhead, 99
old red mill, 26
Oldfield, Lee, 170
Oneida, 7, 22
Oneida Lake, 5, 7, 21, 127
Oneida Nation, 5, 7
Onondaga County, 20
Onondaga County Court House, 37, 126
Onondaga County Poorhouse, 34
Onondaga County War Memorial, 189, 195, 198
Onondaga Country Club, 128
Onondaga Creek, 23, 113
Onondaga Creek floods, 134
Onondaga General Hospital, 187
Onondaga Hill, 20, 34, 40
Onondaga Hollow, 19
Onondaga Lake, 7, 8, 10, 31, 190, 212, 221
Onondaga Long House, 73
Onondaga Nation, 5, 6, 7, 8, 22, 124, 125, 213
Onondaga Pottery Company, 56
Onondaga Register, 35
Onondaga Savings Bank Building, 188
Onondaga Valley, 21, 23
Onondaga Water Authority, 186, 203
Ontario Bank, 33
Orange Bowl, 190
organ grinder, 128
Oswego, 6, 7, 12, 16, 19, 20, 22, 34, 35,

56, 61, 62, 63, 202
Oswego Canal, 23, 110
Oswego Falls, 6
Oswego, fire of, 1850, 42
Oswego snowfall, 191
Oswego Speedway, 222
Oswego-Syracuse Railroad, 34
Owasco Lake, 21, 221
Owasco Lake hermit, 102

P
PGA Seniors tournament, 191
Packwood Hotel, 140
Palladium, 35
Parsons, Chauncey J., 22
Parsons, Johnny, 190
Patriots' War, 34
Peaceable Kingdom, The, 211
Pearl Harbor, 146, 176
Pease, Charles, 35
Peck, Gen. John J., 52
Pei, I. M., 188
People's Hospital, 187
Perry, Col. Walter, 177
Pershing, John J., 148
Peterboro, 36
Phoenix, 6, 62
plank road, 32
Pioneer Homes development, 166
Piskor, Dean Frank, 196
Pompeian Players, 189
Pompey, 6, 20, 22, 200
Pompey Stone, 6, 10
Poncet, Father, 6
Poolo's ice cream parlor, 205
Port Byron, 23, 56, 111
Powell, Harriet, 36, 37
Powell, Lewis, 58
Prescott, 35
Price, Milton S., Store, 85
Prohibition, 143, 147
Prospect Hill, 23, 37, 66

Q
Queen Anne, 6

R
Raffeix, Peter, 11
Rea, Henry B., 146
Reagan, Ronald, 193
Red Badge of Courage, The, 61
Redfield, Lewis H., 35
regional market, 158
Republican party, 37
Reynolds, Steve, 221
Rice, Grantland, 145
Riehlman, R. Walter, 198, 199
Richardson, Judge, 22, 27
Robineau, Adelaide Alsop, 126
Robinson, Jackie, 62
Rockefeller, John D., 33
Rockwell Manufacturing Co., 185
roller skating, 78
Rome, 22, 27
Roosevelt-Barnes libel trial, 100
Roosevelt, Franklin D., 145, 148, 165
Roosevelt, Theodore, 97, 108, 119, 138
Root, Col. Augustus I., 52
Russell, Archimedes, 58, 80, 81, 126
Rusterholtz, Jerome, 186, 187
Ruth, Harold "Babe," 145

S
SUNY Cortland, 187
SUNY Morrisville, 187
SUNY Oswego, 187
SUNY College of Environmental Science and Forestry, 187, 189
Sackett's Harbor, 22, 35
St. Joseph's Hospital, 23, 57, 58, 66, 99, 188
St. Lawrence River, 5
St. Leger, Lt. Col. Barry, 7
St. Mary's Roman Catholic Church, 26, 42
St. Paul's Episcopal Church, 26, 35, 42
SA&K Building, 71
Salina, 20
Salina Street, 174
Salt City Playhouse, 189
Salt industry, 55, 69, 100
salt reservation, 20, 21
Sampson Navy Base, 146

Samuel I. Newhouse Communications Center, 199
Sanderson Brothers Steel Workers, 131
Sanderson-Holcomb Steel, 97
Sanford, C. Harry, 145
Salvation Army, 59
Sandy Creek, 22
Saterlee, George, 101
Sauer, Hank, 190, 207
Saonchiocwa, Chief, 11
Saxton, Johnny, 194
Schayes, Dolph, 195
Schrafft's, 152
Schuyler County, 7
Schwartz, Victor, 145
Schwartzwalder, Floyd, 190, 196
Schwedes, Gerhard, 196
Sears Roebuck, 127
Sears Roebuck homes, 99
Seneca Lake, 146
Seneca Nation, 5
Seneca Turnpike, 20
Seward, William H., 54, 55, 58, 59, 60
Seymour, Paul, 195
Shaeffer, John, 20
Shapiro, Ephraim, 203
Shattuck, Frank G., 152
Shearer, Norma, 154
Shenandoah, 157
shinplasters, 48
Shoppingtown, 189
Shubert Brothers, 99, 189
Sibley's, 160
Sidat-Singh, 145, 173
Sig Sautelle Circus, 101
Sigel's Coffee House, 38
Silsbee, Joseph Lyman, 58, 81
Simmons, Roy, 172
Sitting Bull, 153
Skaneateles, 7, 20, 22, 140, 182, 183
Skaneateles Baptist Society, 35
Skaneateles-Clift Park, 102
Skaneateles Lake, 33
Skaneateles Lake Transportation Co., 105
Skaneateles Lake Water, 60
Smith, Agent Lowell R., 147

Smith, Grant, 36
Smith, Thomas W., 203
Smith, Vivus W., 36, 37
Society of Concord, 36
Soldiers and Sailors Monument, 118
Solebay, Battle of, 22
Solvay, Alfred, 55
Solvay, Ernest, 55
Solvay Process, 55
Solvay Process chimney demolition, 114
Solvay Process Company, 55, 70, 115
Solvay Process locomotive wreck, 115
Solvey Process workers homes, 114
Southern Tier, 7
Spanish-American War, 62, 93
Spanish influenza, 99
Spencer, Mrs. Elmina, 53
Spirit of Light, 163
Split Rock explosion, 100, 140, 141
stagecoach rides, 36
Stanford, Leland, 65
Star Park, 152
state railroad convention, 34
State Tower Building, 160, 163
steam railroads, 34
steam tractors, 87
Stearn's bicycles, 89
Stevens, Oliver, 21
Stevens, William, 20
Stickley, Gustav, 126
Stone, P. Schuyler, 34
Strand Theatre, 155
suburban railways, 57, 98, 116
Sullivan, Gen. John, 7
Sunday, Billy, 137
Superior, 22
Susquehannah River, 5, 19
Sweet, John E., 56, 57
Sweet, William A., 56
Swindell, Sammy, 222
Syracuse and Auburn trolley, 105
Syracuse Automobile Club, 149
Syracuse baseball, 62
Syracuse Bomber Base, 146, 180, 181
Syracuse Bridge Company, 126
Syracuse Chiefs, 146, 190, 207

Syracuse China, 84
Syracuse City Hall, 71
Syracuse Excelsior baseball team, 68
Syracuse House, 26, 34, 37, 61
Syracuse Hotel, 146
Syracuse Nationals, 189, 195
Syracuse Rescue Mission, 59, 76
Syracuse Savings Bank, 48
Syracuse, Sicily, 31
Syracuse snowfall, 191
Syracuse Stars, 62, 68, 125
Syracuse State Fair 1849, 37
Syracuse State Fair, 1858, 37
Syracuse Symphony, 189, 208, 209
Syracuse University, 64, 187
Syracuse University basketball, 220
Syracuse University crew, 212
Syracuse University football, 145, 172, 173, 190, 196, 212
Syracuse University Medical College, 57, 177
Syracuse Stage, 189

T
Taber House, 107
Taft, William Howard, 122
Taughannock Falls, 9
telephone, 57
temperance movement, 75
Thayer, Sanford, 44
Thomas, Jesse, 144
Thomson, Dr. Cyrus, 38, 43
Thruway, 186, 187
Tiffany, Louis Comfort, 126
Tioga County Medical Society, 19
Todd, Amos, 21
Tolley, Chancellor William P., 193
Tories, 6, 7
Tornado of 1912, 123
Treaty of 1784, 15
Treaty of Aix-la-Chapelle, 6
Truax Hotel, 150
Truman, Harry, 193
Truxton, 62, 68, 170, 171
Tubman, Harriet, 37, 47
Tully, 5, 70

Tuscarora Nation, 5
Twenty-seventh Division, 100
Tyler, Comfort, 19, 20

U
Underground Railroad, 36, 37, 47
Udwin, Claude, 144
Union Springs, 6
United States Bank Bill, 33
Upstate Medical Center, 188
urban renewal, 186
Utica, 20, 22

V
Vadeboncoeur, E. R., 176
Valentino, Rudolph, 153
VanBuren, Martin, 22, 37
VanCortlandt, Col. Phillip, 16
Vanderbilt Square, 56
Vanderbilt Station, 56
VanSchaick, Col. Goose, 7, 16
Vietnam, 185
Volstead Act, 143
Von Schoultz, Niles Gustaf, 34, 35
Von Steuben, Baron Frederick William, 20

W
WFBL, 145
WHEN-TV, 185
WMAC, 144
WSYR, 176
Wadsworth, Gen., 20
Wainwright, Gen. Jonathon, 146, 182, 183
Walker, Dr. Mary E., 52, 97
Walsh, William, 203
Walton, Abram, 26
Walton Tract, 23
War Chest, 139
War of 1812, 22, 24, 25
Ward Wellington Ward, 98, 126
Warners Brickyard, 9
Washington, George, 7
Waterloo, 20, 23
Watson, Elkanah, 27, 37, 40
Webster, Daniel, 36
Webster, Ephraim, 19, 20

Weed, Thurlow, 37
Weedsport, 22, 23, 60, 77, 87
Weedsport Fire of 1871, 59
Weighlock Building, 65
Welland Canal, 22
Wells College, 33, 57
Wells & Coverly, 145
Wells-Fargo Express Co., 33
Wells, Henry, 33
Wescott, Edward Noyes, 61, 92
West Street Station, 169
Western Union Telegraph Co., 33
White, Hamilton Salisbury, fire chief, 93
White, Dr. Hiram, 43
White, Horatio N., 58, 81
Whitestown, 20
Wicks, Parke W., 224
Wieting Opera House, 57, 60, 86
Wilkinson, Alfred, 22
Wilkinson, John, 23, 31, 34, 36, 56, 98
Will, Anton, 56
Will & Baumer Candle Co., 56
Willett, Lt. Col. Marinus, 7
Williams, John T., 39
Willow Basket Production, 103
Wise, Mr., 45
Witherill's, 189
Wizard of Oz, 61
Wood, Jethro, 30, 56
Woodland, 5
Woodland Reservoir, 97
Woodruff, Martin, 35
World War I, 101, 139, 140, 141
World War II, 146, 176, 177, 178, 179,
    180, 181, 182, 183
Wright, Gordon, 97

Y
Yates Castle, 158, 159
Yates Hotel, 98
Young, Mayor Thomas, 220

Z
Zeisberger, David, 6

About the Author

Henry W. Schramm, a native of Brooklyn, came to Syracuse in 1941 to attend Syracuse University. Following naval service in the Atlantic and Pacific theaters during World War II, he was graduated from the university in 1948 with a journalism-history degree.

A reporter for the *Post Standard,* Syracuse, and the *Binghamton Press,* he entered the public relations field before being recalled for army service during Korea. He served as a motion picture and photo operations officer in Germany.

He was on the faculty at the State College of Forestry before joining Doug Johnson Associates. While with Doug Johnson, he was a staff member of the New York State Joint Legislative Committee on Metropolitan Area Studies and consultant for the State Natural Beauty Commission. During this period he won four Silver Anvils from the Public Relations Society of America.

He received his M.A. degree from Syracuse University in 1956, and was upstate correspondent for *Business Week* magazine. He also wrote numerous freelance articles.

In 1970 he came with Key Bank as public relations officer. Former president of the Central New York Chapter of the Public Relations Society of America, he also headed the Hiscock Legal Aid Society.

He has written several books, among them *They Built A City* and *Syracuse From Salt To Satellite* both with the late William Roseboom; *The Dynamic Years; Empire Showcase,* a history of the New York State Fair; and, most recently, *A Lamp In The Window* with Richard Palmer.

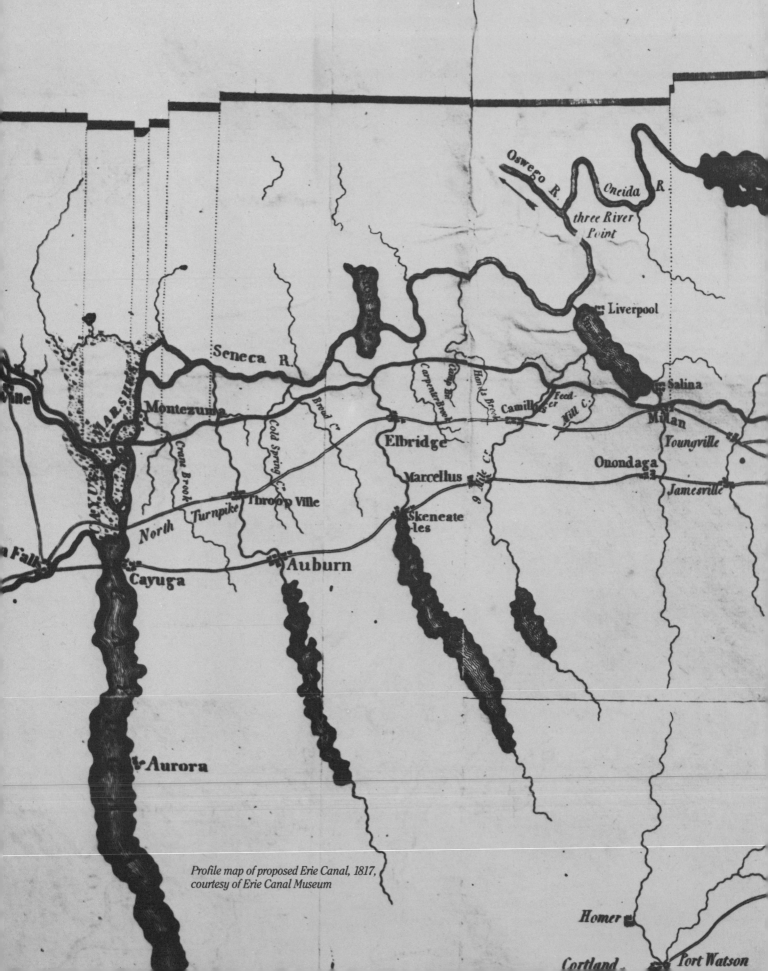

A Profile of the extent of the Levels and of the Places and lifts of the L

Oswego R.

Oneida R.

three River Point

Liverpool

Seneca R.

Carpenter Brook

Camillus

Feed er

Salina

Montezuma

Brud C.

Cold Spring C.

Elbridge

Mill C.

Milan

Youngville

Crane Brook

Marcellus

9 Mile Cr.

Onondaga

Jamesville

North

Turnpike

Throop Ville

Skeneate les

Falls

Cayuga

Auburn

Aurora

*Profile map of proposed Erie Canal, 1817,
courtesy of Erie Canal Museum*

Homer

Cortland

Port Watson